Rights Talk The Impoverishment of Political Dis
34   11953
39204000023582

RIGHTS TALK

The Impoverishment of Political Discourse

Mary Ann Glendon

THE FREE PRESS
A Division of Macmillan, Inc.
NEW YORK

Maxwell Macmillan Canada
TORONTO

Maxwell Macmillan International
NEW YORK   OXFORD   SINGAPORE   SYDNEY

The Free Press
A Division of Macmillan, Inc.
866 Third Avenue, New York, N.Y. 10022

Maxwell Macmillan Canada, Inc.
1200 Eglinton Avenue East
Suite 200
Don Mills, Ontario M3C 3N1

Macmillan, Inc. is part of the Maxwell Communication Group of Companies.

Printed in the United States of America

printing number
1 2 3 4 5 6 7 8 9 10

Library of Congress Cataloging-in-Publication Data

Glendon, Mary Ann
    Rights talk : the impoverishment of political discourse / Mary Ann Glendon.
        p.   cm.
    Includes bibliographical references and index.
    ISBN 0-02-911825-5
    1. Civil rights—United States.   2. Political participation—United States.   3. Political culture—United States.   I. Title.
KF4749.G54   1991
342.73′085—dc20
[347.30285]   91-13723
                                                         CIP

To Leonora Leahy Stanfield

Contents

Preface

In the Spring of 1990, men and women in East Germany and Hungary participated in the first fully free elections that had taken place in any of the East European countries since they came under Soviet control in 1945. Excitement ran high. The last people to have voted in that part of the world were now in their seventies. Some young parents, casting a ballot for the first time, brought their children with them to see the sight. Many, no doubt, will long remember the day as one marked with both festivity and solemnity. Meanwhile, in the United States, public interest in politics appears to be at an all-time low. Two months before the 1988 presidential election, polls revealed that half the voting-age public did not know the identity of the Democratic vice-presidential candidate and could not say which party had a majority in Congress.[1] In that election, only half the eligible voters cast ballots, thirteen percent less than in 1960. Americans not only vote less than citizens of other liberal democracies, they display a remarkable degree of apathy concerning public affairs. Over a period of twenty years, daily newspaper readership has fallen from seventy-three percent of adults to a mere fifty-one percent.[2] Nor have the readers simply become viewers, for ratings of network evening news programs have dropped by about twenty-five percent in the past ten years, and the slack has not been taken up by cable television news. Cynicism, indifference, and ignorance concerning government appear to be pervasive. By all outward indicators, the right and obligation to vote—a subject of wonder to East Europeans, and the central concern of many of us who worked in the civil rights movement in the 1960s—is now held here in rather low esteem.

Poor voter turnouts in the United States are, of course, mere symptoms of deeper problems, not least of which are the decline of broadly representative political parties, and the effect of the "sound-bite" on serious and sustained political discussion. On this deeper level lies the phenomenon with which this book is concerned: the impoverishment of our political discourse. Across the political spectrum there is a growing realization that it has become increasingly difficult even to define critical questions, let alone debate and resolve them.

Though sound-bites do not permit much airing of issues, they seem tailor-made for our strident language of rights. Rights talk itself is relatively impervious to the other more complex languages we still speak in less public contexts, but it seeps into them, carrying the rights mentality into spheres of American society where a sense of personal responsibility and of civic obligation traditionally have been nourished. An intemperate rhetoric of personal liberty in this way corrodes the social foundations on which individual freedom and security ultimately rest. While the nations of Eastern Europe are taking their first risk-laden and faltering steps toward democracy, the historic American experiment in ordered liberty is thus undergoing a less dramatic, but equally fateful, crisis of its own. It is a crisis at the very heart of the American experiment in self-government, for it concerns the state of public deliberation about the right ordering of our lives together. In the home of free speech, genuine exchange of ideas about matters of high public importance has come to a virtual standstill.

This book argues that the prominence of a certain kind of rights talk in our political discussions is both a symptom of, and a contributing factor to, this disorder in the body politic. Discourse about rights has become the principal language that we use in public settings to discuss weighty questions of right and wrong, but time and again it proves inadequate, or leads to a standoff of one right against another. The problem is not, however, as some contend, with the very notion of rights, or with our strong rights tradition. It is with a new version of rights discourse that has achieved dominance over the past thirty years.

Our current American rights talk is but one dialect in a universal language that has developed during the extraordinary era of attention to civil and human rights in the wake of World War II. It is set apart from rights discourse in other liberal democracies by its starkness and simplicity, its prodigality in bestowing the rights label, its legalistic character, its exaggerated absoluteness, its hyperindividualism, its insularity, and its silence with respect to personal, civic, and collective responsibilities.

This unique brand of rights talk often operates at cross-purposes with our venerable rights tradition. It fits perfectly within the ten-second formats currently preferred by the news media,[3] but severely constricts opportunities for the sort of ongoing dialogue upon which a regime of ordered liberty ultimately depends. A rapidly expanding catalog of rights—extending to trees, animals, smokers, nonsmokers, consumers, and so on—not only multiplies the occasions for collisions, but it risks trivializing core democratic values. A tendency to frame nearly every social controversy in terms of a clash of rights (a woman's right to her own body vs. a fetus's right to life) impedes compromise, mutual understanding, and the discovery of common ground. A penchant for absolute formulations ("I have the right to do whatever I want with my property") promotes unrealistic expectations and ignores both social costs and the rights of others. A near-aphasia concerning responsibilities makes it seem legitimate to accept the benefits of living in a democratic social welfare republic without assuming the corresponding personal and civic obligations.

As various new rights are proclaimed or proposed, the catalog of individual liberties expands without much consideration of the ends to which they are oriented, their relationship to one another, to corresponding responsibilities, or to the general welfare. Converging with the language of psychotherapy, rights talk encourages our all-too-human tendency to place the self at the center of our moral universe. In tandem with consumerism and a normal dislike of inconvenience, it regularly promotes the short-run over the long-term, crisis intervention over preventive measures, and particular interests over the common good. Saturated with rights, political language can no longer perform the important function of facilitating public discussion of the right ordering of our lives together. Just as rights exist for us only through being articulated, other goods are not even available to be considered if they can be brought to expression only with great difficulty, or not at all.[4]

My principal aim in the chapters that follow has been to trace the evolution of our distinctive current rights dialect, and to show how it frequently works against the conditions required for the pursuit of dignified living by free women and men. With stories and examples drawn from disputes over flag-burning, Indian lands, plant closings, criminal penalties for homosexual acts, eminent domain, social welfare, child support, and other areas, I have endeavored to demonstrate how our simplistic rights talk simultaneously reflects and distorts American culture. It captures our devotion to individualism and liberty, but omits our traditions of hospitality and care for the community. In the images of America and Americans that it projects, as well as in the ideals to which it implicitly pays homage, our current rights talk is a verbal caricature of our culture—recognizably ours, but with certain traits wildly out of proportion and with some of our best features omitted.

Our rights-laden political discourse does provide a solution of sorts to the communications problems that beset a heterogeneous nation whose citizens decreasingly share a common history, literature, religion, or customs. But the "solution" has become part of the problem. The legal components of political discourse, like sorcerers' apprentices, have taken on new and mischief-making connotations when liberated from their contexts in the speech community of lawyers. (A person has no duty to come to the aid of a "stranger.") With its nonlegal tributaries rapidly dwindling, political rhetoric has grown increasingly out of touch with the more complex ways of speaking that Americans employ around the kitchen table, in their schools, workplaces, and in their various communities of memory and mutual aid.

Under these circumstances, what is needed is not the abandonment, but the renewal, of our strong rights tradition. But it is not easy to see how we might develop a public language that would be better suited in complexity and moral seriousness to the bewildering array of difficulties that presently face us as a mature democracy in an increasingly interdependent world. Nor is it readily apparent how the public forum, dominated as it is by images rather than ideas, could be reclaimed for genuine political discourse.

We cannot, nor would most of us wish to, import some other country's language of rights. Nor can we invent a new rhetoric of rights out of whole cloth. A political Esperanto without roots in a living cultural tradition would die on the vine. Throughout the book, therefore, I have marshalled evidence that Americans do possess several indigenous languages of relationship and responsibility that could help to refine our language of rights. In many settings, employing a grammar of cooperative living, American women and men sound better and smarter than our current political discourse makes them out to be. The best resource for renewing our political discourse, therefore, may be the very heterogeneity that drives us to seek a simple, abstract, common language. The ongoing dialogue between freedom and responsibility, individualism and community, present needs and future plans, that takes place daily in a wide variety of American speech communities could help to revitalize our rights tradition as well as our political life.

It is only by overcoming our disdain for politics, however, that we can tap the reserves of wisdom, virtue, and imagination that Americans still display in their varied communities of memory and mutual aid. The prospects for such a project are not especially bright. The energy, skill, and goodwill required to bring a new sort of dialogue into the public square through the barriers of sound-bites, mutual distrust, and the gridlock of special interests would be formidable. Furthermore, the seedbeds of civic virtue (as many political theorists refer to families, religious communities, and other primary social groups) are not in peak condition. The skills of citizenship, not to mention those of statesmanship, have begun to atrophy. It is not at all clear that Americans really desire to engage in a potentially self-correcting dialogue about the ends of political society and the right ordering of our lives together, or that public officials are ready to take the lead by providing the necessary information, example, and opportunities for discussion. No mere "science" of politics will overcome these impediments. But politics, as recent events in Eastern Europe remind us, is also an art—the art of the impossible—and we spurn its transformative dimension at our peril.

Acknowledgments

I am especially grateful to the three persons who were most closely associated with me in the writing of this book: to my husband, Edward R. Lev, for his unfailing encouragement, advice, humor, and good judgment; to Raul F. Yanes for his intelligent and resourceful research assistance; and to Wendilea Brown for her professional attention to the preparation of the manuscript.

Many friends and colleagues furnished me with helpful comments on various drafts and provided me with valuable information at crucial stages; in particular: Brigitte Berger, David Blankenhorn, Donald Brand, Amitai Etzioni, Robert K. Faulkner, Thomas C. Kohler, Marc K. Landy, John H. Langbein, William F. Maestri, Martha L. Minow, Jennifer Nedelsky, Mark Osiel, Fred Siegel, Aviam Soifer, Judith Wallerstein, Emmy Werner, James Boyd White, and Alan Wolfe. The manuscript also benefited greatly from the expert editing of Joyce Seltzer of The Free Press.

For giving me the opportunity to present and test ideas about rights in workshops, public lectures, and discussions, I am indebted to Roger L. Conner and the American Alliance for Rights and Responsibilities; Bruce Hafen and Brigham Young University; Jack Hitt and *Harper's* Magazine; Harvey C. Mansfield, Jr., and the Harvard John M. Olin Seminar on Constitutional Government; Richard John Neuhaus and the Institute on Religion and Public Life; Katherine V. Lorio and the Loyola University of New Orleans School of Law; Dean Rudolph C. Hasl and the St. Louis University School of Law; Andrew R. Cecil and the University of Texas at Dallas; Thomas L. Pangle and the University of Toronto; Jean Bethke Elshtain and the Robert Penn Warren Center for the Humanities at Vanderbilt University; and Dean Robert Clark and my colleagues at Harvard Law School.

Present in these pages in important ways are the people who

fostered in me, years ago in Berkshire County, an enduring enthusiasm and affection for local politics: friends, teachers, and relatives in my home town of Dalton, and coworkers at *The Berkshire Eagle* where I was apprenticed during the summers of my high school, college, and law school years. At the *Eagle,* I had the good fortune to come under the tutelage of the remarkable woman to whom this book is dedicated, Leonora Leahy Stanfield. As a young housewife in the 1940s, Lee joined with some of her neighbors in what we would now call grassroots organizing; in 1945 she became, by a landslide, the first woman elected to the Pittsfield City Council; and, when I met her in the mid-1950s, she was the librarian and a general reporter at the *Eagle,* for which she still writes a popular weekly column. The grace and good cheer with which she overcame forbidding obstacles as a pioneer working mother in politics and journalism have inspired me and many others whose lives she has touched. Knowing her has also helped me to appreciate the wide and powerful effects that can radiate outward from the exemplary life of a single human being. When I permit myself to hope that politics can be the art of the impossible, a way of transcending as well as advancing self-interest, I do so with Lee Stanfield and Berkshire County in mind, as much as with Vaclav Havel and Eastern Europe.

ONE

The Land of Rights

And where freedom is, the individual is clearly able to
  order for himself his own life as he pleases?
Clearly.
Then in this kind of state there will be the greatest variety
  of human natures?
There will.
This, then, seems likely to be the fairest of states, being
  like an embroidered robe which is spangled with every
  sort of flower.

—Plato, *The Republic*[1]

Our own ways of thinking and speaking seem so natural to us that very often it is only an empathetic outsider who can enter into our view of the world, and spot a peculiarity in it. Thus it took an aristocratic Frenchman, resolved to make the best of living in a democratic age, to notice that the everyday speech of the Americans he encountered on his travels here in 1831 and 1832 was shot through with legalisms. Tocqueville's ten-month journey took him all over what was then the United States, from Massachusetts to Georgia, from New Orleans to the territory that is now Wisconsin. Wherever he went, he found that lawyers' habits of mind, as well as their modes of discourse, "infiltrate through society right down to the lowest ranks."[2] Foreign observers today are still struck by the degree to which law and lawyers have influenced American ways of life.[3]

Tocqueville attributed the legal cast of common parlance to the fact that in America, unlike in Continental Europe, most public men were lawyers.[4] Though skeptical about the power of the law as such to exert much direct influence on human behavior, he regarded this American penchant as a social phenomenon of the utmost importance. For he believed that legal ideas could, under certain circum-

1

stances, help to shape the interior world of beliefs, attitudes, dreams, and yearnings that are the hidden springs of individual and social action. To be sure, he was in general accord with his great predecessor Rousseau that "the real constitution of the State" is composed "of morality, of custom, above all of public opinion."[5] Rousseau had likened a nation's laws to the arc of an arch, with "manners and morals, slower to arise, form[ing] in the end its immovable keystone."[6] But neither Rousseau nor Tocqueville was inclined to underrate the arc's supporting role. As he listened to the speech of Americans in all walks of life, Tocqueville became convinced that law and lawyers had left an unusually strong imprint on the "manners and morals" of the new nation, and therefore on its unwritten constitution. Not only was legal language "pretty well adopted into common speech," but a legalistic spirit seemed to pervade "the whole of society, penetrating each component class and constantly working in secret upon its unconscious patient, till in the end it has molded it to its desire."[7]

Tocqueville's observations are even more pertinent to contemporary American culture than they were to the small democratic republic of our forebears. Americans today, for better or worse, live in what is undoubtedly one of the most law-ridden societies that has ever existed on the face of the earth. The reach of government and law have extended to a degree that Tocqueville and his contemporaries would have found hard to imagine. The proportion of legally trained individuals among our government officials, and in the population at large, moreover, is higher than ever. A great communications and entertainment industry now reports on and dramatizes their doings. We are surrounded by images of law and lawyers.

In addition, middle-class Americans are apt to have many more firsthand contacts with the legal system than did their ancestors. In an earlier day, anyone who was not wealthy, and was able to abstain from violence, had a good chance of living his or her whole life without seeing the inside of a law office or a courtroom. By the middle of the twentieth century, however, Americans commonly had brief dealings with lawyers as they purchased or sold homes, made wills, or settled estates. At the same time, eligibility expanded for jury service, an experience which rarely fails to leave a deep impression even on those who initially view it as a nuisance. When divorce became a mass phenomenon, multitudes of men and women had their own "day in court" of sorts, either as parties or witnesses.

In the phrase of legal historian Lawrence Friedman, life in modern America has become "a vast, diffuse school of law."[8]

This "legalization" of popular culture is both cause and consequence of our increasing tendency to look to law as an expression and carrier of the few values that are widely shared in our society: liberty, equality, and the ideal of justice under law. With increasing heterogeneity, it has become quite difficult to convincingly articulate common values by reference to a shared history, religion, or cultural tradition. The language we have developed for public use in our large, multicultural society is thus even more legalistic than the one Tocqueville heard, and it draws to a lesser degree on other cultural resources. Few American statesmen today are—as Abraham Lincoln was—equally at home with the Bible and Blackstone. Political figures now resort primarily to legal ideas and traditions when they seek to persuade, inspire, explain, or justify in public settings. Legality, to a great extent, has become a touchstone for legitimacy. As a result, certain areas of law, especially constitutional, criminal, and family law, have become the terrain on which Americans are struggling to define what kind of people they are, and what kind of society they wish to bring into being. Legal discourse has not only become the single most important tributary to political discourse, but it has crept into the languages that Americans employ around the kitchen table, in the neighborhood, and in their diverse communities of memory and mutual aid.

The law talk that percolates through American society today, however, is far removed from nineteenth-century versions. For one thing, it has been through the fiery furnace of critical theory, from Oliver Wendell Holmes Jr.'s insistence on strict analytical separation between law and morality, to the "realist" fact-skeptics and rule-skeptics of the 1930s, to their latter-day epigones of the right and left. Secondly, though the legal profession still contains many more planners and preventers than litigators, it is the assertiveness of the latter rather than the reserve of the former that migrates most readily through the media into the broader culture. Finally, law-talk in Tocqueville's day was not nearly so saturated with rights talk as it has been since the end of World War II. In short, legal speech today is a good deal more morally neutral, adversarial, and rights-oriented than it was in 1831.

There is no more telling indicator of the extent to which legal notions have penetrated both popular and political discourse than our increasing tendency to speak of what is most important to us in terms of rights, and to frame nearly every social controversy as a clash of rights. Yet, for most of our history, political discourse was not so liberally salted with rights talk as it is today, nor was rights discourse so legalistic. The high season of rights came upon the land only rather recently, propelled by, and itself promoting, a gradual evolution in the role of the courts.

The marked increase in the assertion of rights-based claims, beginning with the civil rights movement of the 1950s and 1960s, and the parallel increase in recognition of those claims in the courts, are sometimes described as a rights revolution. If there is any justification for using the overworked word "revolution" in connection with these developments, it is not that they have eliminated the ills at which they were aimed. Indeed, the progress that has been made, substantial as it is, serves also to heighten our awareness of how deep, stubborn, and complex are the nation's problems of social justice. What do seem revolutionary about the rights-related developments of the past three decades are the transformations they have produced in the roles of courts and judges, and in the way we now think and speak about major public issues.

At least until the 1950s, the principal focus of constitutional law was not on personal liberty as such, but on the division of authority between the states and the federal government, and the allocation of powers among the branches of the central government. In keeping with Hamilton's observation in *Federalist* No. 84 that "the Constitution is itself, in every rational sense, and to every useful purpose, A BILL OF RIGHTS," the theory was that individual freedom was protected mainly through these structural features of our political regime. The Supreme Court saw far fewer cases involving free speech, association, religion, and the rights of criminal defendants than it does now, not only because such issues were less frequently litigated, but because, until relatively recent times, many important provisions of the Bill of Rights were thought to apply only to the federal government. Gradually, however, the Supreme Court developed its "incorporation" doctrine, through which more and more of the rights guaranteed by the first eight amendments to the Federal Constitution were declared to have been made binding on the states (incorporated) by the Fourteenth Amendment. This process accelerated in the 1960s when the Warren Court vigorously began to exercise the power of judicial review as a means of protecting individual rights from interference by state as well as federal governments.[9] Today the bulk of the Court's constitutional work involves claims that individual rights have been violated.[10] In the 1980s, even though a majority of justices on the United States Supreme Court began to adopt a slightly more deferential attitude toward the elected branches of government, the rights revolution continued, as many state supreme courts began interpreting state constitutions to confer more rights on individuals.[11]

The trendsetters of the legal academic world were quick to recognize the burgeoning of individual rights as the central legal drama of the times. The top legal minds of the New Deal era had been virtuosos of legislation and administrative law; specialists in taxation, antitrust, and labor; architects and engineers of the regulatory state and the new federalism. With the civil rights generation, however, legal attention shifted to the courts. The study and teaching of constitutional law gained in excitement and prestige. Older constitutional law professors who had given pride of place to federal-state relations and the commerce clause were succeeded by men and a few women who focussed on advancing equality and personal liberty by means of rights. To a great extent, the intellectual framework and the professional ethos of the entire current population of American lawyers have been infused with the romance of rights. In legal education, an intense preoccupation with the Bill of Rights and the courts tends to obscure the important roles that federalism, legislation, and the separation of powers still can and must play in safeguarding rights and freedom. The rights revolution has contributed in its own way to the atrophy of vital local governments and political parties, and to the disdain for politics that is now so prevalent in the American scene.

Unlike the New Dealers (who resembled the Founders in their attention to the overall design of government and to the functions and relations among its specialized organs), many bright, ambitious public lawyers of the 1960s had a narrower and less organic view of law, government, and society. They saw the judiciary as the first line of defense against all injustice, and came to regard the test case as preferable to ordinary politics. To no small degree, this shift of the energy and interests of public-law lawyers from legislation and regulation to adjudication reflected growing sensitivity to the obvious and persistent racism of many local laws, institutions, and practices. Encounters with corrupt and prejudiced officials had soured many activists and intellectuals of the civil rights era on legislatures and local governments, while their faith in the judiciary was strength-

ened by a series of bold Supreme Court rulings that seemed to wipe
out ancient wrongs with a stroke of the pen. Landmark cases in
the criminal-law area, and above all, the Court's celebrated 1954
desegregation decision in *Brown v. Board of Education*,[12] shone like
beacons, lighting the way toward an America whose ideals of equal
justice and opportunity for all would at last be realized. Many hope-
ful men and women came to believe that the high road to a better
society would be paved with court decisions—federal court decisions. At the elbow, so to speak, of wise Supreme Court justices,
would be renowned social scientists, lawyers armed with theories
generated in the best law schools, and teams of young law clerks,
fresh from the classroom and bearing the very latest word on constitutional law. The civil rights movement thus did not exploit as
fully as it might have the opportunities opened up by its voter reg-
istration drives and by the historic one-person, one-vote decisions of
the Supreme Court.[13]

Our justifiable pride and excitement at the great boost given to
racial justice by the moral authority of the unanimous Supreme Court
decision in *Brown* seems, in retrospect, to have led us to expect too
much from the Court where a wide variety of other social ills were
concerned. Correspondingly, it seems to have induced us to under-
value the kind of progress represented by an equally momentous
social achievement: the Civil Rights Act of 1964. The time-honored
understanding that difficult and controversial issues should be decided by the people through their elected representatives, except
where constitutional text and tradition clearly indicated otherwise,
began to fray at the edges. A text, it became fashionable to say in the
1970s, has no determinate meaning, and tradition is as likely to be
oppressive as nourishing. To many activists, it seemed more efficient, as well as more rewarding, to devote one's time and efforts to
litigation that could yield total victory, than to put in long hours at
political organizing, where the most one can hope to gain is, typically, a compromise. As the party system gradually fell prey to large,
highly organized, and well-financed interest groups, regular politics
came to seem futile as well as boring, socially unproductive as well
as personally unfulfilling.

Gradually, the courts removed a variety of issues from legislative
and local control and accorded broad new scope to many constitutional rights related to personal liberty. Most dramatic of all, perhaps, from the average citizen's point of view, was the active role
that lower federal court judges assumed in many parts of the coun-

try, using their remedial powers to oversee the everyday operations of prisons, hospitals, and school systems. Court majorities with an expansive view of the judicial role, and their academic admirers, propelled each other, like railwaymen on a handcar, along the line that led to the land of rights. The example of the civil rights movement inspired many other victims of injustice to get on board. In the 1970s, the concerns of women crystallized around the idea of equal rights. Soon, persons and organizations devoted to social and related causes—such as preventing the abuse and neglect of children, improving the treatment of the mentally and physically disabled, eliminating discrimination based on life-style, protecting consumers from sharp practices, preventing cruelty to animals, and safeguarding the environment—began to articulate their concerns in terms of rights.

As we have reconceptualized increasing numbers and types of issues in terms of entitlements, a new form of rights talk has gradually come into being. This change in our habits of thought and speech is a social phenomenon of equal importance to the legal developments whose course it has paralleled. The significance of this aspect of the rights revolution comes into even sharper focus when one takes a comparative perspective.

In the years since the end of World War II, rights discourse has spread throughout the world. At the transnational level, human rights were enshrined in a variety of covenants and declarations, notably the United Nations' Universal Declaration of Human Rights of 1948.[14] At the same time, enumerated rights, backed up by some form of judicial review, were added to several national constitutions. (Great Britain, with neither judicial review nor a single-document constitution, became something of an anomaly in this respect.) Nor was the rush to rights confined to "liberal" or "democratic" societies. American rights talk is now but one dialect in a universal language of rights. The American version of rights talk, however, displays several unusual features. Intriguing differences have emerged between the formulations of rights in American contexts and the ways in which rights are proclaimed and discussed in many other liberal democracies.

We do not, of course, normally think of our own way of speaking as a dialect. But American rights talk does possess certain distinctive characteristics that appear both in our official declarations and in our ordinary speech. As an initial example of the latter, consider the lively discussions that took place in the wake of the Supreme Court's first controversial flag-burning decision in June

1989.[15] On the day after the Court ruled that burning the American
flag was a form of expression protected by the First Amendment to
the Constitution, the *Today* show invited a spokesman for the American Legion to explain his organization's discontent with that decision. Jane Pauley asked her guest what the flag meant to the nation's
veterans. He gave a standard reply: "The flag is the symbol of our
country, the land of the free and the home of the brave." Jane was
not satisfied. "What exactly does it symbolize?" she wanted to know.
The legionnaire seemed exasperated in the way people sometimes get
when they feel there are certain things that should not have to be
explained. The answer he came up with was, "It stands for the fact
that this is a country where we have the right to do what we want."
Of course he could not really have meant to espouse a principle that
would have sanctioned the very act he despised. Given time for
thought, he almost certainly would not have expressed himself in
that way. His spontaneous response, however, illustrates our tendency, when we grope in public settings for the words to express
strong feelings about political issues, to resort to the language of
rights.

Later that same day, a man interviewed on National Public Radio
offered a defense of flag-burning. He said, "The way I see it, I buy
a flag. It's my property. So I have a right to do anything I want with
it." Let us put aside the fact that the flag involved in the case happened to be a stolen one. What is striking about this man's rights talk
is that, like the outburst of the legionnaire, it was couched in absolute
terms. In neither case was the choice of words idiosyncratic. How
often, in daily speech, do all of us make and hear claims that whatever right is under discussion at the moment trumps every other
consideration?

When roused to speak out about issues of great importance, we
often find ourselves repeating the experience of the righteously in-
dignant legionnaire. We are apt to begin, as he did, by speaking from
the heart, choosing some formula that carries a rich train of associations for us personally and for like-minded people. When our spontaneous efforts are challenged, or meet with real or feigned
incomprehension on the part of a listener, we often find that words
temporarily fail us. Like the legionnaire when ordered to "unpack"
the symbol by a television interviewer, we may be temporarily
tongue-tied. On such occasions, we often begin to speak about
rights, and to do so in a distinctive manner that I have called the
American rights dialect. This dialect, whose features are illustrated in

more detail in the chapters that follow, is pervasive. When People for the American Way asked a thousand young Americans what makes America special, most of them quite properly mentioned our famous rights and freedoms.[16] One after another, however, the young men and women expressed themselves in the same language that came so easily to the legionnaire. One said that America's uniqueness lay in "individualism, and the fact that it is a democracy and you can do whatever you want." Another said: "Our freedom to do as we please, when we please." Another: "That we really don't have any limits." And so on.[17]

Yet a moment's reflection tells us that these extravagant beliefs and claims cannot possibly be true. We have criminal laws that put rather decisive limits on our ability to do anything we want. Thus the Supreme Court in the flag case was careful to point out that the First Amendment does not protect verbal incitement to immediate breach of the public peace. As for property, our ownership rights are limited by the rights of our neighbors, by zoning laws, by environmental protection measures, and by countless other administrative rules and regulations. The property-rights enthusiast on public radio probably does not even have the right to burn dead leaves in his own back yard. To speak in this careless fashion is not without consequences; in fact, it sets us up to fail twice over—first, by cheapening or betraying our own meaning (The flag "stands for the fact that this is a country where we have the right to do what we want"), and second, by foreclosing further communication with those whose points of view differ from our own. For, in its simple American form, the language of rights is the language of no compromise. The winner takes all and the loser has to get out of town. The conversation is over.

Plato in *The Republic* made the idea of a state where everyone is free to say and do what he wants sound highly attractive—a "city full of freedom and frankness," with an amazing profusion of life-styles.[18] But as Socrates disingenuously extols the delights of absolute freedom, his interlocutor, Adeimantus, grows uneasy. In such a city, one would not have to participate in government, or even to be subject to government—unless one wished. One would not need to go to war when others did, or even to keep the peace—unless one was so disposed. The "humanity" of such cities, Socrates continues, is "quite charming"—just look at all the persons sentenced to death or exile who are permitted to walk about the streets. And see how indulgent the citizens are toward the character defects of public men—so long as such men profess to be friends of the people.

Plato's image of the city where license reigns supreme makes a
strong initial appeal to that part of us that delights in freedom and
variety. "Just as women and children think an assortment of colors
to be of all things most charming, so there are many men to whom
this state, which is spangled with the manners and characters of
mankind, will appear to be the fairest of states," Socrates observes.
But as its implications unfold, we and Adeimantus begin to suspect
that this sort of freedom may lead straight to the eclipse of anything
we would recognize as meaningful liberty.

Some listeners to American rights talk might reach the conclusion that Americans have nothing in common with those ancient
Greeks who claimed that moderation, balance, and limits were what
distinguished their civilization from the peoples they called barbar-
ians. Others, noting that the Greeks are reputed to have honored
their own ideals quite frequently in the breach, might say that we are
simply less hypocritical. Much that passes for normative in the media, the universities, and the entertainment industry suggests that
modern Americans have rejected many traditional social constraints
in principle and thrown them off in fact. But the total picture is a
good deal more complex. Most American parents, to cite an obvious
instance, remain deeply concerned with setting limits and helping
their children achieve self-control. To some extent, families are aided
in these efforts by the various communities in which they participate.
It seems likely, too, that most Americans agree in principle that our
regime is an experiment in *"ordered* liberty" (in Justice Cardozo's
locution)[19]—though they may not agree on the relative scope to be
given to the two components of that ambiguous concept. Why then
does our public rhetoric so regularly gloss over the essential interplay
between rights and responsibilities, independence and self-discipline,
freedom and order?

The distinctive traits of our American rights dialect can be discerned at both of the great "moments" in the history of human
rights. The first of these moments was marked by the late eighteenth-
century American and French revolutionary declarations, and the
second by the wave of constitution-making and the international
human rights movement that emerged in the wake of World War II.
The language that evolved to promote and implement the rights
proclaimed at those crucial junctures partakes everywhere of certain
common characteristics, but everywhere has its own local accent.
The common features are well-known. From the treatises of
seventeenth- and eighteenth-century philosophers, the ideas of nat-

ural right and equality gave shape, momentum, and a definite direction to scattered and diffuse social forces. They spoke to as yet unnamed longings; they awakened sleeping hopes, fired imaginations, and changed the world.[20] The eighteenth-century "rights of man," like modern "human rights," all mark a stand against the abuse and arbitrary exercise of power. They are landmarks in the recognition of the dignity of the individual human person and of our potential to be free and self-determining. These common characteristics, together with the contemporary thrust toward the internationalization and "universalization" of human rights, give to rights discourse everywhere a superficial appearance of unity. The path of the United States diverged somewhat from those of most other Atlantic-European nations, however, at each of these great watersheds in the history of rights.[21] The parting of the ways was already evident in 1789 when the French *Declaration of the Rights of Man and the Citizen,* in contrast to the *Declaration of Independence,* emphasized that individuals have duties as well as rights.[22]

In the years since the end of World War II, "rights" have entered importantly into the cultural schemes of meaning of peoples everywhere. But rights were imagined differently from one place to another. And even slight divergences in such matters are of potentially great interest, for the world of meanings is where we human beings spend most of our lives, "suspended in webs of significance" that we ourselves have spun.[23] The way we name things and discuss them shapes our feelings, judgments, choices, and actions, including political actions. History has repeatedly driven home the lesson that it is unwise to dismiss political language as "mere rhetoric." When Vaclav Havel in 1989 gained a platform from which to address the world, he chose to deliver one of his first major speeches on "the mysterious power of words in human history."[24] The Czech president's message was a somber one, for his purpose was to remind us that while exhilarating words like "human rights" recently have electrified society "with their freedom and truthfulness," one need not look far back into the past to find words and phrases whose effects were as deadly as they were hypnotic. Most sobering of all, said Havel, the very same words that can at some times be "rays of light," may turn under other circumstances into "lethal arrows."

It thus seems worthwhile—as well as interesting—to try to identify those characteristics that make our version of rights talk a special dialect; to explore the differences in shades of meaning between our own and other forms of rights discourse; and to probe the discrep-

ancies as well as the similarities between our public rights talk and
the ways we speak at home, at work, in the neighborhood, and in the
church or mosque or temple. The contrast with other countries is not
a dramatic one, but rather a matter of degree and emphasis. American rights talk is set apart by the way that rights, in our standard
formulations, tend to be presented as absolute, individual, and independent of any necessary relation to responsibilities. The simplicity
and assertiveness of our version of the discourse of rights are more
noticeable when viewed in the light of the continuing dialogue about
freedom and responsibility that is taking place in several other liberal
democracies.

All over the world, political discourse is increasingly imbued
with the language of rights, universal, inalienable, inviolable. Yet,
subtle variations in the way rights ideas are presented can have broad
and far-reaching implications that penetrate nearly every corner of
the societies involved. Take, for example, the way a country depicts
itself to new citizens in naturalization proceedings. When my adopted
Korean daughter, Sarah, became an American citizen, our country's
official national symbolism was on prominent display at her naturalization ceremony. That day, Sarah and several hundred other immigrants heard a solemn recital in Boston's famed Faneuil Hall of all
the rights and freedoms that would henceforth be theirs. As a sou-
venir of the occasion, she was given a red-white-and-blue pamphlet
in which the Commissioner of Immigration and Naturalization explained "The Meaning of American Citizenship:"

> This citizenship, which has been solemnly conferred on you, is a thing
> of the spirit—not of the flesh. When you took the oath of allegiance to
> the Constitution of the United States, you claimed for yourself the
> God-given unalienable rights which that sacred document sets forth as
> the natural right of all men.[25]

Rights dominate the notion of citizenship from the top to the bottom
of the American system, from the literature distributed at federal
buildings throughout the country to the pronouncements of the
United States Supreme Court (which once referred to citizenship as
"the right to have rights").[26]

Our close neighbor, Canada, presents quite a different face to its
new citizens. To be sure, Canadian citizenship literature, and Citizenship Court judges, prominently mention rights, but they lay still
greater stress on the importance of participation in the political life of

a multicultural society.[27] The great writer on cities, Jane Jacobs, delights in telling how, when she became a citizen of Canada, she was instructed by the judge that the most important thing about being a Canadian is learning to get along well with one's neighbors. Just talk? Perhaps. But it is the kind of talk we do not easily forget. Words spoken in a formal setting, on a day marking an important change of status, carry a special charge. Like the words of the marriage ritual, they etch themselves on our memories.

Formal proclamations of fundamental rights, too, have a different flavor from country to country. Without falling into the error of equating official statements of aspirations with representations of reality, one learns what the drafters of such documents deemed important, and what ideals have become part of the state-sponsored folklore. Try, for example, to find in the familiar language of our Declaration of Independence or Bill of Rights anything comparable to the statements in the Universal Declaration of Human Rights that "Everyone has duties to the community," and that everyone's rights and freedoms are subject to limitations "for the purposes of securing due recognition and respect for the rights and freedoms of others and of meeting the just requirements of morality, public order and the general welfare in a democratic society."[28]

These differing official pronouncements do not spring from nowhere. The language of the United Nations Declaration is a melding of the Anglo-American rights tradition with the more nuanced dialect of rights and responsibility associated with the Romano-Germanic legal traditions. These traditions in turn are informed by a somewhat different amalgam of Enlightenment political philosophy from that which inspired the American founders. It made a considerable difference, for example, that natural rights theories were elaborated for us principally by Hobbes and Locke, without the glosses added within the continental tradition by Rousseau and Kant.

To be sure, ideas that are absent from the text of our foundational documents can be, and often are, supplied by interpretation in court decisions. Thus, American lawyers know that, from the very beginning, the United States Supreme Court has acknowledged implicit limits on our constitutional rights and has imposed obligations on citizens to respect each other's rights. Jurists are also well aware that ordinary private law—contracts, torts, domestic relations—is replete with reciprocal duties. Nevertheless, it is the language emblazoned on our monumental public documents, far more than the numerous limitations buried in the text of individual court decisions, that lodges in the collective memory, permeates popular discourse, and enters into American habits of mind.

The most distinctive features of our American rights dialect are the very ones that are most conspicuously in tension with what we require in order to give a reasonably full and coherent account of what kind of society we are and what kind of polity we are trying to create: its penchant for absolute, extravagant formulations, its near-aphasia concerning responsibility, its excessive homage to individual independence and self-sufficiency, its habitual concentration on the individual and the state at the expense of the intermediate groups of civil society, and its unapologetic insularity. Not only does each of these traits make it difficult to give voice to common sense or moral intuitions, they also impede development of the sort of rational political discourse that is appropriate to the needs of a mature, complex, liberal, pluralistic republic.

Our rights talk, in its absoluteness, promotes unrealistic expectations, heightens social conflict, and inhibits dialogue that might lead toward consensus, accommodation, or at least the discovery of common ground. In its silence concerning responsibilities, it seems to condone acceptance of the benefits of living in a democratic social welfare state, without accepting the corresponding personal and civic obligations. In its relentless individualism, it fosters a climate that is inhospitable to society's losers, and that systematically disadvantages caretakers and dependents, young and old. In its neglect of civil society, it undermines the principal seedbeds of civic and personal virtue. In its insularity, it shuts out potentially important aids to the process of self-correcting learning. All of these traits promote mere assertion over reason-giving.

For a heterogeneous country committed to an ongoing experiment in ordered liberty, these are grave matters. Obstacles to expression and communication can hobble a collective enterprise which depends heavily upon continuing public deliberation. Our rights talk is like a book of words and phrases without a grammar and syntax. Various rights are proclaimed or proposed. The catalog of individual liberties expands, without much consideration of the ends to which they are oriented, their relationship to one another, to corresponding responsibilities, or to the general welfare. Lacking a grammar of cooperative living, we are like a traveler who can say a few words to get a meal and a room in a foreign city, but cannot converse with its inhabitants.

Our communicative deficiency is more serious than a mere traveler's, however, for it seals us off from our fellow citizens. By indulging in excessively simple forms of rights talk in our pluralistic society, we needlessly multiply occasions for civil discord. We make it difficult for persons and groups with conflicting interests and views to build coalitions and achieve compromise, or even to acquire that minimal degree of mutual forbearance and understanding that promotes peaceful coexistence and keeps the door open to further communication. Our simplistic rights talk regularly promotes the short-run over the long-term, sporadic crisis intervention over systemic preventive measures, and particular interests over the common good. It is just not up to the job of dealing with the types of problems that presently confront liberal, pluralistic, modern societies. Even worse, it risks undermining the very conditions necessary for preservation of the principal value it thrusts to the foreground: personal freedom. By infiltrating the more carefully nuanced languages that many Americans still speak in their kitchens, neighborhoods, workplaces, religious communities, and union halls, it corrodes the fabric of beliefs, attitudes, and habits upon which life, liberty, property, and all other individual and social goods ultimately depend.

Yet this need not be so. There are several indications that our rights-dominated public language does not do justice to the capacity for reason or the richness and diversity of moral sentiments that exist in American society. If this is the case, we could begin to refine our rhetoric of rights by recognizing and drawing on our own indigenous resources. A refined rhetoric of rights would promote public conversation about the ends towards which our political life is directed. It would keep competing rights and responsibilities in view, helping to assure that none would achieve undue prominence and that none would be unduly obscured. It would not lend itself to the notion that freedom is being able to do anything you want.

The critique of the American rights dialect presented here rejects the radical attack on the very notion of rights that is sometimes heard on both ends of the political spectrum. It is not an assault on specific rights or on the idea of rights in general, but a plea for reevaluation of certain thoughtless, habitual ways of thinking and speaking about rights. Let us freely grant that legally enforceable rights can assist citizens in a large heterogeneous country to live together in a reasonably peaceful way. They have given minorities a way to articulate claims that majorities often respect, and have assisted the weakest members of society in making their voices heard. The paradigms of civil rights at home and universal human rights around the world undoubtedly have helped to bring to light, and to marshal opinion against, oppression and atrocities. We Americans justifiably take a great sense of pride in our particular tradition of political liberty. Many of us harbor, too, a patriotic conviction that, where freedom is concerned, the United States was there first with the best and the most. From there, however, it is but a step to the more dubious proposition that our current strong, simple version of rights is the fulfillment of our destiny toward freedom, or to the still more questionable notions that, if rights are good, more rights must be even better, and the more emphatically they are stated, the less likely it is that they will be watered down or taken away.

In a reflective mood, even the most ardent rights enthusiast must concede some substance to the persistent critiques from right and left[29] that trace their origins, respectively, to Edmund Burke's concern about the social costs of rights,[30] and Karl Marx's dismissal of rights as mostly smoke and mirrors.[31] The prevailing consensus about the goodness of rights, widespread though it may be, is thin and brittle. In truth, there is very little agreement regarding *which* needs, goods, interests, or values should be characterized as "rights," or concerning what should be done when, as is usually the case, various rights are in tension or collision with one another. Occasions for conflict among rights multiply as catalogs of rights grow longer. If some rights are more important than others, and if a rather small group of rights is of especially high importance, then an ever-expanding list of rights may well trivialize this essential core without materially advancing the proliferating causes that have been reconceptualized as involving rights. Can it really be the case, as an article in *The New Republic* suggested in 1990, that "so long as I eat tuna fish and support the use of primates in AIDS research," my endorsement of the idea of human rights is rendered problematic?[32] At some point one must ask whether an undifferentiated language of rights is really the best way to address the astonishing variety of injustices and forms of suffering that exist in the world.

On the bicentennial of our Bill of Rights, Americans are struggling to order their lives together in a multicultural society whose population has grown from fewer than four million in 1791 to over 250 million men, women, and children. No longer "kindly separated" (as Jefferson put it) "by nature and a wide ocean" from much of the world,[33] we are now acutely conscious that we spin through time and space on a fragile planet where friend and foe alike are locked in ever-tighter webs of interdependence. Creative, timely, and effective responses to the social and environmental challenges presently facing us will not easily emerge from habits of thought and discourse that are as individualistic, rights-centered, and insular as those now current in the United States. Until recently, we have stood in this respect at the opposite pole from the Soviet Union and the countries that were within its political sphere of influence. In those nations, political discourse was long characterized by excessively strong and simple duty talk. Civic responsibilities and the general welfare were officially exalted at the expense of rights, the individual, and particular communities. Now, however, in one of the most remarkable political upheavals in history, public discourse in those countries has begun to correct for exaggerated and impoverished notions of duty and community. The discourse of rights and the idea of civil society have become important elements of experiments in democratic socialism and social democracy. The doors and windows of the East are opening to winds bearing seeds of change from all directions.

No one knows how these processes will play out in the new Europe. One thing is certain, however. As Paul wrote to the Corinthians, the world as we know it is continually passing away. The question for Americans therefore is not whether our own rights tradition will change, but what it will become. Like Moses, who never entered the promised land, but glimpsed it from afar, our Founding Fathers had a vision of an America where all citizens were endowed with certain inalienable rights, but they lived in a country where this vision was only partially realized. In recent years, we have made great progress in making the promise of rights a reality, but in doing so we have neglected another part of our inheritance—the vision of a republic where citizens actively take responsibility for maintaining a vital political life. The rights tradition we have constructed on the foundation laid by those who have gone before us has served the nation well in many ways. From what springs of meaning can it be nourished and renewed?

TWO

The Illusion of Absoluteness

The third absolute right, [after life and liberty] inherent
in every Englishman, is that of property: which
consists in the free use, enjoyment and disposal of all
his acquisitions, without any control or diminution,
save only by the laws of the land. . . . So great
moreover is the regard of the law for private property
that it will not authorize the least violation of it; no,
not even for the general good of the whole community.
—William Blackstone, *Commentaries on the Laws of England*[1]

A man's home is his castle. That maxim, traditionally attributed to Sir Edward Coke, was the defense offered by Marvin
Sokolow, when he was hauled into a Queens County court by his
landlord after his downstairs neighbors complained that their peace
and quiet were being destroyed by the Sokolow children, ages two
and four. The landlord sought to evict the Sokolows on the basis of
a clause in their lease providing that no tenant shall make, or permit
any members of his family to make, "disturbing noises," or otherwise
interfere with the "rights, comforts or convenience of other tenants."
Trial Judge Daniel Fitzpatrick went right to the heart of the matter.
"The difficulty of the situation here," he said, "is that Mr. Sokolow's
castle is directly above the castle of Mr. Levin."[2] The judge sympa-
thized with the Levins, a middle-aged working couple who cherished
a quiet evening at home after a grueling day in Manhattan. He was
understanding about the Sokolows' predicament as well. The judge
opined that "children and noise have been inseparable from a time
whence the mind of man runneth not to the contrary." He took a dim
view, however, of Mr. Sokolow's claim that "This is my home, and
no one can tell me what to do in my own home." The judge pointed
out the obvious fact that modern apartment house living brings us into

18

a kind of "auditory intimacy" with our neighbors. Apartment dwellers in urban America are in a different relation with each other than lords and ladies living in an age "when castles were remote, separated by broad moors, and when an intruder had to force moat and wall to make his presence felt within," said the judge.

Though he rejected the notion that Mr. Sokolow had the right to do anything he wanted in his home, the judge did not accept the equally extreme position of the landlord and the Levins that, under the lease, *any* disturbing noise provided grounds for throwing a family out of their apartment. Neither the property interest claimed by the tenant nor the contract language relied on by the landlord could be treated as giving rise to absolute rights. Both were subject to evaluation in the light of reason, and in that light the judge found that the noise made by the Sokolows was neither excessive nor deliberate. Noting that the Christmas season was approaching ("a time for peace on earth to men of good will"), Judge Fitzpatrick announced his solution to the problem: "They are all nice people and a little mutual forbearance and understanding of each other's problems should resolve the issues to everyone's satisfaction."

Nice people all over the United States, like Mr. Sokolow and his neighbors, often deploy the rhetoric of rights as though they and their particular interests trumped everything else in sight. Most of us can recognize ourselves at times in the young people interviewed by People for the American Way who said that freedom means there really are no limits. So far as property is concerned, few of us have not maintained at one time or another that, "It's mine and I can do what I want with it"—whether the "it" be a flag, a back yard, or our own bodies. If a neighbor complains about our stereo, our noisy party, or our late-night piano practicing, our automatic reaction is apt to be that we have a right to do as we please in our own homes. When Boston University sought to placate its neighbors by attempting to regulate parties held by its students living in off-campus apartments, many students angrily resisted. Students interviewed by *The Boston Globe* asserted that persons who did not like late night noise should not have chosen to rent in a university area.

In these sorts of situations, like Mr. Sokolow, we often try to clinch the argument by appealing to the ancient property rights of Englishmen, and by invoking these rights in the strongest possible way. Yet this careless manner of speaking cannot be blamed on our English legal inheritance, or even on the American frontier mentality. Neither in England, nor even in Canada (where conditions historically were more similar to ours) is the idea of property or the discourse of rights so extravagant. Indeed, a prominent officially sponsored value in Canada is learning to get along with others in a multicultural society—a society which in many ways resembles a large multiple dwelling, with all the stresses and strains that living in such close quarters implies.

The exaggerated absoluteness of our American rights dialect is all the more remarkable when we consider how little relation it bears to reality. There is a striking discrepancy, as the *Sokolow* case illustrates, between our tendency to state rights in a stark unlimited fashion and the common sense restrictions that have to be placed on one person's rights when they collide with those of another person. On any given day, in courtrooms all over the nation, at all seasons of the year, when harried judges handle garden-variety disputes, they use a chastened, domesticated, concept of rights. Landlords' contract rights do not extend to evicting tenants for any disturbing noise; but tenants cannot make as much noise as they wish in the enclosed space that belongs to them.

Property, historically the paradigmatic right for England and the United States, has always been subject to reasonable regulation, despite the excited rhetoric that often attends its assertion. Blackstone tells us in the epigraph above that the law's regard for property is "so great . . . that it will not authorize the least violation of it; no, not even for the general good of the whole community." But Blackstone himself had just defined this "absolute" right as one which cannot be controlled or diminished "save only by the laws of the land." In a country (like England) with legislative supremacy, a whole regiment could march through this saving clause. In the United States as well, common-sense limitations on all sorts of individual rights have long been accepted in law and practice. How, then, can we explain the persistence of absoluteness in our property rhetoric, and in our rights rhetoric in general? To find the beginnings of an answer, we must go back to the first great "moment" in the history of rights, when property became the template from which other American rights were cut.

THE PROPERTY PARADIGM

The American property saga starts with John Locke—not with Locke the philosopher or Locke the political theorist, but with Locke the story-teller. Property acquired its near-mythic status in our legal tradition, in part, because the language and images of John Locke played such a key role in American thinking about government. The centerpiece of Locke's *Second Treatise of Government* was the chapter on property where he presented his famous account of the origin of individual ownership in an imaginary "state of nature."[3] Like the story of Adam and Eve, Locke's fable is set in a time and place when the good things of the earth were available in abundance: "all the World was America." In the beginning, said Locke, God gave the world to men in common. In the "state of nature," no one originally had dominion over the plants, animals, and land to the exclusion of others. Yet even then, Locke asserted, there was property—for "every Man has a Property in his own Person," and in the "Labour of his Body, and the Work of his Hands." When a man "mixed" his labor with something by removing it from its natural state, Locke argued, he thereby made that acorn, or apple, or fish, or deer, his property—"at least where there is enough, and as good left in common for others." The same was true, Locke said, for appropriation of land by tilling, planting, and cultivating.

Locke did not give any supporting reasons for his fateful decision to characterize one's interest in one's own person in terms of ownership. He seems to have expected his readers to accept without question that proprietorship of one's body was a God-given right, as natural as breathing. That this proposition is less self-evident than Locke maintained, however, is apparent from the fact that continental Europeans find the notion startling, accustomed as they are to another idea, fundamental to their legal systems, that a human body is not subject to ownership by anyone.[4] But the Lockean terminology still echoes in American speech. After his "demonstration" that individual property rights were anterior to government, Locke went on to his next proposition, namely, that the essential reason human beings submit to government is to safeguard their "property." In a move that was to have great significance for Americans, he announced that he would use the word "property" to designate, collectively, "Lives, Liberties, and Estates."[5] According to Locke, the preservation of property, in this capacious sense, is "the great and *chief end*" for which men come together into commonwealths.[6]

No political philosopher of the continental branch of the Enlightenment accorded such a high place to property. Indeed, as Rousseau imagined human beings in the "state of nature," they had "neither houses, nor huts, nor any kind of property whatever."[7] But it is important to remember that Locke, in the *Second Treatise,* was engaged in no mere abstract philosophical exercise. His aim was less to propound a rigorous theoretical treatment of the origins of government than it was to marshal persuasive arguments to legitimate the transition from unfettered royal power to constitutional monarchy. The *Second Treatise* is in many ways more like a lawyer's brief than a learned tract, though it is not always read that way. As an advocate, Locke knew the case against the divine right of kings would be strengthened if he could persuasively establish that there are natural rights that exist prior to and independent of the sovereign state. In the agrarian society of seventeenth-century England, property was the most appealing candidate for such a right. Locke's inspired choice of property as *the* prototypical natural right served simultaneously to delegitimate the monarchy as it then existed, and to buttress the political power of both the landed gentry and the rising merchant classes. Property was the linchpin in his foundations for government based on consent. Once the goal of parliamentary supremacy was established in England, the Lockean property story faded into the background there. Property rights continued to be subject to significant limitation by custom and positive law. This has also been the case in Canada and other countries whose political systems were patterned on the English model.

In the United States, for a variety of reasons, Locke's ideas about property fell on different soil, and his tale of property in the state of nature was interpreted more literally than he probably meant it to be. His property theory entered, with other elements, into a distinctively American property story. The philosopher's influence in this respect was mediated and reinforced by that of a renowned English jurist, William Blackstone, whose lectures on law were much more widely read and consulted in the United States than in his native country.

Blackstone was less concerned with what he called the "airy metaphysical notions" of "fanciful writers" on property in the state of nature than he was with the solid fact of property in civil society.[8] When the inhabitants of the earth "increased in number, craft, and ambition", he wrote, it became necessary to replace natural rights with civil rights, that is, rights under law. This step was required in order to avoid "tumult" and to promote conditions for commodious living.[9] Ranking high among these conditions, in Blackstone's estimation, was the need for stability and permanence in ownership: "Necessity begat property; and in order to insure that property, recourse was had to civil society, which brought along with it a long train of inseparable concomitants; states, government, laws, punishments, and the public exercise of religious duties."[10]

Blackstone, unlike Locke, was interested in property for its own sake. In fact, interested is too bland a word for the way Blackstone felt about property. It stirred his lawyerly soul. "There is nothing which so generally strikes the imagination and engages the affections of mankind," he wrote, "as the right of property; or that sole and despotic dominion which one man claims and exercises over the external things of the world, in total exclusion of the right of any other individual in the universe."[11] In this apostrophe to property, we find no ifs, ands, or buts. A property owner, Blackstone tells us, rules over what he owns, not merely as a king, but as a despot. Property rights are absolute, individual, and exclusive.

As fate would have it, Blackstone's *Commentaries* was *the* law book in the United States in the crucial years immediately preceding and following the American Revolution. Although English law was not binding as such in our courts after the break with the mother country, it was (except for a brief period of patriotic rejection) long considered relevant and helpful by lawyers and judges. Even if there had been a strong desire to refer to American law, no published reports of the decisions of American courts were produced until the early nineteenth century. But English court reports were not always available either, especially away from major cities. Blackstone's systematic treatment of English law, therefore, was not only a source of great importance, but the only reference work that many lawyers had. According to Daniel Boorstin, "In the first century of American independence, the *Commentaries* were not merely an approach to the study of law; for most lawyers they constituted all there was of the law."[12]

For this reason, Blackstone's work was much more fully absorbed into legal thinking here than in England, where legal resources were both more diverse and more readily available. It would be hard to exaggerate the degree of esteem in which the four compendious volumes of the *Commentaries* were held. Thomas Jefferson, when he drew up recommendations for a course of legal studies, prescribed "the inimitable *Commentaries*" of Blackstone as "the last perfect digest" of both common law and equity.[13] Nearly a century later, Abraham Lincoln advised a correspondent who had inquired about the best way to learn the law to begin by reading Blackstone all the way through, and then to read it carefully a second time.[14] In the late nineteenth century, when the *Commentaries* were of little more than historical interest in England, Blackstone was still being touted here as the font of legal wisdom. John B. Minor of the University of Virginia replied to a request in 1870 in essentially the same fashion as Jefferson and Lincoln had, adding that the student would be surprised, when he turned to other more recent law books, "at the multiplied forms of knowledge supplied by Blackstone and his annotators."[15] Successive annotated American editions of Blackstone remained a working part of lawyers' libraries here until the end of the nineteenth century.

Blackstone's *Commentaries* were more than just a handy reference work. His excursions into political and legal theory, his disquisitions on natural law, and his samplings from the writings of political philosophers, made the *Commentaries* a major channel for the migration of ideas from one realm of discourse to another. Most American lawyers learned of natural rights, not from the original works in which they had been expounded, but in the genial, garbled, and simplified version of Blackstone. The men of learning among the Founders knew their Blackstone through and through. As Robert Ferguson has written, "All of our formative documents—the Declaration of Independence, the Constitution, the Federalist Papers, and the seminal decisions of the Supreme Court under John Marshall—were drafted by attorneys steeped in Sir William Blackstone's *Commentaries on the Laws of England*."[16]

What is of importance to our inquiry here is that the strong property rights talk of Locke and Blackstone was in the air at the right moment to fuse with certain political factors that helped to make property the cardinal symbol of individual freedom and independence in the United States. Chief among these factors was the uneasiness felt by the framers of our Constitution concerning the potential threat posed to certain kinds of property rights by popularly elected legislatures.[17] The statesmen who gathered in Philadelphia in 1787 had had a glimpse of pure democracy at the state and local levels in the 1770s and 1780s, and were alarmed at what they saw. What mainly aroused their fears was the passage by state legislatures of debtor relief legislation, and the issuance of paper money that resulted in devaluation of outstanding debts. The principal means the drafters of the Constitution chose to protect transactions from legislative depredation was to build into the framework of government our familiar system of checks and balances. The design of government, rather than any enumerated right, was meant to constitute the main protection for individual or minority rights from tyranny by the majority. Thus the very structure of our government was developed around the problem of protecting private property. Property was taken by the Founders as "the central instance of rights at risk in a republic governed by popularly-elected legislatures."[18]

Property, Locke's clever choice for legitimating the power of the rising classes in seventeenth-century England, was also a convenient symbol, in the early years of our republic, for the principle that individual rights must set limits to the power of popular government. In late eighteenth-century United States, where landholding was characterized by "a pattern of modest-sized, widely dispersed, individually owned, farms," and where the large majority of white males could aspire to landownership at some point in their lives,[19] private property was the perfect example of a protected sphere into which the state could not enter. What J. G. A. Pocock has written about property in late seventeenth-century England was even more true of the United States a hundred years later: "The point about freehold in this context is that it involves its proprietor as little as possible in dependence upon, or even in relations with, other people, and so leaves him free for the full austerity of citizenship in the classical sense."[20] This was a vision of freedom that appealed to Federalists and Anti-Federalists alike. In a very concrete way, property could be seen to promote independence and personal security for the majority of white male inhabitants. A man's home was his sanctuary and his castle.

RHETORIC AND REALITY

From the very beginning, the absoluteness of American property rhetoric promoted illusions and impeded clear thinking about property rights and rights in general. The framers' efforts to directly and indirectly protect the interests of property owners were never meant to preclude considerable public regulation of property. The Fifth Amendment expressly recognized the federal eminent domain or "takings" power (a traditional prerogative of sovereignty). In the nineteenth century, the takings authority was liberally invoked, especially at the state level, to promote economic development, and notably to aid railroads in acquiring land. Furthermore, traditional flexible legal limitations on the rights of owners (such as the broad principle that one should not use one's property to inflict harm on others) were applied routinely in the capillaries of private law. And, early on, Supreme Court decisions made it clear that property rights, though of high importance, were not, and could not be, absolute. In the *Charles River Bridge* case (1837), a corporation that had been chartered by the State of Massachusetts to operate a profitable toll bridge from Cambridge to Boston sued to invalidate the charter of a new public corporation set up to build a second bridge (a few hundred yards from the old) that would be free to the public after its construction costs were paid. The majority opinion of the United States Supreme Court upholding the constitutionality of the new charter stated: "While the rights of private property are sacredly guarded, we must not forget that the community also have rights, and that the happiness and well being of every citizen depends on their faithful preservation."[21]

Despite many limitations on property rights in practice, the paradigm of property as a specially important, and very strong, right continued to exert a powerful influence on the law. The two most important legal issues before the Court in the second half of the nineteenth century were both treated as involving "property," with disastrous results in the first instance and unfortunate ones in the second. In 1856, Dred Scott, who had entered federal court in Missouri as a man, left it as a piece of property, when the Missouri Compromise (prohibiting slavery in the new territories) was held unconstitutional.[22] From the latter years of the century up to the 1930s, the Supreme Court repeatedly invoked property rights (in an expansive form) to strike down a series of laws that, taken together, might have served to ease the transition here, as similar legislation did in Europe, to a modern mixed economy and welfare state.

The reason the Court gave for invalidating statutes that attempted to promote health and safety in the workplace,[23] to protect female and child laborers,[24] and to encourage the nascent labor movement[25] was that these laws interfered with contractual and property rights of employer and employee alike. In these cases, "property" and "liberty" remained closely allied, but the meanings of both expanded and converged in the notion of freedom of contract—"the right to make contracts for the acquisition of property."[26] One of the most important of these agreements, the Court said, was that of employment. If the Court were to permit legislatures to interfere with contracts between employers and employees in the name of protecting workers' health or safety or promoting workers' organizations, there would be "a substantial impairment of liberty in the long-established constitutional sense."[27] In the view then prevailing in the Court, freedom of contract was "as essential to the laborer as to the capitalist, to the poor as to the rich; for the vast majority of persons have no other honest way to begin *to acquire property,* save by working for money."[28]

While the Supreme Court was thus according a high level of protection to the interests of owners of productive property, courts at the state level were diligently erecting a protective shield around another kind of property—the family home. Using the law of trespass, judges strengthened the rights of homeowners to exclude others from their premises. They extended criminal and civil penalties for intruding on premises used for residential purposes even when the person who entered was a landlord seeking to make repairs, or a process-server, or a person trying to recover goods belonging to him but detained on the homeowner's property.[29] Judges and juries showed themselves willing to tolerate the use of force, including deadly force, in support of a property owner's right to exclude others. There were, to be sure, certain legal restrictions on the use of self-help in the defense of property. Nevertheless, as one writer summed up the situation: "In court, defense of the castle may have had its limits, but in public opinion it was an absolute right."[30] Legal historian Aviam Soifer has written that "the rhetoric surrounding legal doctrine from the middle to the end of the nineteenth century tended to reinforce [beliefs of most white male Americans that they were] entirely free to contract for, hold, and devise property as they saw fit."[31]

Vigorous and direct constitutional protection for entrepreneurial property rights began to decline when the Supreme Court, under heavy pressure to uphold the economic and labor legislation of the Depression and New Deal period, repudiated several earlier cases where it had sacrificed progressive legislation on the altar of a broad notion of "property." Though the Court did not begin to defer regularly to legislative judgment where economic rights were concerned until the late 1930s, portents had existed for over a decade. Zoning laws—representing the potentially vast governmental authority to restrict a landowner's use of his property—passed constitutional muster in 1926.[32] Another early warning signal of property's shifting rank among constitutional values appeared in a 1934 decision where the Court remarked, while upholding a statute regulating the price of milk, that:

neither property rights nor contract rights are absolute; for government cannot exist if the citizen may at will use his property to the
detriment of his fellows, or exercise his freedom of contract to work
them harm. Equally fundamental with the private right is that of the
public to regulate it in the common interest.[33]

The decisive turning point came in the 1937 Supreme Court term,
when the Court upheld the National Labor Relations Act and a state
law establishing minimum wage levels for women and children,
overruling earlier decisions that were squarely to the contrary.[34]

The Court's interpretation of the "eminent domain" clause began to shift as well. The relevant portion of the Fifth Amendment
reads ". . . nor shall private property be taken for public use, without just compensation." From the early years of the republic, it had
seemed settled that this language meant that the federal government
could not take property *except* for a public use. In other words, the
government had no power to force a transfer of wealth from one
private individual to another, to take (as Justice Chase had put it in
1798) property from A and give it to B.[35] Even while this understanding endured, there was considerable elasticity in the eminent
domain clause, depending on how broadly or narrowly the Court
would construe "public," and the extent to which judges were prepared to second-guess the judgment of legislators regarding (1)
whether a proposed use was "public," and (2) whether the means
chosen by the legislature were appropriate to the public end it had in
view. Beginning in the 1950s, the elastic turned to Silly Putty. The
Court began to adopt a highly deferential posture toward legislative
decision-making on ends as well as means in the area of takings.
Public use, which long had been understood as meaning that the
property must be taken either for actual use by a segment of the
public (e.g., a park, highway, or school), or to eliminate a public evil
(e.g., flood danger, urban blight), took on a broader, more vague,
sense of "public purpose."[36]

It began to seem that the only practical limit on the power of eminent domain was the requirement of just compensation. The culmi-
nation of these cases at the Supreme Court level was a unanimous 1984
decision upholding an extensive reorganization of land ownership in
Hawaii.[37] Over 90 percent of the privately owned land in that state
had been concentrated in the hands of a small group of large proprietors. These owners rented land under long-term leases to persons
who then built homes on the rented ground. In 1967, the State of Ha-

waii authorized the Hawaii Housing Authority, upon request of such lessees, to exercise the power of eminent domain to take property from the landlords, pay them compensation, and sell it to the lessees. This certainly appeared to be a public taking for a private use, a classic forced transfer from A to B, and it was challenged as such in the courts. The opinion of the Court by Justice O'Connor, however, stated that, "where the exercise of the eminent domain power is rationally related to a conceivable public purpose, the Court has never held a compensated taking to be proscribed by the Public Use Clause."[38] The purpose that the Court accepted as "conceivable" was a vague aim to counter "oligopolistic" tendencies.[39]

Another line of cases decided under the takings clause reduced the constitutional status of property still further. It had long been recognized by the Court that government, without condemning property outright, might so diminish its value by regulation as to effect a de facto "taking" for which compensation ought to be paid. Since every regulation diminishes to some extent the value of the property that is affected, and since government could not operate if it had to pay compensation each time it exercised what Oliver Wendell Holmes, Jr., once called "the petty larceny of the police power,"[40] the Supreme Court has to engage in some delicate line-drawing. The Court has never developed a fully coherent test for determining when regulation goes so far that it is to be considered a taking. Not surprisingly, however, the Justices over time have adjusted their perspectives to the growth in America of a vast regulatory state. In general, the Court has been increasingly ready to accept legislative judgments in these "regulatory takings" cases, expressing only some mild reservations concerning what it has considered to be excesses of regulatory zeal.

The most striking example of how low the right of property has sunk in the official hierarchy of constitutional values is a case decided at the state level in 1981. It is a case that illustrates dramatically how cramped and impoverished American rights talk can be. In order to induce General Motors Corporation to build a new Cadillac assembly plant that was projected to bring 6,000 jobs to the area, the City of Detroit agreed to use its power of eminent domain to acquire a site that GM wanted. This was not just another forced transfer from one private owner to another: The land in question was an entire ethnic neighborhood known as "Poletown," complete with 1,400 homes, schools, 16 churches, 144 local business, and a neighborhood organization that begged the Michigan Supreme Court to save the com-

munity from the wrecker's ball and the bulldozer.[41] Originally a
place where generations of Polish immigrants had made their home,
Poletown was, by the time it was marked for destruction, one of
Detroit's oldest racially integrated communities. The neighborhood
residents—with the combined power of City Hall, General Motors,
the United Auto Workers, the banks, and the news media arrayed
against them—naively thought that the courts would protect their
property rights. No amount of compensation, they pointed out,
could repair the destruction of roots, relationships, solidarity, sense
of place, and shared memory that was at stake.

But our legal system did not afford them a ready way of talking
about such harms. Pathetically, they tried to construct an argument
by analogy to environmental protection. But the environmental argument did not register in the minds of judges trained in a legal
system that has difficulty both in dealing with long-term effects and
with envisioning entities other than individuals, corporations, and
the state. As for the property rights of the Poletown residents, the
day was long gone when such rights could prevail against a "public
use." It was enough, said a majority of the Michigan Supreme Court
justices, that Detroit's purpose was to alleviate unemployment and
fiscal distress. The benefit to a private entity, GM, was merely "in-
cidental" to the public scheme. Nor would the Court second-guess
the highly problematic judgment that handing Poletown over to GM
was likely to serve Detroit's stated purpose of saving jobs and promoting the economic health of the region. General Jaruzelski himself
could not have been more implacable. In the end, the Cadillac plant
failed to produce the economic benefits that had been glowingly
predicted. But 4,200 people had been displaced in "the most massive
and rapid relocation of citizens for a private development project in
U.S. history."[42]

This apparent decline in overt legal solicitude for traditional types
of property rights does not mean that property, more broadly understood, has ceased to command the respectful attention of the
American legal system. Supreme Court decisions holding corporations to be "persons" with constitutional speech rights, and striking
down state and federal efforts to restrain corporate influence in elections, have indirectly (though less visibly) fortified protection of
productive property.[43] With constitutional reinforcement of their
already superior access to the marketplace of ideas, corporate persons
now have less need of the old-fashioned straightforward protection
of economic rights they enjoyed in the early part of this century.

Although the heyday of the absolutist property paradigm came and went more than fifty years ago, the paradigm persists in popular discourse and still occasionally receives lip service even from the Supreme Court. The Court's now common subordination of property to other rights makes it all the more remarkable that property continues to cast its spell, and to entrance the minds of legal scholars as well as laypersons. In America, when we want to protect something, we try to get it characterized as a right. To a great extent, it is still the case that, when we *specially* want to hold on to something (welfare benefits, a job), we try to get the object of our concern characterized as a property right. At a recent public hearing on a proposed reform of Massachusetts divorce law, a representative of a fathers' rights group argued against improving the economic position of the custodial parent, saying, "The woman already gets the most important property of the marriage—the children—why should she get the other property as well?" Blackstone's treatise lies a'mouldering in the stacks, but its rhetoric marches on.

There are traces of John Locke's myth-making, too, in our relentless tendency to "propertize" things, particularly his decision to begin the story of natural right with the bald assertion that ". . . every Man has a Property in his own Person."[44] Certainly, many Americans speak of owning their bodies and body parts. Property theories have been prominent also in the arguments advanced in disputes over the legal status of frozen embryos produced in the *in vitro* fertilization process.

There are further Lockean echoes in the efforts of many persons on both the left and right of the American political spectrum to link "property" with liberty and independence. Each camp, of course, has a different understanding of property. Since land ownership can no longer serve to provide the majority of citizens with a protected sphere, jobs with their associated benefits, especially pensions, are the principal bases for whatever economic security most middle-class people possess. Welfare benefits have become the meager counterpart for a large part of the poverty-level population. As the importance of employment and social assistance for status and security came to be appreciated, Thurman Arnold, Charles Reich, and other legal theorists began to try to reconceptualize jobs and welfare as new forms of property.[45] In the 1960s, reformist lawyers launched a campaign to persuade the Supreme Court that welfare benefits, social security, and government jobs should be treated as property for constitutional purposes.[46] This effort had only limited success in a series of cases establishing that one could not be deprived of welfare benefits and certain other statutory entitlements without an opportunity to be heard.[47] Conservative lawyers, for their part, have had equally modest success in trying to convince the Court that the takings clause should accord more protection to the type of property that interests them—the wealth produced by the free operation of market forces.[48]

From time to time, isolated Supreme Court decisions have led wishful or fearful commentators to believe that property rights are making a comeback in constitutional law. Indeed, the Court in recent years does seem to be according a slightly higher degree of protection to certain types of property rights (homes, property used for charitable purposes, individual inheritance) in its takings cases. In general, however, ownership (especially ownership of productive property) remains subject—and properly so—to a network of restrictions that make life possible in a complex, interdependent, modern society. In Continental legal systems, these sensible sorts of distinctions and accommodations have been easier to achieve because the property right, and rights in general, were imagined from the beginning within a slightly different narrative.

THE PARADIGM OF INHERENT LIMITS

There are several historical reasons why a significantly different discourse on property and rights developed on the European continent in the early modern and the modern periods. To begin with, Jean-Jacques Rousseau, whose language and ideas had an even greater influence on continental political theory and rhetoric than John Locke's had on ours, held no particular brief for private property, though he did accord a place to private ownership in his theory of government. Whereas Locke's chapter on property was the very centerpiece of his *Second Treatise,* Rousseau devoted only a few pages to property in *The Social Contract.* Furthermore, some of Rousseau's ideas about ownership—and, what is of special interest to us here, his manner of expressing them—were quite dramatically at variance with those of Locke, as well as with the thinking of the stolid English and Scottish writers of "republican" persuasion for whom private property was the necessary base for the virtuous independent-minded citizen. In a memorable passage of his discourse on the origins of inequality, Rousseau had written:

The first man who, having enclosed a piece of ground, bethought himself of saying 'This is mine,' and found people simple enough to believe him, was the real founder of civil society. From how many crimes, wars, and murders, from how many horrors and misfortunes might not any one have saved mankind, by pulling up the stakes, or filling up the ditch, and crying to his fellows: 'Beware of listening to this imposter; you are undone if you once forget that the fruits of the earth belong to us all, and the earth itself to nobody.'[49]

In this 1754 essay, Rousseau, characteristically, mentioned the unmentionable: the relationship of property to selfishness, greed, power, and violence. With a few deft strokes, he painted a serpent in the midst of Locke's garden of peaceful labor. After reading Rousseau, we can't help noticing that Locke is quite vague about the transition from the state of nature to civil society; he never tells us precisely how property acquired in the former state came to be matched up with particular owners in the latter.

Rousseau shouted from the rooftops what other astute (but more discreet) observers had thought fit only for discussion over port in the drawing room. In Blackstone's lectures—designed, as he said, for "gentlemen" who needed to know enough law to act responsibly in Parliament or to manage their own estates—the great admirer of property admitted that the subject of its origins was not for everyone:

Pleased as we are with the possession [of property], we seem afraid to look back to the means by which it was acquired, as if fearful of some defect in our title. . . . These inquiries, it must be owned, would be useless or even troublesome in common life. It is well if the mass of mankind will obey the laws when made, without scrutinizing too nicely into the reasons for making them.[50]

If we were to inquire very far into the history of any given item of property, Blackstone speculated, what we would find might not correspond in all particulars with the Lockean vision of men hunting, fishing, and otherwise mingling their labor with objects removed from the common stock. Not only is it likely that our ancestors in the forest primeval sometimes took things away from each other by force or cunning, but even within recent memory "civilized" folk had gained territory by "seizing on countries already peopled, and driving out or massacring the innocent and defenseless natives."[51] But Englishmen need not worry too much about such matters anymore, Blackstone concluded reassuringly, for "the legislature of England has universally promoted the grand ends of civil society, the peace and security of individuals, by steadily pursuing that wise and orderly maxim, of assigning to everything capable of ownership a legal and determinate owner."[52]

Rousseau's less admiring, and potentially destabilizing, notions about property had their greatest influence in countries where constitutional government had not been established, and where land ownership was not so widely distributed as it was in the United States. In *The Social Contract,* Rousseau wrote that property rights are always subordinate to the overriding claims of the community; that an owner is a kind of trustee or steward for the public good; and that human beings have a natural right to what they need for their subsistence.[53] These fertile and suggestive ideas were hardly original with Rousseau. Their roots were in two traditions that Hobbes and Locke had done much to exclude from Anglo-American political discourse: the classical and the Biblical. In neither of these traditions was property disdained as such, but in neither was it exalted. As the ancients thought of these matters, what got in the way of virtue was not property itself, but human proclivities toward immoderation or greed. The classical writers, however, deemed the possession of certain external goods important as a means to the end of leading a virtuous life. As Aristotle put it, "it is impossible, or not easy, to do noble acts without the proper equipment."[54] Consistently with this tradition, Rousseau gave the ownership of private property entrance to his political theory, but not the keys to the city.

Rousseau's view that all human beings have a natural right to what is necessary to them for subsistence had some support in Biblical traditions. Significantly, however, in the Book of Deuteronomy, the notion does not appear as a right of the needy, but rather as an obligation of the property owner.[55] The ideas of stewardship, of property as inherently entailing obligations, and of subsistence needs as taking precedence over property rights, became major themes of Christian ethics, figuring prominently today in the programs of Christian labor organizations and political parties on the European continent, as well as in the social encyclicals of the modern Popes.

Arguably, the most important contribution of Rousseau to modern European political discourse was to keep alive classical and Biblical treatments of great perennial issues.[56] True, these remained only subthemes and countercurrents, but they were strong enough to keep European liberalism in dialogue with Athens and Jerusalem.

Rousseau, by using the classical authors as touchstones even when he resisted or rejected them,[57] influenced the political discourse of later European generations in ways that he may not have expected.

A variety of political and economic factors rendered continental Europe especially receptive to certain Rousseauean themes, and at the same time prevented exaggerated notions of property from dominating the development of rights ideas there. Prior to the French Revolution, there was no country in Europe where land ownership was as widely or evenly distributed as it was in the United States. A major element of the program of the French revolutionaries was to bring about a broader distribution of land through extensive confiscation and sale of properties belonging to the royal family, the Church, and the nobility. Through sale and resale, most of this land did eventually pass from speculators into the hands of peasant farmers,[58] who then held it as tightly as had the proprietors in the old regime. The legal treatment of property in the great law-making period that began under Napoleon both furthered the revolutionary aim of breaking up the power of the landed aristocracy (by forced division of all estates in the inheritance laws) and consolidated the new ownership rights of the farming and merchant classes.[59] The French Civil Code of 1804 left no doubt about the degree to which the rising classes valued private property. Yet Napoleon's codifiers were equally firm about the need to regulate ownership in the public interest. After pronouncing that "Ownership is the right to enjoy and dispose of things in the most absolute manner. . . ," the Code goes on to say, "provided that they are not put to a use prohibited by statutes or regulations."[60]

In the turbulent period of the French "Founding," with a bloody forced reorganization of property relationships fresh in everyone's memory, property was a central preoccupation, but it could hardly become, as it had in the United States, the leading symbol of individual security and independence. The French Declaration of the Rights of Man and the Citizen lists property, along with liberty, security, and resistance to oppression, as a natural right that government must preserve. But in the French context, these rights could not be conflated, Lockean fashion, into the general name, "property," as a catch-all for one's person, labor, and everything else of importance.

After the overthrow of Napoleon, the precariously reestablished French monarchy made no attempt to restore confiscated estates to their prerevolutionary owners. But the fact that most of the land in

France had been wrested only recently from one group of proprietors and transferred to new ones loomed silently over all discussions of property and of law. This was the case, not only in France, but throughout Europe. In the various regions of what is now Germany, the greatest legal scholars of the century devoted the best part of their energies to questions suggested by events in France. On the surface, the great debate seemed to be a dispute over whether systematic French-style codification of the laws should be sought as a means of promoting German political unification. All the positions in this scholarly jousting, however, had grave implications regarding the dominant political issue that had emerged in every part of Germany in the late eighteenth century: land reform to end feudalism in the German countryside.[61] In the 1830s, a clever law student in Berlin initially threw himself into the controversies that occupied his professors, but at a certain point he wrote to his father that he was dropping the law because it all seemed "false" to him: "A curtain had fallen, my holy of holies had been shattered, and new gods had to be found."[62] It must have appeared to the young Karl Marx that the endless arguments about the proper legal approaches to possession, prescription, and ownership were, to a great extent, disguised disputes over the validity of titles obtained by force and legitimized after the fact by laws enacted by the victorious side.

Though a strong concept of property was at an apogee in the thinking of many German jurists in the latter part of the nineteenth century, it never quite assumed American dimensions. Savigny, the most influential scholar of his time, had, it is true, described property as "the unlimited and exclusive domination of a person over a thing."[63] But when the main lines of modern German property law were finally worked out in the late nineteenth century, the draftsmen of the Civil Code (like their French counterparts) opted for a strong right with inherent limitations: "The owner of a thing may, except where contrary to the law or the rights of third parties, deal with the thing as he pleases and exclude others from any interference."[64]

Another factor that helped set European thinking about property and rights on a somewhat different course from our own was the emergence, as early as the late eighteenth century, of early forerunners of the modern welfare state. The Prussian Code of 1794 proclaimed that the welfare of the commonwealth and its inhabitants is the aim of society and marks the limit of law.[65] This code, a pet project of Frederick the Great, recognized an obligation on the part of the state to provide food, work, and wages for all who could not support themselves, and who had no claim for support upon their lord or the local community. In addition, it obliged the state to provide establishments for relieving the poor. As Tocqueville noticed, this code of an enlightened monarch bore a curious resemblance in these respects to the French Declaration of the Rights of Man as well as to the French Constitution of 1791.[66] Such provisions were not simply the trophies of revolution in France, or mere attempts to ward off violent social change in Prussia. Nor were they just functional analogues to the Elizabethan poor laws. Unlike their Anglo-American counterparts, which left poor relief up to local or private entities, they recognized an affirmative obligation on the part of the state to provide for the unemployed and needy. They emerged from and embodied feudal notions of sovereignty as involving obligations,[67] and they were the ancestors of modern European regimes of social and economic rights. The European welfare idea is a curious amalgam of modern socialist thought and premodern understandings of the protection that an overlord owed to his dependents, transposed to the sovereign in the emerging nation states of the eighteenth century.

Rousseauean rhetoric, classical notions of virtue, Biblical injunctions, and feudal vestiges are thus entwined in the roots of some of the most important contemporary differences between continental and Anglo-American attitudes toward government, including the lesser degree of mistrust of government that is still observable in the former. These elements all combined to form part of the background for the social upheavals of 1848; helped to prepare the way for the development of modern European versions of the welfare state; and subdued the thrust of property rights toward absoluteness.

After Germany was politically unified in the late nineteenth century, Bismarck established a rudimentary social security system in an effort to cut the ground out from under the Social Democratic party which, since its founding in 1875, had become the largest and best organized socialist party in Europe.[68] Elsewhere in Europe, including England, "universal" (male) suffrage, and the growing power of labor movements, led to the adoption of a wide variety of social legislation. Meanwhile, in the United States, moderate social legislation, such as health and safety laws for workers, was regularly being held unconstitutional in the courts. In countries without judicial review, and where the property paradigm was not so strong as it was here, the basic foundations of the welfare state were thus established quite early. In most of Europe, the process of striving for a prudent mix in the mixed economy and for a reasonable balance between social assistance and private initiative proceeded on the basis of a firm commitment to the relief of man's estate. Today, as William Pfaff has written, "The limits of nationalized enterprise are generally conceded, but it is still taken for granted [in the majority of European nations] that governments must be held responsible for employment and public welfare. It is expected that health, employment, and retirement will be insured at levels that many Americans still find scarcely credible."[69]

In the post–World War II period, the various streams of ideas about rights that had been agitating Western minds for over 200 years coalesced into a universal language of rights. In the United States, legal and popular rights discourse intensified in the 1950s and 1960s. The contemporaneous developments in post-war Europe appear broadly similar from a distance but, again, it is the nuanced differences that are intriguing. The United States Supreme Court, which had retrenched from its strong defense of economic liberties in the 1930s, began in the 1950s to expand the constitutional protection of a broad range of personal rights—freedom of expression, equal protection of the laws, and various rights of criminal defendants. Meanwhile, all Europe was reexamining fundamental legal ideas in the light of the experience with National Socialism. Legal positivism, the notion that one's rights are no more or less than what the law says they are, now seemed untenable. The Third Reich, after all, had adhered for the most part to legally "correct" procedures in adopting laws and regulations that snuffed out lives and stifled liberties. The idea of prepolitical "human" rights thus came to have wide appeal, although there was no consensus on any secular foundation for such rights, or on their precise content. In the realm of practical politics, traditional European forms of parliamentary supremacy also came into question. Judicial review in some form began to seem desirable as a way of backing up human rights and checking abuses of majoritarian rule. Accordingly, most of the new constitutions that have appeared in the West since World War II have included lists of rights and have established tribunals with varying degrees of power to review legislative and executive action for conformity to norms of "higher law." It is a striking feature of these postwar constitutions, however, that few of the rights they establish are presented in such a way as to lend themselves to the interpretation that they are absolute.

The Canadian Charter of Rights and Freedoms of 1982, the prod-

uct of much reflection on the constitutional experience of both Western Europe and the United States, affords a good example of how,
even in a country within the Anglo-American legal orbit, rights can
appear in strong, but not absolute, form. The very first section of the
Charter states that it guarantees the rights and freedoms set out in it
"subject only to such reasonable limits prescribed by law as can be
demonstrably justified in a free and democratic society."[70] Further
on, the Charter establishes a legislative override procedure through
which the entire group of what we would call First Amendment
rights, as well as a wide range of other rights including equality and
the rights of criminal defendants, may be limited by Parliament or
the legislature of any province. Finally, several Charter rights, such
as the right to travel and pursue a livelihood, are expressly subjected
to limitations in the very paragraphs where they appear. Property as
such is not even mentioned as a basic right, though it is expressly
protected under the 1960 statutory Canadian Bill of Rights.

The West German Basic Law of 1949 (applicable since October
1990 to all of reunified Germany) affords yet another, and somewhat different, example of a framework for an adequately complex
discourse about property and rights. Its main section dealing with
property reads in pertinent part:

ARTICLE 14.
  (1) Property and the right of inheritance are guaranteed. Their
content and limits shall be determined by law.
  (2) Property imposes duties. Its use should also serve the public
weal.
  (3) Expropriation shall be permitted only in the public weal. It may
be effected only by or pursuant to a law which shall provide for the
nature and extent of the compensation. . . .[71]

Here one notes, first, the familiar strong liberal commitment to
private ownership. But this is immediately qualified by the "content
and limits" clause. In the second paragraph appears the Biblical and
feudal notion (taken up by several modern natural law theorists) that
the privilege of having one's property guaranteed by the state entails
obligations. The third paragraph contains the eminent domain power
with the usual limitations on its exercise. The Social Democratic
input is most evident in two other articles: Article 15 which expressly
authorizes and regulates nationalization of land and the means of
production, and Article 20, which declares that the Federal Republic
is a social welfare state (*Sozialstaat*).

In theory it might seem that cramming socialist, Biblical, and feudal notions together in the formulation of constitutional property rights would involve the law in hopeless internal contradictions. But forty years of experience indicates that the tension among principles in this area has been a fruitful one.[72] At the very least, we may observe that these postwar constitutions lend no legitimacy whatsoever to statements such as, "This is a country where I can do anything I want"; or, "It's my property, so I can do what I want with it." It is difficult to imagine any serious contemporary European legal philosopher saying, as Ronald Dworkin did in *Taking Rights Seriously,* that "if someone has a right to something, then it is wrong for government to deny it to him even though it would be in the general interest to do so."[73] It has proved difficult even for those American legal scholars who, like Dworkin, vehemently reject Blackstone's complacent world view, to escape from Blackstone's spell.

WHAT DIFFERENCE DOES A STORY MAKE?

The historic rise and decline of property rights in our constitutional scheme has been outlined here not only in order to further illustrate our American tendency to formulate rights in a stark, unqualified, fashion, but to suggest how such habits of exaggeration can foster the illusion that the rights in question are more secure than they are in fact. It has been many a day since property was king in the American legal system. And, as we have seen, the idea of absolute property rights was misleading even in its heyday. How little we learned from this experience with one right that was historically touted as natural, prepolitical, and absolute, is apparent from our more recent fumbling with the privacy right. Much of the attention the Supreme Court once lavished on a broad concept of property, including the freedom of contract to acquire it, it now devotes to certain personal liberties that it has designated as "fundamental."[74] Remarkably, the property paradigm, including the old language of absoluteness, broods over this developing jurisprudence of personal rights. The new right of privacy, like the old right of property, has been imagined by the Court and lawyers generally as marking off a protected sphere surrounding the individual. As we shall see in the following chapter, much of the old property rhetoric has been simply transferred to this new area, and the Court has reexperienced familiar difficulties in working out principled limitations on a right that seemed for a time to have no bounds.

Though the "preferred" rights change from time to time, American legal discourse still promotes careless habits of speaking and thinking about them. Mr. Sokolow spoke for many of us when he claimed that no one could tell him what not to do in his own home. He must have known perfectly well that he could not print dollar bills, raise chickens, commit mayhem, or even have a late-night jam session in his Queens castle. When he spoke as he did, he was not speaking the language of the Founders. Still less was he speaking the language of the early colonists who accepted much official (and officious) intrusion into their personal lives. The frontier offered more scope, perhaps, for the illusion of absoluteness, but the circumstances of those who opened the West were also conducive to a vivid awareness of human vulnerability and interdependence. Where then, does this tough talk come from? Why do Americans like Mr. Sokolow and the legionnaire in the flag-burning dispute habitually exaggerate the absoluteness of the important rights they legitimately claim?

Tocqueville's sensitive ear picked it up—this tendency of Americans, "whose language when talking business is clear and dry," to indulge on other occasions in exaggerations and overdrawn descriptions.[75] As usual, he had a theory about it. His explanation, in a chapter titled, "Why American Speakers and Writers are Often Bombastic," is not very convincing, however. It is basically that citizens of a democracy (unlike aristocrats) are preoccupied with their own "paltry" everyday concerns. Their attention, he continued, cannot be drawn away from themselves except by the contemplation of "some prodigious subject." Writers in such a society are glad to pander to the popular taste for "vast conceptions and descriptions out of proportion," since they share that propensity anyway. Neither writers nor the public, Tocqueville said, take the time to measure things accurately, nor do they possess the taste to discern when something is out of proportion. In other words, he supposed our bombastic habits of speech to be part and parcel with our liking for tall tales and Bunyanesque heroes, and to follow from our mindless absorption in the details of material life.

If Tocqueville's theory were correct, however, we would expect to see people in all nations where aristocratic virtues have disappeared engaging in hyperbolic rights talk. Yet this is clearly not the case, even in countries like Sweden that are even more "democratic" than the United States. There must be a more specifically American explanation, therefore, for the persistent absoluteness in rights talk that is still more common in the United States than elsewhere. The way that rights are formulated in the Declaration of Independence and in the Bill of Rights may be one element in the story. Proclamations of rights in most postwar constitutions, like the Canadian and West German examples cited above, avoid giving even the appearance of absoluteness. Certain provisions of the American Bill of Rights, however, are categorical in form. The stark unqualified language of our First Amendment's speech provisions, notably, has given a cast to contemporary debates about hate-speech and pornography that is peculiarly our own.[76] It has also led some eminent jurists to claim that practically no limits can be imposed on speech and other forms of expression. Thus, Justice Hugo Black, viewed by many to have been the most influential judge on the Supreme Court during his long tenure there, once said: "It is my belief that there *are* 'absolutes' in our Bill of Rights, and that they were put there on purpose by men who knew what words meant, and meant their prohibitions to be 'absolutes.' "[77] Justice Black's literal approach to the protection of free speech has been defended by Professor Charles Black, on the ground that explicit judicial recognition that the right needs to be balanced on occasion against competing considerations could lead down the slippery slope to its erosion.[78] The professor went so far as to imply that it is better for the courts to perform any necessary balancing in a covert manner by manipulating the definition of speech. For example, he wrote, a lawyer or judge might say: " 'What we are doing is not an abridgment of freedom of speech; it is something else'—and offer reasons for this conclusion that can be swallowed by people who speak standard English."[79]

The unexpressed premises of this argument—that Americans cannot be trusted to respect a right that is subject to reasonable limitations, and that they can be deceived by judicial finagling in the service of the illusion of absoluteness—are hard to reconcile with democratic values. It is both paternalistic and elitist to suppose that important rights are safer when judges and scholars pretend they are absolute, than when they stress how very substantial must be the reasons that must be given for limiting them.[80] If we really believe that freedom of speech is "the Constitution's most majestic guarantee,"[81] suggestions that judges should dissemble in their reasoning about it ought to give us pause. The prominence given to free speech in the Bill of Rights and in our constitutional jurisprudence is the

outward and visible sign of the essential dependence of our democratic political order upon ongoing reasoned deliberation. Respect
for that process of deliberation would seem to require truth-telling
about rights.

The language of the second amendment ("A well regulated Militia, being necessary to the security of a free state, the right of the
people to keep and bear Arms, shall not be infringed") has similarly
promoted the belief in many quarters that an absolute, or nearly absolute, individual right was thereby created. Here the political positions are often reversed, with many of the same people who claim that
the right of free expression trumps a community's interest in regulating pornography, arguing that the right to keep and bear arms has
to be regulated for the sake of the general welfare. Although the constitutional language in both cases may seem unqualified, the courts
consistently have upheld certain legislative regulations of pornography and weapons. The only point to be made here is that the starkness
of some of the language in the Bill of Rights has helped to legitimate
intemperate arguments made by those who have a particular attachment to one of the rights framed in such terms.

But stark constitutional formulations alone cannot explain our
fondness for absolute rights talk. For property rights appear in the
Constitution only in an oblique and implicitly qualified form: "No
person . . . shall be deprived of . . . property, without due process of
law; nor shall private property be taken for public use, without just
compensation."[82] In the case of property, it was not the Fifth
Amendment, but the Lockean paradigm, cut loose from its context,
that became part of our property story as well as of our rights discourse. Blackstone's flights of fancy about property as absolute dominion stuck in American legal imaginations more than his endless
boring pages on what property owners really may and may not do
with what they own. Blackstone's popular rendition of the theory of
natural liberty did nothing to tame lawyers' rhetoric of rights either.
Natural liberty, he wrote, consists in "a power of acting as one
thinks fit without any restraint or control, unless by the law of
nature."[83] Though human beings exchange *part* of their natural liberty for civil liberty (liberty under law) when they enter society,
good government restrains their natural liberty only so far as is
necessary for the general welfare.[84] The three great rights of life,
liberty, and property, Blackstone proclaimed, are nothing more than
the *"residuum"* of natural liberty—the part which is not required to be
sacrificed to public convenience.[85] "The principal aim of society," he

wrote, echoing Locke, "is to protect individuals in the enjoyment of those absolute rights which were vested in them by the immutable laws of nature."[86]

However, neither Lockean rights rhetoric as mediated by Blackstone, nor constitutional language, can account directly or fully for the illusions of absoluteness that are promoted by American rights talk. Another key piece of the puzzle is the pervasiveness of legal culture in American society. The strong language Mr. Sokolow and the rest of us so frequently use is remarkably similar to a certain type of lawyers' talk that has increasingly passed into common speech. A large legal profession whose most visible members habitually engage in strategic exaggeration and overstatement already was having a substantial effect on popular discourse in Tocqueville's day. The rank-and-file of the legal profession, it is true, spend the greatest part of their professional lives in the humdrum business of adjusting one person's rights with another's. But we are not only the most lawyer-ridden society in the world, we are also the country where the roles of lawyers are most adversarial.[87] The careful, precise professional jargon of the workaday office lawyer appears in popular discourse mainly in caricature ("whereas hereinbefore provided"), while the highly colored language of advocacy flows out to the larger society through the lips of orators, statesmen, and flamboyant courtroom performers. Courtroom law talk, it should be noted, rests on an assumption that is not generally to be commended for civil conversation: that when each of two disputants pushes his or her version of the facts and theory of law to the ethically permissible limit, some third party will be smart enough to figure out from two distorted accounts what probably happened and how the law should be brought to bear on the case. Needless to say, opinions differ on how much exaggeration or omission is ethically permissible. One of my old law professors used to say, "There's a big difference between honesty and blurting out the truth!"

What's wrong with a little exaggeration, one might ask, especially in furtherance of something as important as individual rights? If we always took care to note that rights are qualified, would we not risk eroding them altogether? There are a variety of ways to respond to these concerns. In the first place, no one can be an absolutist for *all* our constitutionally guaranteed rights, because taking any one of them as far as it can go soon brings it into conflict with others. Secondly, the rhetoric of absoluteness increases the likelihood of conflict and inhibits the sort of dialogue that is increasingly necessary in a pluralistic society. In the common enterprise of ordering our lives together, much depends on communication, reason-giving, and mutual understanding. Even the legal profession is beginning to question the utility and legitimacy of the traditional strategic adoption of extreme positions by lawyers. Lawyers, as well as clients, are reckoning the social costs of our unique brand of adversary litigation. How ironic it would be if, after the American legal profession had become more sophisticated about alternative methods of dispute resolution, the old hardball litigators' talk lingered on in the rest of society, making it more difficult than necessary for neighbors and family members to deal with the friction inherent in everyday living.

Claims of absoluteness have the further ill effect that they tend to downgrade rights into the mere expression of unbounded desires and wants. Excessively strong formulations express our most infantile instincts rather than our potential to be reasonable men and women. A country where we can do "anything we want" is not a republic of free people attempting to order their lives together.

Absoluteness is an illusion, and hardly a harmless one. When we assert our rights to life, liberty, and property, we are expressing the reasonable hope that such things can be made more secure by law and politics. When we assert these rights in an absolute form, however, we are expressing infinite and impossible desires—to be completely free, to possess things totally, to be captains of our fate, and masters of our souls. There is pathos as well as bravado in these attempts to deny the fragility and contingency of human existence, personal freedom, and the possession of worldly goods. As John Updike recently observed, a certain unreflective Utopianism has undeniably been an important part of the American experience—Utopianism that, as it crumbles in our own time, gives way to "a naive, unending surprise and indignation that life is as it is. We cannot, unlike the Europeans, quite get over it."[88]

The exaggerated absoluteness of our American rights rhetoric is closely bound up with its other distinctive traits—a near-silence concerning responsibility, and a tendency to envision the rights-bearer as a lone autonomous individual. Thus, for example, those who contest the legitimacy of mandatory automobile seat-belt or motorcycle-helmet laws frequently say: "It's my body and I have the right to do as I please with it." In this shibboleth, the old horse of property is harnessed to the service of an unlimited liberty. The implication is that no one else is affected by my exercise of the individual right in question. This way of thinking and speaking ignores the fact that it is a rare driver, passenger, or biker who does not have a child, or a spouse, or a parent. It glosses over the likelihood that if the rights-bearer comes to grief, the cost of his medical treatment, or rehabilitation, or long-term care will be spread among many others. The independent individualist, helmetless and free on the open road, becomes the most dependent of individuals in the spinal injury ward. In the face of such facts, why does our rhetoric of rights so often shut out relationship and responsibility, along with reality?

THREE

The Lone Rights-Bearer

That the individual shall have full protection in person
and in property is a principle as old as the common
law; but it has been found necessary from time to time
to define anew the exact nature and extent of such
protection. . . . Gradually the scope of these legal
rights [to life, liberty, and property] broadened; and
now the right to life has come to mean the right to
enjoy life,—the right to be let alone.
—Warren and Brandeis, *The Right to Privacy*[1]

The American dialect of rights talk implicitly encodes an
image of the possessor of rights. His qualities, or lack of them, help
to explain why our rights claims are so stark and our responsibility
concepts so inconspicuous. To the extent we recognize ourselves in
the rights-bearer, our current rights discourse may seem to be our
mother tongue. To the extent he seems strange, or only a partial or
lesser version of ourselves, we will often feel ignored, left out, or
misrepresented by political discourse. As with other aspects of our
rights dialect, the implied image of the rights-bearer is an exaggerated form of a common modern ideal that has many attractive
features.

The eighteenth-century rights of life, liberty, and property, as
Karl Marx was the first to note, are preeminently rights of separated,
independent, individuals. The liberty vaunted by revolutionaries in
France and North America, he wrote, was the freedom of "man
regarded as an isolated monad, withdrawn into himself."[2] It was
"founded . . . upon the separation of man from man"; indeed, it was
the very "right of such separation."[3] Nowhere, however, is that
separation so pronounced as in the rights discourse of the United
States, where "liberty," and "equality" did not rub shoulders with

47

"fraternity," and where, at the end of the nineteenth century, the essence of the right to life would be reconceptualized as "the right to be let alone."

No aspect of American rights discourse more tellingly illustrates the isolated character of the rights-bearer than our protean right of privacy. Though the United States Supreme Court has been accused of fashioning this right from whole cloth, the notion was already implicit in the stories and images that migrated from the works of Hobbes, Locke, and Blackstone into American legal and popular culture. The United States is only one of many countries that have accorded constitutional protection to individuals in their private life, but it is unique in the number and types of uses to which the concept has been put. Unusual, too, is the way the American legal system imagines the person endowed with such protection. Constitutional and international privacy norms elsewhere present both the right and the right-bearer as having a social dimension. England, though home of the myths portraying man as radically solitary in the state of nature, has never made privacy the subject of a general "right." Thus the history of the American version of privacy should shed light on yet another distinctive feature of the American rights dialect—its extraordinary homage to independence and self-sufficiency, based on an image of the rights-bearer as a self-determining, unencumbered, individual, a being connected to others only by choice.[4]

The lone rights-bearer of American political discourse is an admirable figure in many ways. Yet he possesses little resemblance to any living man, and even less to most women. When did he ride into town? Where did he come from? And how did he become the protagonist of the American rights story?

THE RIGHT OF PRIVACY

The origin of all rights, in the Lockean fable, was the "property" a man possessed in his own person in the state of nature. When man enters civil society, the story goes, he gives up only so much of his natural liberty as is necessary for the sake of comfortable self-preservation. As Blackstone retold the story for generations of American lawyers, the primary end of government is to protect individuals in the enjoyment of their "absolute" rights—which are none other than the "residuum" of natural liberty. A subsidiary task

of law (the one that keeps most lawyers busy) is to regulate the rights
and duties of individual members of society in their relations to one
another. Beyond that, Blackstone explained, the law has no concern
with how individuals conduct themselves: "Let a man . . . be ever so
abandoned in his principles, or vicious in his practice, provided he
keeps his wickedness to himself, and does not offend against the rules
of public decency, he is out of the reach of human laws."[5]

At first, then, it was the tradition of limited government, rather
than the value of personal privacy as such, that made the idea of an
inviolable private sphere a cornerstone of Anglo-American liberalism. As John Stuart Mill pointed out in the introduction to his essay
On Liberty, England, more than most other countries of Europe, had
traditionally refrained from legally interfering with private conduct.
But this abstention, he said, was "not so much from any just regard
for the independence of the individual," as from "the still subsisting
habit of looking on the government as representing an opposite interest to the public."[6]

The major impetus for recognizing a legal *right* to privacy was
the invention, in the nineteenth century, of instantaneous photography, and the development of rapid means of communication. The
camera permitted unprecedented intrusions into private life, and the
appearance of advertisements, newspapers, and magazines aimed at
mass audiences facilitated broad dissemination of personal images
and information. The first to feel the rude effects of these innovations
were the rich and powerful. Difficult as it may be to imagine now,
the respectable press at the turn of the century was sympathetic to the
plight of public figures subjected to the "ordeal of the camera." *The
New York Times* was among those deploring the impudence of photographers seeking to capture the likenesses of famous people:

> The present President of the United States [Theodore Roosevelt] has
> been so much annoyed by photographers who have attended his
> down-sittings and his uprisings and spied out all his ways, for the
> purpose of making permanent pictorial record of the same, that it is
> reported that only his respect for the dignity of his office has upon one
> or two occasions prevented him from subjecting the impertinent
> offender to the appropriate remedy . . . of personal chastisement.
>
> Mr. J. Pierpont Morgan, we read, was so beset by "kodakers"
> lying in wait to catch his emergence from his office on the day of his
> return from Europe that he was actually held a prisoner for some
> time.[7]

Aggressiveness in using the new technology was not confined to the United States. In Germany, upon the death of Bismarck in 1899, avid photographers burst into the Iron Chancellor's death chamber to obtain pictures of the body—to the great distress of his family.[8]

Many victims of pioneering paparazzi turned to the legal system for help in preventing their likenesses from being reproduced in the mass media. A New York judge, though denying relief in an early case, sympathetically captured the essence of these calls for some legal remedy. He described them as based on the belief that, "A man has the right to pass through this world, if he wills, without having his picture published, his business enterprises discussed, his successful experiments written up for the benefit of others, or his eccentricities commented upon either in handbills, circulars, catalogues, periodicals or newspapers."[9] Though a few of the initial cases involved women plaintiffs, the person who demanded protection against such intrusion was usually, as the judge said, "a man,"—a man, moreover, with a certain standing, habituated to controlling his environment and information about himself, and with an interest in continuing to do so.[10]

The legal systems of the industrial world were not slow in responding to the desires of such people. As has so often been the case, however, the United States took a distinctive approach, one which later turned out to have been laden with unforeseen consequences and burdened with an inheritance of deeply flawed assumptions about human beings. The American version of the "right to privacy," in the end, protected neither the important men for whom it was originally devised nor the women upon whom it was eventually bestowed as effectively as did several legal devices developed for the same purposes elsewhere.

The emergence of the distinctive American approach to privacy exemplifies the innovating role that legal scholarship has often played in the development of our ideas about rights. In 1890, a lawyer from a prominent Boston family, Samuel D. Warren, and his onetime law partner, Louis D. Brandeis, coauthored a *Harvard Law Review* article in which they undertook to produce a theory that could ground legal causes of action for intrusions into personal life. They had no doubts about the gravity of the new social problem. As they saw it:

> The press is overstepping in every direction the obvious bounds of propriety and of decency. Gossip is no longer the resource of the idle and of the vicious but has become a trade, which is pursued with

industry as well as effrontery. To satisfy a prurient taste the details of sexual relations are spread broadcast in the columns of the daily papers. To occupy the indolent, column upon column is filled with idle gossip, which can only be procured by intrusion upon the domestic circle. The intensity and complexity of life, attendant upon advancing civilization, have rendered necessary some retreat from the world, and man, under the refining influence of culture, has become more sensitive to publicity, so that solitude and privacy have become more essential to the individual; but modern enterprise and invention have, through invasions upon his privacy, subjected him to mental pain and distress, far greater than could be inflicted by mere bodily injury.[11]

To the rescue of the victims of such unseemly prying, the two lawyers brought time-honored methods of common-law reasoning. They pored over court decisions involving analogous issues (libel, slander, property rights in literary and artistic creations) in search of some implicit underlying principle that could be extended to cover the novel situations then arising. They found such a principle, they thought, in a group of English and American cases permitting individuals to enjoin the publication of etchings and drawings made for their own amusement, the contents of private letters, lecture notes, and so on. Although the courts in all these cases had rested their decisions on property rights, Warren and Brandeis claimed to have discerned that what was *really* being protected was the "inviolate personality" of the artist or author, a personal right rather than a property right. They named their article after the latent principle they believed they had discovered: "The Right to Privacy."

> The principle which protects personal writings and any other productions of the intellect or of the emotions is the right to privacy, and the law has no new principle to formulate when it extends this protection to personal appearance, sayings, acts, and to personal relations, domestic or otherwise.[12]

Warren and Brandeis acknowledged that it would not always be easy to determine when "the dignity and convenience of the individual must yield to the demands of the public welfare or of private justice," but they noted that the law had dealt with problems of establishing limits on tort recovery before, and they expressed confidence that it could do so here.[13] Privacy was thus, quite literally, pulled from the hat of property. Summoning up the Lockean trilogy of life, liberty, and property, the authors explained that, through the right of privacy, the right to life had now blossomed into "the right to enjoy life,—the right to be let alone."[14]

What made it especially easy for Warren and Brandeis to think they saw a "right to be let alone" as the silver thread running through a group of literary and artistic property cases were two powerful intellectual paradigms then operating in the American legal milieu. The first was the traditional idea of property as marking off a sphere around the individual which no one could enter without permission, and as providing the most reliable basis for individual independence. If the protected sphere extended to the fence around the farm, *a fortiori* it must surround the man in the farmhouse, and his interior life. Warren and Brandeis harnessed the idea of a man's home as castle, and put it to work in the service of privacy. In the modern world, take away the fence around the forty acres, take away the farmhouse, and an invisible shield nevertheless remains:

> The common law has always recognized a man's house as his castle, impregnable, often, even to its own officers engaged in the execution of its commands. Shall the courts thus close the front entrance to constituted authority, and open wide the back door to idle or prurient curiosity?[15]

To American lawyers in 1890, it must have seemed the most natural thing in the world to fashion protection for the personal sphere on the model of property protection then at its apogee.

Warren and Brandeis went a step further, however, and welded these traditional American ideas about property to certain of John Stuart Mill's enormously influential views about personal liberty. In 1859, Mill had contended, in his essay *On Liberty,* that the ancient question of the nature and limits of the power that society may legitimately exercise over individuals urgently needed to be taken up once again.[16] Under modern democratic governments, he wrote, the main threat to liberty was no longer oppression by a tyrant or an oligarchy, but the power of the people themselves, the tyranny of the majority. Like Tocqueville, Mill was concerned that majority power over individuals could be exerted insidiously through social pressure, as well as overtly by public force.

Using hard-edged terminology that resonated better with American than English legal culture, Mill asserted his famous principle that in what "merely concerns himself," the independence of the individual "is, of right, absolute."[17] The true domain of human liberty, he said, is one's own conscience, thoughts, feelings, expression, tastes, and pursuits. Interference with individual freedom in these areas is justified only to prevent harm to others. "Over himself, over his own body and mind, the individual is sovereign."[18] This broad idea of liberty represented a quantum leap in the history of rights. Hobbes had considered that only the right to life was retained after man entered civil society. For Locke, only life, liberty (in a narrow sense), and property were exempt from governmental intrusion. Mill, however, was proposing to put a vast area of conduct and opinion off limits from regulation—and to do so by virtue of a *right*.

The chapter of the essay *On Liberty* where Mill develops the notion that an individual's conduct should be as free as his opinions is titled "Of Individuality." Though the positions taken in that chapter regarding what we would now call life-style liberties are widely accepted today, the arguments Mill advanced in support of them have been largely forgotten. They are worth recalling, however, for they are surprisingly at odds with the egalitarian sentiments avowed by most contemporary rights enthusiasts. Here is the gist of Mill's case for maximizing individual freedom of action:

> Genius can only breathe freely in an *atmosphere* of freedom. Persons of genius are . . . more individual than any other people—less capable, consequently, of fitting themselves, without hurtful compression, into any of the small number of moulds which society provides in order to save its members the trouble of forming their own character. . . .
>
> In sober truth, whatever homage may be professed, or even paid, to real or supposed mental superiority, the general tendency of things throughout the world is to render mediocrity the ascendant power among mankind.[19]

The qualities of the ordinary men and women whose opinions thus threaten to stifle the development of gifted persons may vary from time to time and place to place, Mill says, but "they are always a mass, that is to say, collective mediocrity."[20] In his day, as Mill saw it, society was in a bad way. The vote had been extended to a broad range of people, the "masses." These newly enfranchised electors were forming their political opinions under the influence of a growing mass communications industry. This, Mill pointed out, meant that they were listening to "men much like themselves, addressing them or speaking in their name, on the spur of the moment, through

the newspapers.''[21] Can a country with mass media and democrat-
ically elected leaders avoid domination by mediocre majorities?

Fortunately they can, said Mill, giving reasons that must have
warmed the hearts of high-minded and self-satisfied intellectuals on
both sides of the Atlantic:

> The initiation of all wise or noble things comes and must come from
> individuals; generally at first from some one individual. The honor
> and glory of the average man is that he is capable of following that
> initiative; that he can respond internally to wise and noble things, and
> be led to them with his eyes open.[22]

Essential to the project of bringing the "average man" to desire "wise
and noble things" was the leadership and example of people who are
not "average." Such people, said Mill, cannot flourish except with a
great deal of personal freedom. To the vulgar, many of these gifted
persons might appear eccentric or even wicked; hence the need to protect and foster their "individuality." Looking around him, Mill
gloomily observed that "All the political changes of the age . . . tend
to raise the low and lower the high."[23] It seemed obvious to him that,
for the good of everyone, "exceptional individuals" needed to be
especially encouraged.

Oliver Wendell Holmes, Jr., Louis D. Brandeis, and other eminent American jurists were much taken by the essay *On Liberty*.
Through them, many of Mill's ideas were turned into catchphrases
of American constitutional law (the marketplace of ideas, clear and
present danger, consenting adult), especially in free speech cases.
The right of privacy as imagined by Brandeis and Warren also fit
neatly into the framework of justification that Mill had advanced for
personal liberties, though Mill is not among the authorities cited in
their article.

The theory advanced by the two Boston lawyers made slow but
steady progress after its elaboration in the *Harvard Law Review*. Gradually, over the next thirty years or so, several state courts developed
a body of privacy law within tort law. Privacy did not, however,
become a general unified right in tort law. It was rather the notional
basis in principle for a cluster of causes of action protecting individuals from intrusion by others into their personal affairs, from public
disclosure of personal information, and from commercial appropriation of their name or likeness. Protection against publicity—the
aspect of privacy that was the main subject of Warren and Brandeis—

remained the least developed of these areas, largely because it was here that privacy notions collided with freedom of the press. Brandeis himself, we now know, had serious reservations about the appropriate scope of privacy rights in this context. The ink was barely dry on "The Right to Privacy" when he confided in a letter to his fiancée that he really should have written a "companion piece" on "The Duty of Publicity."[24] A staunch believer in the necessity of a free press for an informed citizenry, Brandeis first articulated in these letters a theme he would sound later as a Supreme Court justice: "If the broad light of day could be let in upon men's actions, it would purify them as the sun disinfects."[25]

The privacy idea did not reveal its full expansive force until it migrated from torts into constitutional law. The point of entry was hardly noticeable, except in retrospect. Again the stimulus was a problem created by new technologies. In 1928, a majority of the Supreme Court held that wiretapping by federal officers did not violate the constitutional rights of a criminal defendant against unreasonable search and seizure because the wiretap did not involve a *physical* invasion of the suspect's person or property, and what was obtained was not a *tangible* object.[26] In retrospect, the decision seems clearly wrong—an example of the sort of temporary difficulty courts sometimes have in adapting legal principles to new situations. The case was eventually overruled, and would have been forgotten but for an eloquent dissenting opinion. The dissenter argued that the Fourth Amendment to the Constitution, which protects the "right of the people to be secure in their persons, houses, papers, and effects, against unreasonable searches and seizures" should be understood, together with the Fifth Amendment, as implicitly securing a more general "right to be let alone—the most comprehensive of rights and the right most valued by civilized men."[27] The dissenter was Louis D. Brandeis.

In the American legal system, it is not unusual for transformative new ideas to make their debut in a losing brief or a dissenting opinion. Certain novel ideas, even in defeat, can begin to change the way that judges and lawyers look at a problem. Eventually, they may be connected with other more familiar ideas, altering old legal categories from within, and forging new ones.[28] In the years after the Brandeis dissent, references to privacy interests began to appear sporadically in Supreme Court opinions.[29] The hold that the Brandeis formulation had taken in the minds of members of the legal elite can be seen in a 1950 speech on the Fifth Amendment by the then Dean of the Harvard Law School. Erwin Griswold (later to serve under two presidents as Solicitor General of the United States) titled his speech, "The Right to be Let Alone."[30] This right, he claimed, was nothing less than "the underlying theme of the Bill of Rights," essential to the integrity and autonomy of the individual, to the life of the "inner man." The audacious Warren and Brandeis project of "defining anew" the scope of our constitutional rights had found a prominent disciple.

The decisive moment for the emergence of privacy as a constitutional right did not occur, however, until much later. Most lawyers would put the date at 1965, when one of the last states with a statute restricting the use of contraceptives was obliged to defend the constitutionality of its law before the Supreme Court. The question was whether this "uncommonly silly law" (as Justice Stewart called it)[31] had to remain on the books—as most other obsolete laws do—until the Connecticut legislature repealed it, or whether it should be struck down by the Supreme Court.

There was ample basis in previous Court decisions for invalidating the Connecticut law. One line of cases protected families from interference with their internal decision-making processes.[32] Another decision protected convicts from forced sterilization, which was seen as an interference with a vital personal liberty.[33] For two of the majority justices in *Griswold v. Connecticut,* the family protection and personal liberty cases were authority enough.[34] The other members of the majority, however, adduced a further justification in their opinions. Mr. Justice Douglas found in the "penumbras" of the Constitution, "a right of privacy older than the Bill of Rights" protecting the "intimate relation of husband and wife" and the "bilateral loyalty" of that relationship from state interference.[35] Justices Goldberg and Brennan, and Chief Justice Warren, thought that there was a "right of marital privacy" in the concept of liberty in the Fourteenth Amendment and in the "retained" rights of the people in the Ninth Amendment.[36]

There was nothing in *Griswold v. Connecticut* to suggest that the privacy right accepted there was envisioned as an individual right. *Griswold* seemed at the time merely to consolidate in the Supreme Court's case law the kind of protection for marriage and family life that, by 1965, was the subject of express provisions in more modern constitutions. Many constitutions and most international human rights declarations contain language to the effect that the state must provide special protection for marriage and the family. The opinions of Justices Douglas and Goldberg, especially, seemed to be in that mode. Justice Goldberg repeatedly characterized the right involved as "the right of marital privacy."[37] He noted that prior court decisions had recognized a private realm of family life which the state could not enter, and he expressed his agreement with the views of Justice Harlan in an earlier dissenting opinion that:

> Certainly the safeguarding of the home does not follow merely from the sanctity of property rights. The home derives its pre-eminence as the seat of family life. . . . Of this whole 'private realm of family life' it is difficult to imagine what is more private or more intimate than a husband and wife's marital relations.[38]

Griswold v. Connecticut was just another step in the construction of constitutional protection for American families through case law. It pointed toward the partial liberation of privacy from the property paradigm.

Or so it seemed until 1972, when the Court abruptly severed the privacy right from its attachment to marriage and the family and launched it as a full-fledged *individual* right. Again, the context was a state law relating to contraception. Massachusetts by then was the only state that still prohibited the sale of contraceptives to unmarried persons. When an abortion rights activist, William Baird, challenged the Massachusetts law on constitutional grounds, the Court took a fresh look at the privacy right and decided that it was not a marital or family right after all, but "the right of the *individual,* married or single, to be free from unwarranted governmental intrusion into matters so fundamentally affecting a person as the decision whether to bear or beget a child."[39]

The practical impact of declaring the obsolete statute unconstitutional was almost negligible. But in declaring privacy an individual right, the Court had taken a momentous step. *Eisenstadt v. Baird* not only put the right squarely on an individual basis, but it marked a shift from privacy as "freedom from surveillance or disclosure of intimate affairs," to privacy as "the freedom to engage in certain activities" and "to make certain sorts of choices without governmental interference."[40] *Eisenstadt* not only marked the elevation to constitutional status of an individual's right to be let alone, but it represented substantial acceptance of Mill's ideas about freedom of conduct. Just how momentous the shift had been became apparent one year later in a case that precipitated the most intense social controversy of the 1970s and 1980s.

In the spring of 1970, Norma McCorvey, a 20-year-old Dallas waitress, found herself poor, unmarried, and pregnant. With no idea of where to turn for help, she sought an abortion. In her desperation, and believing it might aid her to circumvent the strict Texas abortion law, she fabricated a story that she had been gang-raped by three men and a woman.[41] Her invention was to no avail, because, as her doctor informed her, Texas permitted an abortion only to save the life of the pregnant woman. Lacking funds to travel to California, the nearest state where abortions were readily available, she next turned to a lawyer for help in arranging an adoption. The attorney, aware that preparations to challenge the Texas law were underway, gave Ms. McCorvey's name to two other lawyers who were looking for someone to be the plaintiff in a test case. Norma McCorvey consented to play that role, as Jane Roe, and the suit was duly filed. In 1973, the Supreme Court of the United States held in *Roe v. Wade* that the constitutional right of privacy was "broad enough to encompass a woman's decision whether or not to terminate her pregnancy."[42] The Court proceeded to strike down, not only the old strict Texas law, but also the more liberal abortion laws toward which legislatures in other states were tending.[43]

Norma McCorvey thus won the right that had been understood from its earliest appearance in the American legal system as "the right to be let alone." And let alone she was. No one, apparently, had been willing to help her either to have the abortion she desired, or to keep and raise the child who was eventually born. While the litigation was pending, she surrendered the infant for adoption. Years later, she was fruitlessly searching for her son or daughter (she never was told which it had been).[44]

The judicially announced abortion right in 1973 brought to a virtual halt the process of legislative abortion reform that was already well on the way to producing in the United States, as it did all over Europe, compromise statutes that gave very substantial protection to women's interests without completely denying protection to developing life.[45] In the abortion cases that followed and enlarged the scope of *Roe*, privacy began to show the same thrust toward absoluteness that had characterized property rights in an earlier era. Rather than trying to articulate the basis and purpose of the privacy right, the Justices simply laid down a set of rules: there could be no regulation of abortion at all in the interest of protecting the fetus until viability; measures to protect the health of the pregnant woman could be put in place beginning with the second trimester, but could not unduly burden her privacy interest; after viability (roughly in the third trimester), the states might legislate to protect what the Court called "potential" life, but only if such regulations did not infringe the health of the woman. In striking contrast to the situation in other nations, health was so broadly defined in *Roe's* companion case, *Doe v. Bolton,* that few limits could be placed on the abortion right even in late pregnancy.[46]

Even such a staunch defender of the *Roe* decision as Professor Laurence Tribe was troubled by its grant of an absolute right to abortion during the first two trimesters, with hardly any limitation in the third. He took the Court to task for "reaching beyond the facts of the case to rank the rights of the mother categorically over those of the fetus, and to deny the humanity of the fetus. . . ,"[47] and he expressed regret that Justice Blackmun did not manifest "a more cautious sensitivity to the *mutual* helplessness of the mother and the unborn that could have accented the need for affirmative legislative action to moderate the clash between the two."[48]

Although Justice Blackmun's majority opinion in *Roe v. Wade* had disingenuously recited that the abortion right was not absolute,[49] the Court in fact could not contain it. No rights could be asserted on behalf of the developing fetus as such, even close to the time of birth, because, as Justice Blackmun explained, "the word 'person', as used in the Fourteenth Amendment, does not include the unborn."[50] Even the slight room that *Roe* had left open for state regulation of abortion in the late stages of pregnancy was progressively narrowed in later cases.[51] In effect, a system of abortion on request, covering the entire nine months of pregnancy, was put in place for any woman who could find a doctor to agree with her assessment of the degree of her distress.

In *Roe,* Justice Blackmun had stated reassuringly that the pregnant woman was not to be "isolated" in her privacy.[52] But when the Court faced the issue head-on in actual cases concerning whether abortion funding should be available to her,[53] or whether states could require that women seeking abortions be provided with information regarding alternatives such as adoption, or assistance available to them if they wished to bring the pregnancy to term,[54] the paradigm of the lone rights-bearer prevailed. The only instances where notification to, or consultation with, others could be required were those involving unmarried pregnant teenagers aged 17 and under.[55] The right to privacy, the quintessential right of individual autonomy and isolation, seemed indeed to be, as Brandeis had claimed, "the most comprehensive of rights." Although its career in tort law was unremarkable, in constitutional law it became one of the most absolute rights known to the American legal system.

It began to appear that there were no bounds to its expansive potential until 1986, when the Court decided by a narrow margin in *Bowers v. Hardwick* that an old Georgia statute criminalizing homosexual activity was constitutional.[56] Never having established the theory on which the right of privacy was based, nor what end it was supposed to serve, the Court was not at its best when it finally attempted to figure out how to limit the principle. The majority merely announced in *Bowers* that "there is no fundamental right to commit sodomy" without explaining *why* it was treating sexual activity between consenting adults in the home of one of them as less "private" than abortions of human fetuses performed in busy clinics. The Supreme Court's decisions in *Bowers* and *Roe,* as we shall see in Chapter Six, both contrast strikingly with the resolutions of these issues reached by leading courts elsewhere.

The privacy cases have generated political controversy and acrimony to the point where they overshadow many other important aspects of the Court's work. When Robert Bork, who had been highly critical of the reasoning of the privacy decisions, was nominated to replace Lewis Powell, a *Roe v. Wade* supporter, on the United States Supreme Court, his judicial confirmation hearings became the political event of the season. In the rhetoric of most opponents of Judge Bork's nomination, privacy was not just one right among many. Similar to property in its heyday, privacy was vaunted as a superright, a trump.

When, however, the Supreme Court, with a new conservative member, next heard an abortion case in 1989, it left both *Roe v. Wade* and the right of privacy in place.[57] (Though widely interpreted as signalling that a new majority on the Court is prepared to accord somewhat more leeway to state legislatures in regulating abortion, the only immediate legal effect of *Webster v. Reproductive Health Services* on the trimester scheme of *Roe* is that it permits a state to require testing to determine whether a fetus is viable.)

In the hundred years that have passed since Warren and Brandeis took up their pens to help shield prominent individuals from excessive public scrutiny, the "right to be let alone" has become firmly entrenched in our legal system. Was the "right most valued by civilized men" the best device available to protect the interests of the powerful individuals for whom it was first devised, or the vulnerable pregnant women upon whom it was eventually bestowed? Or were there other ways to safeguard their freedom, privacy, and personal dignity? Let us consider the experience of some other countries where the rights-bearer is imagined as a person situated within, and partially constituted by, her relationships with others.

RIGHTS OF PERSONALITY

Photography and mass communications generated similar legal problems all over the industrialized world in the nineteenth century. In Europe, as here, the incidents that provoked the most outcry involved the unauthorized taking or use of the likenesses of famous people—photographs of the corpse of Bismarck, a drawing of the deathbed scene of Rachel, the greatest French actress of the day. The initial French response was an 1881 statute on the press, eliminating truth as a defense to defamation in certain situations.[58] Thereafter, the French courts developed further protection for personal likenesses and correspondence by analogy to property rights. In Germany, the legislature forbade the publication or distribution of a private individual's picture without his or her consent.[59] As in the United States, no specific causes of action based on privacy appeared in either country's tort law until many years later. In both France and Germany, however, when such rights appeared, they were formulated as rights of "personality," qualified in their inception, and resting on a rather different notion of human personhood from that implicit in the right to be let alone.

Just as one may date the migration of the "right to be let alone" into American constitutional law from Brandeis's dissent in the 1928 wiretapping case, one can locate the birthplace of personality rights as a *constitutional* idea in Europe in the 1949 West German Basic Law. That constitution, written under the watchful eyes of the Allied powers, and drawing on an eclectic assortment of legal sources, made respect for and protection of "human dignity" the foremost duty of the state. This obligation was placed at the very apex of the hierarchy of constitutional values in the first article of the new Constitution. Then, in the second article, the Basic Law went on to provide:

> 2 (1). Everyone shall have the right to the free development of his personality in so far as he does not violate the rights of others or offend against the constitutional order or the moral code.[60]

It is worth noting that the German word used here for "development" is not the usual *Entwicklung,* but rather, *Entfaltung,* whose literal meaning is "unfolding"—as in the opening of a rosebud, or the unfurling of a flag. The choice of words alone suggests that the notion at the core of the right of personality is an outward-turning one. Early judicial interpretations confirmed that the personality right is not to be envisioned as a right to be barricaded against the world. The *Bundesgerichtshof* said, for example, in a 1957 case: "The free development of the personality consists precisely in the individual's reaching out beyond himself."[61]

Like American privacy, the German right of personality is unmistakably an *individual* right, and its evolution affords especially instructive comparisons with the development of the privacy concept in the United States. (The absence of formal constitutional review in England, and its highly limited scope in France, have precluded the appearance of a constitutional law of privacy in those countries.[62]) In German law, however, we can see clearly how a modern legal system, facing a common social problem, developed an approach that diverges slightly yet significantly from our own. In the German Civil Code of 1896, effective in 1900, the basis of most tort actions was (and still is) a code section which provides in very general fashion:

ARTICLE 823.

(1). Whoever intentionally or negligently injures the life, body, health, freedom, property or other right of another contrary to law, is obligated to the other to make good the resulting damage.

(2). The same obligation is imposed on one who violates a statute intended to protect another. . . .

For decades, German courts and scholars maintained that the language "or other right" in §823 (1) was not broad enough to encompass injuries to personality. As in France, protection of interests such as those represented by one's likeness was afforded initially mainly by special legislation.

The great turning point occurred in 1954, when the *Bundesgerichtshof* held that the standard interpretation of Article 823(1) had to be reexamined in light of the 1949 constitution's commitment to respect for the worth of the individual in Article 1, and the personality right established in Article 2.[63] By the end of the 1950s, court decisions made it clear that the constitutional right of personality had infused new content into the language "other right" in Article 823(1) of the Civil Code.[64] Accordingly, private citizens were afforded greater opportunities to seek legal redress against other individuals for unauthorized publication or disclosure of personal material, such as private letters or personal medical information.

Working with a clearer statement of the principle on which the right was founded and the end it was to serve, the West German courts found it somewhat easier than did their American counterparts to delineate its contours and limits. That the principle of Article 2 was an individualistic one was stressed in an early case, where the *Bundesgerichtshof* said: "Articles 1 and 2 of the Basic Law protect . . . what is called human personhood, . . . that inner sphere of personality which is in principle subject only to the free determination of the individual."[65] But the social dimension of the individual rights-bearer was kept in view as well. The right of personality was limited in the Basic Law by "the rights of others," the "constitutional order," and the "moral code." The courts acknowledged that some balancing would be required: "The limits of the right of personality are imposed by the fact that the individual must integrate himself into society and respect the rights and interests of others. . . . In the case of conflicting interests, it may be necessary to weigh one against the other."[66] In the tort area, where an individual's interest in preventing public disclosure of personal data must often be balanced against freedom of information, German courts, like their American counterparts, give great weight to speech rights, but accord somewhat greater attention than our courts do to the protection of personal reputation.[67]

As in the United States, the most dramatic instance of conflict between personality rights and other constitutional values occurred in a case challenging the validity of a statute regulating abortion. The case, which reached the West German Constitutional Court in 1975, was a mirror image of *Roe v. Wade* in the sense that the statute in question was new and permissive, rather than archaic and restrictive.[68] The German statute permitted elective abortions in the first trimester of pregnancy and was challenged on the ground that it violated the right to life of the fetus. The constitutional texts that seemed to bear most directly on the issue of abortion were: (1) the commitment to human dignity in Article 1; (2) the right to personality in Article 2(1); (3) the provision of Article 2 (2) that "Everyone shall have the right to life and to inviolability of his person"; and (4) the provisions of Article 3 mandating equal rights for men and women.

In the United States, the abortion issue is typically framed as pitting two interests against each other in an all-or-nothing contest: the right to life of the fetus against the pregnant woman's right to privacy and self-determination. The West German Constitutional Court, however, declined to rest its decision either on the right to life claimed for the fetus or on the woman's personal liberty rights. In bringing the various elements of the constitutional background to bear on the issue before it, the Court began by recalling that the 1949 Basic Law places one value, the protection of human dignity, on a higher footing than the others. In the light of Germany's "spiritual-moral confrontation with National Socialism," respect for human dignity suggested another priority: the protection of human life in Article 2 (2) had to be given precedence over the personality rights of Article 2 (1).

To give a principle priority, however, does not mean that it must be permitted to override everything in sight. The legislature had violated the command to respect and protect human dignity when it permitted abortion on demand, the Court ruled, because the absence of any legal disapproval at all gave citizens the impression that abortion was no longer to be disapproved even from an ethical point of view.[69] The fact that the legislature must accord priority to human dignity, the Court went on, does not mean that important interests of women can be ignored. Nor does it mean that criminal punishment has to be the principal technique employed to carry out the duty of protecting life. The Court suggested, in fact, that educational efforts and social assistance to pregnant women should be *foremost* among the means used to protect developing life. Within broad limits, the Court then gave the legislature free scope to devise a system to regulate the termination of pregnancy. Though it could not fail to express legal censure of abortion, the legislature was left free to *exempt* abortion from criminal punishment when the circumstances were such that carrying the pregnancy to term was not reasonably to be demanded from the woman in question.[70]

The West German Court's approach diverged from that taken by the United States Supreme Court in three principal ways. First, it was less rigid. Second, it brought more of the relevant elements of the legal and constitutional background into play, giving each a certain role and weight in shaping the resolution of the problem before the Court. Third, by resting its decision on the relatively narrow ground that the legislature could not completely exempt abortion from legal disapproval, it left the task of fashioning abortion regulation basically up to the legislature and the ordinary political process. The legislature then proceeded to enact a compromise statute— resembling those in place in most other countries—making early abortions relatively easy to obtain, and imposing more safeguards for the fetus as the pregnancy nears term.[71]

Under the statute adopted in West Germany in 1976, when Norma McCorvey's counterpart initially requests an abortion (in the first twelve weeks of pregnancy), she is provided with counseling where she is advised of the benefits and services available to her, especially those that would facilitate continuation of the pregnancy. These services include medical care in pregnancy and childbirth and generous social assistance to single mothers, as well as a highly efficient system of imposition and collection of child support. Except in an emergency, she must then observe a three-day waiting period. If, after informed reflection, the woman still wishes to terminate her pregnancy, she obtains a document from a doctor stating "whether" her pregnancy poses a serious danger to her physical or mental health—a danger that cannot be averted by any other means she can reasonably be expected to bear. Since this documentary requirement does not give the doctor a veto over the woman's decision (it is only an opinion on *whether* she is subject to serious hardship), the step is best understood as one more procedure required in view of the gravity of the decision. With the doctor's certificate, the woman can obtain an abortion within the national health insurance system. Similar, but on the whole less restrictive, statutes are in force in other West European countries, coupled with educational and social welfare systems that are meant to reduce the occasions where abortion will be considered necessary.

In the United States today, by contrast, poor, pregnant women in Norma McCorvey's position have their constitutional right to privacy and little else. Meager social support for maternity and child-raising, and the absence of public funding for abortions in many jurisdictions, do in fact leave such women largely isolated in their privacy. Justice Blackmun's assertion that privacy protects a woman's relationship with her doctor has an especially hollow ring now that most abortions are performed in high-turnover clinics where the woman does not even meet "her" doctor until she is already on the table. As for other potential sources of support and help, the Supreme Court has struck down requirements that pregnant women even be informed of them, saying such laws impermissibly "wedge" the state's message favoring childbirth into the woman's sphere of privacy.[72]

Not only has the Court ruled out mandatory provision of information to women seeking abortions about whatever support, services, and alternatives are presently available to them, its language and characterizations helped to turn the abortion debate into a deadlocked clash of rights. The Court's conceptual framework affected the way that legislators and the public see the issues in more subtle ways as well. By making abortion a woman's prerogative, the Court has made it easier to treat it as a woman's problem. Since contraception and abortion are entirely within a woman's control, the argument runs, pregnancy, childbearing, and child rearing are her responsibility. Extending the right to be let alone to abortion makes it seem legitimate, not only for taxpayers but also for the fathers of unborn children, to leave the freely choosing right-bearer alone. It is no wonder the right is still so "highly valued by civilized men."[73] Interestingly, women activists on both sides of the abortion debate have not made much of the privacy rhetoric used by lawyers and the courts in dealing with that issue. Prolife and prochoice advocates alike have overwhelmingly opted for rights talk, a choice that has forced the debate into a seemingly nonnegotiable deadlock between the fetus's "right to life" and the pregnant woman's "right to choose."

LEGAL IMAGES OF THE PERSON

The American right of privacy, and the continental rights of personality, yield similar legal results in a broad range of situations. Some of the more striking divergences seem attributable to the differing weight attached in various legal systems to one or another aspect of privacy. The United States Supreme Court has, for example, demonstrated a greater readiness to protect individuals from constraints on their sexual and reproductive liberty than from unauthorized publication of personal information or from the gathering and storage of personal information by government. Recent decisions have barred damages against newspapers that have published a rape victim's name,[74] and have upheld state regulations requiring doctors to report the names of patients for whom they prescribe certain drugs.[75] The West German Constitutional Court, by contrast, regularly exhibits more concern about the kind of journalistic intrusiveness that Warren and Brandeis decried,[76] and about the dangers to privacy posed by governmental possession of modern data-processing systems. Taking note of the "practically unlimited" technical means of storing and retrieving personal information that are now at the disposal of governments, the *Bundesverfassungsgericht* delayed a federal census for nearly four years because of the potential for abuse it perceived in certain provisions of the Census Act of 1983.[77]

In many instances, however, different legal consequences flow from another source: the image of the rights-bearer encoded in the laws. The rights of privacy and personality—like all other individual rights—presuppose a legal subject with definite characteristics. The diverse ways of imagining the possessors of rights in the world's legal systems no doubt reflect underlying cultural differences. But they seem to be related as well to the different ways in which philosophical understandings of human nature—with many slips of meaning—have been absorbed into the law in one or another part of the world. In no other country have attempts to regulate the purchase and possession of firearms provoked the kind of outcry that they do here. The intensity of feeling that such issues generate among Americans arises not only from our hair-trigger rights consciousness, but also from a certain American self-understanding: "Don't tread on me."

The differing attributes of rights-bearers in modern legal systems, are, to be sure, variations on a single theme. The hallmark of modernity in law is, as Sir Henry Maine pointed out in 1861, that, "The Individual is steadily substituted for the Family as the unit of which civil laws take account."[78] What distinguishes American law is not its "individualism," but its view of what the individual is. The comparative perspective suggests that our image of the lone rights-bearer has predisposed us to an unnecessarily isolating version of privacy. Where did this strange anthropology originate? And why did it take hold here more firmly than elsewhere?

Practically every seventeenth- and eighteenth-century philosopher spun a tale of what human beings were like in the so-called state of nature. What most of these stories have in common is that they depict "natural man" as a solitary creature. This notion not only marked a departure from the learning of the ancients, but is at variance with what we now know about the protohuman hominids, as well as about life in simple societies. The early modern accounts of human nature differed in details, however. Hobbes saw man in his natural state as driven by fear and desire, engaged in a perpetual state of war with others like himself, and entering society only for the sake of self-preservation. In Locke's more placid scenario, men were not always and everywhere at war with each other. They hunted, fished, and otherwise mixed their labor with the goods of the earth. But Locke's man, too, was a loner. He entered society to preserve his life, liberty, and property, because, though the state of nature is not identical with the state of war, it does have an alarming tendency to degenerate into one when, say, two hunters are chasing the same animal.

On the continent, Rousseau heaped scorn on the efforts of Hobbes and Locke to describe the nature of man. He pointed out that though many philosophers felt the need to go back to the state of nature, none of them had ever arrived at their destination. The reason was that they lacked a historical sense. And he argued that those of his predecessors who claimed to show us man in his original state had only succeeded in describing man as he had become, as civilization had made him. Rousseau's own account of the "true" origin of mankind has a kind of dreamy sweetness. He imagined our remote ancestors as leading lazy, sensual, unreflective lives, enjoying a pure sensation of being that can never be known again. Neither naturally warlike nor naturally fearful, they inflicted harm on others only when threatened, and were capable of a certain compassion for the suffering of other sentient beings.[79] When all is said and done, however, Rousseau's natural man is a solo operator, too, a creature whose chief concern is self-preservation.

One important touch that Rousseau added to the emerging modernist portrait of the human person was to postulate as "natural" a condition that he also believed to be the *sine qua non* for a life of philosophy: self-sufficiency. His noble savage was a strong, healthy, solitary wanderer, who mated casually without bonding. Rousseau himself saw clearly that once human beings were "civilized," self-sufficiency would elude most of them forever. This condition could be achieved in society only by a rare few, philosophically inclined, individuals. So far as those few were concerned, Rousseau shared and perpetuated Plato's austere ideal of the man who "will be especially sufficient unto himself for good living, and above all other men will have the least need of anyone else."[80] Not all of Rousseau's readers, however, observed his careful distinctions between early and modern man, or between bourgeois and philosopher.

Another important Rousseauean theme—man's free agency, his capacity to change and develop—was taken up by one of his great admirers, Immanuel Kant. But where Rousseau had emphasized the transformative power of feeling and imagination, Kant stressed the role of man's reason and will, his quality as a freely choosing, rational actor. To the emerging modernist concept of man it only remained to add the traits of *homo economicus* as they appeared in the writings of Adam Smith and, more especially, in those of Smith's followers who dispensed with his acute moral sensibility. Though intensely involved in social activities like buying and selling, producing and consuming, economic man, too, was essentially a loner. Calculating and self-interested, he represented a kind of independence that was more attainable by the average person than the philosophers' version—self-sufficiency based on property.

It may be noted that the philosophers who elaborated the individualistic basic understandings of human nature that still inform modern legal systems dwelt little on family life or on what women might have been doing in the state of nature. Furthermore, their generic images of "man" as a radically free and independent individual necessarily implied the rejection of many traditional views about what was "natural" in the relations between the sexes and between parents and children. The natural-right philosophers did accept as a given that sexual desire was among the appetites that moved our remote ancestors. Once having paid their respects to the mating impulse, however, the authors of the great works on natural right gave short shrift to the subject of family relations in "nature." They envisioned the dependency of infants as a quickly passing stage, and accorded hardly any attention at all to the mother's circumstances. Since it could not be known who was the father of a child, children were seen as under the power (Hobbes) or care (Rousseau) of their mother until they were able to fend for themselves, when they would forsake her of their own accord.[81] Rousseau described the family as a "natural" society, but portrayed family relations in the state of nature as instinctive and fleeting.[82]

Locke, for his part, was at pains to undercut any justification of monarchy based on analogy to a supposedly benevolent "natural" dominion of parents over their children. He thus took up the subject of the family mainly to attack it. He treated his readers to an alarming catalog of hearsay instances of parents exposing, selling, castrating, or otherwise abusing their children. In "some Provinces" of Peru, he claimed, citing a "history" of the Incas, people had been known to beget children "on purpose to Fatten and Eat them."[83] Thus, at the very heart of the modern tradition of natural right, there was a repudiation of the idea of the human person as "naturally" situated within and constituted through relationships of care and dependency. And in the Anglo-American branch of that tradition, Locke built the case for mistrust of government by casting suspicion on traditional assumptions about the benevolence of parents.

One element of this common inheritance that has been absorbed into the working legal systems of all Western countries is the idea of the human person as a free, self-determining individual. In the continental systems, however, this idea did not displace older understandings of personhood so completely as in the Anglo-American tradition. It seems to have made a difference that the common law systems drew more heavily from the Scottish and English branches of the Enlightenment. Romano-Germanic jurists were more influenced by the continental branches, and especially by Rousseau, who, when he turned from natural man to the subject of man in society, lavished attention, as Plato had, on nurture and education. All along the line, the Romano-Germanic legal systems retained more of an inheritance of older images of the human person: Aristotle's assertion that "man is by nature a political animal";[84] his wry observation that a man "who is in need of nothing through being self-sufficient . . . is either a beast or a god";[85] and the Judeo-Christian teaching that human beings were fashioned in the image and likeness of a loving Creator.

Continental legal systems were more affected, too, by certain post-Enlightenment conceptions of personhood. Karl Marx's excoriating attack on individualistic rights theories was in the name of man's natural sociality. "None of the supposed rights of man," he wrote, "go beyond the egoistic man, man as he is, as a member of civil society; that is, an individual separated from the community, withdrawn into himself, wholly preoccupied with his private interest and acting in accordance with his private caprice."[86] Man's essential nature, Marx claimed, was that of a "species-being," who had become self-centered only in the course of historical development. Socialist, labor, social democratic, and the various Christian political parties in Europe have all helped to temper the effects of radical individualism with both modern as well as premodern counterweights.

The ability of various influential thinkers to capture diffuse thoughts and sentiments in a memorable turn of phrase often seems to have played a role, as well, in determining which ideas took root in a particular legal tradition and which were rejected. We have seen how privacy in American law came to be imagined as a sphere enclosing an isolated individual. It was largely due to Immanuel Kant's influence that the concept of personhood came to be associated in continental law with the more outward-turning idea of free development. The Kantian contribution was indirect, partial, and heavily mediated. In 1791 and 1792, a 24-year-old Prussian youth, captivated by Kant's teaching on the human person, wrote a short book on the proper limits of the power of the state.[87] Wilhelm von Humboldt, who is remembered today in Germany chiefly as an educational reformer, tried to draw out the political implications of Kant's idea of the self as capable of freely and rationally choosing the best means for its own development. He advanced the thesis that the highest purpose of the state was to promote conditions favoring the free and harmonious unfolding of individuality.[88] As the years went by, von Humboldt's thought underwent significant modifications, but that does not concern us here, any more than does the evidence that Brandeis had second thoughts about his privacy article.[89] The genie in each case was out of the bottle.

The idea of freely unfolding development, as we have seen, eventually found its way into Article 2 of the 1949 Basic Law. The right to the free development of one's personality was described by one of the Bonn draftsmen as representing a "fundamental break with the official maxims of the National Socialist period," while the qualification of that right in the interests of the rights of others, the constitutional order, and the moral code, simultaneously represented "a turn away from pure liberalism."[90] Consistent with those views, the West German Constitutional Court in a 1970 decision firmly rejected any notion that the lone-rights bearer of Hobbes and Locke could be the legal subject of the 1949 Constitution: "The concept of man in the Basic Law is not that of an isolated, sovereign individual; rather, the Basic Law resolves the conflict between the individual and the community by relating and binding the citizen to the community, but without detracting from his individuality."[91] As a leading German constitutional commentator put it, "This implies a departure from classical individualism, but at the same time it is a rejection of any form of collectivism."[92]

The views expressed by the West German Constitutional Court in 1970 on the social dimension of personhood correspond almost exactly to those reached by von Humboldt in his mature years. The

Prussian baron's early work, however, found an enthusiastic apostle in England. John Stuart Mill chose as the epigraph for his essay *On Liberty* the following quotation:

> The grand, leading principle, towards which every argument unfolded in these pages directly converges, is the absolute and essential importance of human development in its richest diversity.—Wilhelm von Humboldt: *Sphere and Duties of Government.*[93]

In his chapter on liberty of conduct, Mill gave fulsome credit to von Humboldt for having discovered the importance of the concept of individuality.

> Few persons, out of Germany, even comprehend the meaning of the doctrine which Wilhelm von Humboldt . . . made the text of a treatise—that 'the end of man, or that which is prescribed by the eternal and immutable dictates of reason is the highest and most harmonious development of his powers to a complete and consistent whole;' that, therefore, the object 'towards which every human being must ceaselessly direct his efforts . . . is the individuality of power and development.'[94]

Like von Humboldt's youthful monograph on the role of government, Mill's essay *On Liberty* had its most lasting influence outside his own country. To a greater degree than any other, the American legal system has accepted Mill's version of individual liberty, including its relative inattention to the problem of what may constitute "harm to others" and unconcern with types of harm that may not be direct and immediate. Indeed, we took Mill's ideas a step further than he did. For, when Mill's ideas about liberty of conduct were taken into American constitutional law, they underwent a sea change. His stern sense of responsibility to family and country, and his decided rejection of any notion that all life-styles were equally worthy of respect, largely dropped out of sight. His elitist justification for fostering individuality was never mentioned (and presumably today would be disavowed by most proponents of life-style liberties).

As American law recognized an ever wider range of personal liberties, it also refined the implicit image of the person who possesses these liberties, accentuating his independence and autonomy. But the philosophical ideal of self-sufficiency that we have thus democratized is a state to which few men, and even fewer women, can aspire.[95] By making a radical version of individual autonomy normative, we inevitably imply that dependency is something to be avoided in oneself and disdained in others. American distinctiveness in this regard is most evident and problematic with respect to laws in the areas of procreation, family relations and child raising. As cross-national studies repeatedly have documented, the new freedom to terminate marriage is accompanied to a lesser degree in the United States than in most other Western countries by legal protections and social programs that respond to the needs of a spouse who has become dependent for the sake of child raising.[96] Similarly, in the construction and operation of our welfare programs, and with respect to parental leave, child care, and other forms of family assistance, the United States lags behind many other liberal democracies in protecting motherhood and childhood.

A significantly different context for envisioning the bearer of individual rights is provided in most of the post-1945 West European constitutions, as well as in several international declarations. In these documents, the individual is treated as having a social dimension, and the family is treated as a fundamental social unit. For example, the preamble to the 1946 French Constitution (incorporated by reference in the current French Constitution) provides that "The nation shall ensure to the individual and the family the conditions necessary to their development."

The West German Basic Law of 1949 devotes an entire Article to the protection in principle of family relationships:

ARTICLE 6.

(1) Marriage and family shall enjoy the special protection of the state.

(2) The care and upbringing of children are a natural right of, and a duty primarily incumbent on, the parents. The national community shall watch over their endeavors in this respect.

(3) Children may not be separated from their families against the will of the persons entitled to bring them up, except pursuant to a law, if those so entitled fail or the children are otherwise threatened with neglect.

(4) Every mother shall be entitled to the protection and care of the community.

(5) Illegitimate children shall be provided by legislation with the same opportunities for their physical and spiritual development and their place in society as are enjoyed by legitimate children.

The family as a group is said to have rights in the 1948 Universal Declaration of Human Rights (repeated in the 1966 U.N. International Treaty Relative to Civil and Political Rights):

> The family is the natural and fundamental group unit of society and is entitled to protection by society and the state.[97]

The European Social Charter has numerous articles on the family including:

> I–I6. The family as a fundamental unit of society has the right to appropriate social, legal, and economic protection to ensure its full development.
> I–17. Mothers and children, irrespective of marital status and family relations, have the right to appropriate social and economic protection.[98]

What is noteworthy about these common types of constitutional provisions (for purposes of our examination of forms of rights discourse) is that they help to domesticate the lone rights-bearer by situating him in a context. As guides for legislation and policy, they make it difficult to sustain radically isolating interpretations of the important individual rights protected in all modern constitutions. In the implicit anthropology, so to speak, of these charters, each human being's freedom and individuality is recognized as entitled to the highest respect. But men and women are also seen as essentially social beings, situated within relationships. People do not "enter" society; they are constituted in part by society and in turn constitute it.

The fact is that the philosophers' austere ideal of self-sufficiency cannot be successfully democratized. A large collection of self-determining, self-sufficient individuals cannot even be a society. Nor could such a crowd of monads reproduce itself, for there would be no one to engage in child-raising. (Furthermore, it is far from clear how we can tell whether someone who appears to have attained this exalted state is a great philosopher, or a person suffering from a character disorder.) But the ideal cannot be dismissed as a harmless fantasy. By exalting autonomy to the degree we do, we systematically slight the very young, the severely ill or disabled, the frail elderly, as well as those who care for them—and impair their own ability to be free and independent in so doing. Our insistence, even in divorce law, that self-sufficiency should be the goal for everyone, in practice leaves women bearing the brunt of responsibility for children and other persons in need of care, while running the main risk of family dissolution.

Parents—and others whose notion of self may be inextricable from relationships of caretaking and dependency—are poorly served by a legal-political discourse that exalts self-sufficiency and that treats their relationships as merely freely chosen "life-styles." Ill-served, too, are American traditions of hospitality and concern for the community. When, in our legal and political discourse, we pay homage to radical autonomy and self-sufficiency we are not speaking the language of the frontier or of the Founders. Nor are we using the second languages we still employ (to varying degrees) in the neighborhood, in religious communities, or around the kitchen table. We are adopting, rather, the language and images of certain philosophers and lawyers who, initially at least, were not proposing the product for general consumption. John Stuart Mill's view of the leading role of elites in a democracy was highly congenial to Oliver Wendell Holmes, Jr., and to other intellectuals who played leading roles in shaping American law in the early years of this century;[99] and unavowed Millean premises still seem to be operating in the minds of many contemporary jurists. Unfortunately, by embracing the notion of individual autonomy as fully as they did, by making the concept gender-neutral, and by ignoring or downgrading healthy forms of interdependence, they have distanced legal—and therefore, political—discourse from the everyday lives of most Americans.

The exceptional solitariness of the American rights-bearer is but one aspect of the hyperindividualism that pervades our American rights dialect. Another is our relative inability to focus, in political discourse, upon the institutions of civil society. Lacking an adequate linguistic or conceptual apparatus to deal with the intermediate institutions that stand between the individual and the state, we regularly overlook the effects of laws and policies upon the environments within which sociality flourishes, and the settings upon which individuals depend for their full and free development. The oversight is not inconsequential. For by designing rules and institutions as though human beings were a certain way, we tend to perpetuate that way of being, while rendering ever more difficult the existence of those whose modes of living were of little interest to the philosophers of natural right.

FOUR

The Missing Language
of Responsibility

[T]he law has persistently refused to impose on a
stranger the moral obligation of common humanity, to
go to the aid of another human being who is in danger,
even if the other is in danger of losing his life.
                    —*Prosser and Keeton on the Law of Torts*[1]

The American rights dialect is distinguished not only by
what we say and how we say it, but also by what we leave unsaid.
Each day's newspapers, radio broadcasts, and television programs
attest to our tendency to speak of whatever is most important to us
in terms of rights, and to our predilection for overstating the absoluteness of the rights we claim. Our habitual silences concerning
responsibilities are more apt to remain unnoticed. People for the
American Way expressed surprise when their research revealed that
our nation's young people are well aware of their rights, but "fail to
grasp the other half of the democratic equation," which the researchers defined as "meeting personal responsibilities, serving the community, and participating in the nation's political life."[2] Yet it is
hardly astonishing that the survey results reflect the relative proportions of attention generally accorded in public discourse to rights and
responsibilities.

Within the world of legal discourse, the silence partially lifts.
Here we find that our acts or agreements do involve us in all sorts of
duties—to compensate the persons we injure; to keep the promises
we make in contracts, or pay damages for failing to do so.[3] The
absence of a duty to act, however, has been elevated by lawyers into
a principle that—to most citizens—may even appear to condone irresponsibility. Thus, in the epigraph to this chapter, the authors of

the leading treatise on torts categorically declare that one has no legal duty to come to the aid of another person in mortal danger. Unless we have entered into a relationship (like employment) that gives rise to duties, the law treats us as "strangers" to one another. A variant of this no-duty principle recently achieved constitutional status when the Supreme Court announced that the Constitution imposes no obligation on government or on government employees to assist distressed individuals—"even where such aid may be necessary to secure life, liberty or property interests of which the government itself may not deprive the individual."[4]

Once again we are in the presence of American distinctiveness. Comparison renders some of our legal silences deafening. For most European countries *do* impose a legal duty on individuals to come to the aid of an imperiled person where that can be done without risk of harm to the rescuer. And the constitutions of many other liberal democracies *do* obligate government to protect the health and safety of citizens. This chapter continues the inquiry along the fault line between common American understandings and what we officially proclaim—this time in the realm of responsibility. Buried deep in our rights dialect is an unexpressed premise that we roam at large in a land of strangers, where we presumptively have no obligations toward others except to avoid the active infliction of harm. This legalistic assumption is one that fits poorly with the American tradition of generosity toward the stranger, as well as with the trend in our history to expand the concept of the community for which we accept common responsibility. Like a sorceror's apprentice, the assumption—when freed from legal contexts where it made a certain kind of sense—makes mischief in political discourse.

By tracing the no-duty-to-rescue rule from its ancient origins in tort law to its recent appearance in constitutional law, we can gain some insight into why American law has failed to develop a more expansive conception of what citizens owe to one another, individually and collectively. This examination of American law in turn sheds some light on why our fluency in rights talk has no counterpart when responsibilities are the subject. As in previous chapters, we will see how our legalistic rights dialect can simultaneously diverge from popular discourses, yet have a colonizing effect on them. Let us begin by considering the story American law tells concerning the obligations of fellow citizens, policemen, social workers, and the welfare state itself toward people in desperate circumstances.

THE (MISSING) DUTY TO RESCUE

Lamentably frequent newspaper accounts of bystanders who fail to summon help for victims of accidents or violent crimes continue to revive a question that has been sporadically debated for decades in the law journals: should there be a legal duty to come to the aid of another in peril? If civic responsibilities are going to receive more legal attention in coming years, the negative answer that American law has traditionally given to this question will probably be reexamined. Certainly, a strong case exists for taking a new look at the "bad Samaritan" cases. Though the body of law in question is relatively small, its importance cannot be gauged merely by counting court decisions. For one thing, it is part of the intellectual baggage of nearly every American lawyer. Furthermore, it furnishes the underpinning for several recent constitutional decisions regarding the duties of public servants. Generations of first-year law students have been introduced to basic elements of the law through one or another variant of the following hypothetical case: An Olympic swimmer out for a stroll walks by a swimming pool and sees an adorable toddler drowning in the shallow end. He could easily save her with no risk to himself, but instead he pulls up a chair and looks on as she perishes. When beginning law students learn that the despicable athlete was perfectly within his legal "rights," their reaction is generally one of surprise and disbelief. Yet the "facts" of the classroom example are no less bizarre than those of many real cases where the rule has been applied.[5] Consider, for example, *Yania v. Bigan.*

In Western Pennsylvania, on a September day in 1957, Joseph Yania, a strip-mine operator, and a companion, Boyd Ross, visited a strip-mining operation run by John Bigan to discuss a business matter. While they were there, Bigan asked his visitors to help him start a pump to drain water from a trench where coal was being extracted. Ross accompanied Bigan to one end of the trench where the pump was located. Yania remained standing beside the trench, a deep cut in the earth with eight to ten feet of water at its bottom, and embankments rising to a height of eighteen feet. Then, as the Pennsylvania Supreme Judicial Court later put it, something "bizarre and most unusual" happened. Yania, teased or taunted by Bigan, jumped into the trench and drowned. Neither Ross nor Bigan did anything to help him.

Later, when Yania's widow sued Bigan for failing to take reasonable steps to save her husband's life, her action was dismissed on the ground that the law imposes no duty on us to rescue another person if we are not responsible for his peril.[6] In the court's view, Bigan did not "cause" the death of his visitor. Yania, a 33-year-old man in full possession of his faculties, brought about his own predicament by his foolhardy leap into the trench. Bigan was not obliged to come to his aid, even though he might have done so without risk or cost to himself.

The *Yania* case was indeed bizarre, and fortunately such cases do not arise frequently. But there was nothing unusual about its legal outcome. The Pennsylvania courts, at trial and upon appeal, applied a well-settled rule of American law to deny relief to his widow. In a long line of decisions, bystanders consistently have been exempted from any duty to toss a rope to a drowning person, to warn the unsuspecting target of an impending assault, or to summon medical assistance for someone bleeding to death at the scene of an accident.[7] In one well-known case, the operators of a boat-rental service sat on the shore of a lake on the Fourth of July and watched as an inebriated customer slowly lost his grip on his overturned canoe and drowned. A unanimous Massachusetts Supreme Judicial Court confirmed that the defendants were not obliged to heed the drowning man's screams for help. As for the allegation that the canoe they had rented him was "frail and dangerous," the Court's opinion dryly observed that this "appears to be a general characterization of canoes."[8]

Judges in such cases often point out, correctly, that the law cannot provide a remedy for every harm, or even for every breach of what most people would consider a moral obligation. Still, the language they choose to make the point can sometimes be shocking to a layperson. Consider the following passage in which one judge stressed that, no matter how strongly our moral sentiments might dictate a response, a person has no legal duty to rescue a "stranger:"

> I see my neighbor's two-year-old babe in dangerous proximity to the machinery of his windmill in his yard, and easily might, but do not, rescue him. I am not liable in damages to the child for his injuries . . . because the child and I are strangers, and I am under no legal duty to protect him.[9]

Some of these cases, to be sure, are period pieces. In the Massachusetts of 1928, it cannot have aided the cause of the survivors of the drowned canoer that their deceased, with a companion named Ryan, had been celebrating the nation's birthday by getting pie-eyed in the early morning. And the more grotesque hypotheticals do tend to appear in turn-of-the-century decisions.

But the rule they stand for is still firmly established. As recently as 1980, it was held that an aunt had no duty to warn her eleven-year-old nephew that the seat on a power mower was loose.[10] The standard hornbook, from which the epigraph to this chapter is taken, sums up the state of the current law concisely, and adds a few more gruesome illustrations to emphasize the point:

> [T]he law has persistently refused to impose on a stranger the moral obligation of common humanity to go to the aid of another human being who is in danger, even if the other is in danger of losing his life. Some of the decisions have been shocking in the extreme. The expert swimmer . . . who sees another drowning before his eyes, is not required to do anything at all about it, but may sit on the dock, smoke his cigarette, and watch the man drown. . . . [One is not] required to play the part of Florence Nightingale and bind up the wounds of a stranger . . . , or to prevent a neighbor's child from hammering on a dangerous explosive . . . or even to cry a warning to one who is walking into the jaws of a dangerous machine.[11]

One might view these cases as mere curiosities on the periphery of tort law. But given the large proportion of public officials in the United States who have had legal training, it would be imprudent to minimize the significance of the lessons they communicate. As part of the process through which young men and women are socialized into the legal profession, they have entered into the mental horizon of many American public officials. Year in and year out, all over the country, in a kind of initiation rite, first-year law students have been challenged by their professors of torts or criminal law to come up with a theory to support legal redress against the swimmer who watches while the toddler drowns. The class labors mightily, but in vain. One by one, their ideas are shot down. They are made to see at last that there is no peg in our legal system on which to hang a duty to rescue another person in danger (if we are not in a "special relationship" with the person or did not cause the peril). They are introduced to the concept of *damnum sine injuria,* the class of harms which do not constitute injuries recognized by the law. One of the lessons law students are expected to take to heart from this exercise is that the law distinguishes, for many purposes, between acts and omissions. Another is that they should not make the mistake of confusing their personal notions of morality with what is legal or illegal.

The rule applied in the rescue cases now has many critics and few defenders. Yet it shows remarkable staying power. It not only has resisted a general trend toward expansion of causes of action in tort law, but it continues to govern the outcomes of cases where the judges themselves profess to be dismayed at the defendant's callousness. Furthermore, as mentioned, the no–duty–to–rescue rule has migrated in recent years from a part of tort law affecting relatively few people to a rather prominent position in constitutional law. Federal courts have used the odd rescue cases as a starting point for their analysis of the issues in constitutional tort litigation involving whether local government officials can be held responsible for the failures of policemen, firefighters, social workers, and the like, to come to the aid of persons in danger. What is at stake in these newer decisions is nothing less than the courts' presentation of an image of what type of government we have. It thus seems worthwhile to inquire further into the usual explanations of the rule, America's persistence in clinging to it, and the relationship it bears to the issue of public duties to act.

As mentioned, the standard formulation of the rule under discussion is that there is no duty to come to the aid of an endangered person, except when the potential rescuer is responsible for that person's situation or distress, or when the two are linked in a "special relation".[12] But the law's idea of special relationship is not the one that might first occur to a person in the street if she were asked what persons she is legally obliged to aid. The first group of situations in which the courts recognized a duty to rescue involved providers of various services, such as transportation, to the public. This category was later expanded to include certain other relationships, usually where there was some expectation of protection on one side and some potential or existing financial benefit on the other. To date, the special relationships that have been recognized on a case-by-case basis arise mainly from employment, contractual, or other economic arrangements: shipmaster and crew, innkeeper and guest, shopkeeper and customer, carrier and passenger, educator and pupil, employer and employee.[13] In this world of discourse, one's nephew, one's neighbor (and the neighbor's baby) are "strangers."

Yania v. Bigan came close to being within traditional exceptions to the no-duty-to-rescue rule. If Bigan had shoved Yania into the trench, or if Yania had been working for Bigan, Bigan would have been obliged to take reasonable steps to try to save Yania from drowning. It seems plain that, if the Pennsylvania judges had wished to do so, it would have been relatively easy to fit the *Yania* case at least within the "special relationship" exception. Yania was, after all, on Bigan's land with Bigan's permission, and Bigan had taken advantage of the business visit to get some help with the job of draining his trench. Some courts, in fact, have broadened the list of special relationships to include the connection between an owner or occupier of land and his invitee.[14]

Considering the overall success of American lawyers in persuading the courts to recognize new causes of action for personal injury, it is striking how hesitant the courts have been to stretch the exceptions in the rescue cases. Why, one wonders, has the time-honored process of adapting judge-made tort law to changing social needs and expectations stalled with this set of issues? If tort law is indeed, as an American Bar Association report has described it, "a mirror of morals and a legal vehicle for helping to define them,"[15] what set of beliefs is so strong as to require "common humanity" to be subordinated to them?

The answers to these questions are not easy to find in the legal literature. Among the explanations frequently put forward for the no–duty–to–rescue rule, there is one that seems plainly mistaken: that which locates the origins of the rule in the "extreme individualism typical of Anglo-Saxon legal thought."[16] In fact, there is nothing especially individualistic or Anglo-Saxon about the *origins* of the rule. Affirmative legal duties to come to the aid of another were unknown, not only in early English law, but to most other primitive legal systems. In simple societies where law—and law enforcement mechanisms—exist in but rudimentary form, they are typically concerned with the limited objectives of preventing and punishing—or making restitution for—concrete acts like murder and theft.[17] The encouragement of affirmative acts of good behavior, and sanctions for their omission, are left to other social norms—custom, convention, and religion. In early stages of legal development, the absence of an existing legal pigeonhole is often seen as a sufficient reason in itself for refusing to allow a new type of claim. Thus a primitive distinction between the active infliction of harm and the failure to prevent it was long considered satisfactory as both an explanation and a justification of the rule denying civil damages for failures to rescue. Prosser and Keeton put the matter as follows:

[T]he courts were far too much occupied with the more flagrant forms of misbehavior to be greatly concerned with one who merely did nothing, even though another might suffer harm because of his omission to act. Hence there arose very early a difference, still deeply rooted in the law of negligence, between "misfeasance" and "nonfeasance"—that is to say, between active misconduct working positive injury to others and passive inaction or a failure to take steps to protect them from harm. The reason for the distinction may be said to lie in the fact that by "misfeasance" the defendant has created a new risk of harm to the plaintiff, while by "nonfeasance" he has at least made his situation no worse, and has merely failed to benefit him by interfering in his affairs.[18]

The traditional line between acts and omissions, grounded in "deeply rooted intuitions about causation,"[19] still runs through much of the law and gives many American scholars pause about reexamining the rescue rule. Modern defenders of the rule argue, as well, that the law should not attempt to provide a remedy for every wrong. The absence of a legal obligation in rescue cases, one scholar maintains, is appropriate because realistic distinctions have to be made between the sort of conduct that can reasonably be required, and that which is above and beyond the call of duty.[20] Other commentators, while not attempting to defend the rule in principle, have expressed concerns about formulating a workable alternative:[21] What if the rescuer is clumsy and worsens the situation? What if the rescuer himself is injured while trying to help? How would one apportion responsibility if, as in the notorious 1964 case of Kitty Genovese, not just one but thirty-eight people watched or listened for forty minutes as a woman was murdered?

From a comparative perspective, a telling characteristic of American discussions of the problem is that they are conducted almost exclusively within the framework of tort, the body of law concerned with compensation for personal injury. Thus, American critics of the status quo, with rare exceptions, have been able to envision only one concrete change: a new tort action that would permit victims or their survivors to sue unhelpful bystanders for damages. Yet, if we were to hazard a guess about what troubles most people when they learn about the current state of the law, it is probably not that persons who are not rescued (or their survivors) are unable to collect money from the individuals who ignored their plight. What is more likely to surprise and disappoint an average citizen is the sense that the law appears to condone particularly shocking forms of anti-social behavior: failures to warn, or act, or summon aid.

In Continental European legal systems, when the discrepancy between legal rules and common moral standards came to be perceived as jarring, the problem was approached from quite a different angle. The problem was seen in European countries as one involving civic duties rather than private rights—and thus the natural solution seemed to be to establish criminal sanctions for failure to rescue.[22] With regard to the subsidiary question of whether a violation of this civic obligation should, in addition, be grounds for a lawsuit by particular individuals, some countries—France, for example—do permit private actions for damages, but most do not.[23] A person who fails to come to another's aid in Europe is thus answerable to the public. But he is not necessarily required to compensate the victim or the victim's survivors, as he would be if he had actively harmed the other person, or if he had created the situation of peril. Maximum fines in the European statutes are set low enough to emphasize that the purpose of the legislation is chiefly hortatory. The European statutes have been in force long enough to permit the observation that making the failure to come to the aid of a person in peril a criminal offense has not given rise to any special difficulties in practice.[24] The duty imposed, after all, is not one of heroism, but a moral minimum, requiring people to take only such measures as do not involve significant cost or risk, such as calling the proper authorities. The problems envisioned by some American commentators relating to calculation of damages do not arise where tort liability is excluded.

The question we started with, then, becomes: why, as the absence of a legal duty to rescue began to be widely perceived as anomalous, did most American critics of the status quo seek to find a new approach exclusively within the framework of tort law? Perhaps this represents, in part, a traditional American preference for private, rather than public, initiatives; or for judicial rather than legislative development of the law. No doubt the tort solution, and the lack of enthusiasm for it in many quarters, reflect as well a division of view regarding the vagaries of the American jury system. But another element in the explanation seems to be that, in the legal discourse of the Romano-Germanic systems of Continental Europe, the notion of criminal law as reflecting and reinforcing widely shared minimal standards of behavior is much more prominent than it is in the United States or in England. Continental European commentators take it for granted that making the failure to rescue at least a *public* wrong will operate to encourage compliance with certain basic duties attaching to good citizenship. As a leading French legal scholar put it, the rescue laws serve as reminders that we are members of society and ought to act responsibly.[25] Many American jurists, by contrast, are somewhat uncomfortable with the idea that law, in addition to all the other things it does, has a role in forming or reinforcing a common moral sense. An exceptional voice in this respect has been that of Anthony D'Amato, who has argued in favor of introducing a duty to rescue in the criminal law to encourage responsible civic behavior, but who counsels against a tort remedy that could render a potential rescuer "an insurer of every reckless act that he happens to see."[26]

The failure of most American theorists to even consider such an approach seems to be attributable in part to the fact that American legal education for much of the twentieth century has placed heavy stress on the distinction between law and morality. In a laudable effort to teach students to keep their personal views or prejudices from interfering with their duties as officers of the law, law schools often unintentionally promoted the notions that morality was essentially arbitrary or unknowable; and that law and morality were not only distinguishable, but entirely separate. A moment's reflection suffices to remind us of how much of American criminal law, like criminal law everywhere, has traditionally been, and remains, a repository of moral norms. But this expressive aspect of law has been downplayed to a great extent in mainstream American legal education. I do not wish to suggest that the criminal law today can or should be the energetic civic schoolteacher it was in colonial times. As a wise nineteenth-century English jurist wrote:

> You cannot punish anything which public opinion, as expressed in the common practice of society, does not strenuously and unequivocally condemn. To try to do so is a sure way to produce gross hypocrisy and furious reaction. . . . Law cannot be better than the nation in which it exists, though it may and can protect an acknowledged moral standard, and may gradually be increased in strictness as the standard rises.[27]

The dismay that law students and others typically express on hearing of the no–duty–to–rescue rule, however, suggests that American law could set its sights a little higher here without violating any canons of prudence.

The difficulty that the American legal system has with such matters reflects not only our cultural pluralism, but distant divergences in the attitudes toward law taken by English and continental philosophers of natural rights. Rousseau's vigorous embrace—at a crucial juncture in European history—of the classical notion that law can and should help to shape society and to make good citizens of the individuals who compose it, together with Kant's emphasis on the ability of human beings to create and follow ethical norms, still figure importantly in the intellectual horizon of continental jurists.[28] American lawyers, by contrast, have more fully accepted the Hobbesian idea of law as command, together with the strict separation—postulated by Hobbes and elaborated by John Austin—between law and morality.

Thanks largely to its acceptance and promotion by Oliver Wendell Holmes, Jr., this constricted idea of law was even more influential in the United States than it was in England. In the single most widely quoted legal article ever written by an American, Holmes roundly denounced the "confusion between legal and moral ideas," and asserted that a distinction between them was "of the first importance for the . . . right study and mastery of the law."[29] "If you want to know the law . . . ," he said, in a sentence that is etched in the memory of nearly every American lawyer, "you must look at it as a bad man, who cares only for the material consequences which such knowledge enables him to predict. . . ."[30]

Holmes doubted, furthermore, whether any meaningful content could be assigned to morality. In another speech that has passed into American legal folklore, he debunked "natural law" theories, observing that we all have "preferences" and beliefs which we are dogmatic about, but that other people are equally dogmatic about theirs. This, he said, "means skepticism":

> Not that we would not fight and die . . . to make the kind of world that we should like—but that we have learned to recognize that others will fight and die to make a different world, with equal sincerity or belief. . . . [W]hen differences are sufficiently far reaching we try to kill the other man rather than to let him have his way. But that is perfectly consistent with admitting that, so far as appears, his grounds are as good as ours. . . . It is true that beliefs and wishes have a transcendental basis in the sense that their foundation is arbitrary.[31]

As for legal rights, Holmes said, they are part of living by consent in a political order where officials "tell me that I must do and abstain from doing various things or they will put the screws on to me." A right, for legal purposes, is only a "prophecy" that the public force will be applied to those who contravene it. No doubt, the Civil War hero acknowledged, many rights are backed up by intense emotion—"the fighting will of the subject to maintain them." But that, he said, does not supply them with a natural foundation. After all, "A dog will fight for his bone."

This century's most influential American jurist went so far as to deplore the fact that much legal phraseology has moral connotations—right, duty, malice, and so on—commenting that, "For my own part, I often doubt whether it would not be a gain if every word of moral significance could be banished from the law altogether, and other words adopted which should convey legal ideas uncolored by anything outside the law."[32] Holmes, who died in 1935, never considered the effect that legal language and ideas already were having outside the legal community, an effect that became steadily more significant with the passage of time. His fellow justice, Louis Brandeis, however, had seen a bit further. For "good or ill," he remarked, "Our government is the potent, the omnipresent teacher."[33] Today, the explosion of law and its pervasiveness in our culture make it clear that, in this respect, Brandeis was the more prescient.

In places and times where law is only one of many coexisting systems of social norms—and not the most important one among them—the silence of the law on many subjects is of no particular importance. In societies where the common sense of the community is expressed in various customary, religious, or conventional understandings, it would be redundant to pile legal sanctions on top of social ones. In heterogeneous modern states, however, common values are harder to identify, while law and its official enforcement apparatus are more universal and highly developed than other forms of social regulation. Nowhere is this more so than in the United States. Whether meant to be or not, law is now regarded by many Americans as the principal carrier of those few moral understandings that are widely shared by our diverse citizenry. In these circumstances, legal silences can acquire unintended meanings. The absence of a legal obligation to come to the aid of another in peril can begin to miseducate a public which incorrigibly refuses to draw the line between law and morality as neatly as Holmes taught generations of American lawyers to do.

Yet, precisely because our society is so legalistic, the chances are reasonably good that a new and forceful legal statement of minimal standards of helping behavior could reinforce and value the deeds of those who already practice the ethic involved, while encouraging the broader development of similar behavior and attitudes. No one can say for sure, of course, just how, or how much, a change in the rescue rule would affect conduct and opinion. Such a change would, of course, have to be well-publicized and widely discussed to have any significant influence.[34] Still, the European experience is encouraging.[35] And, an interesting American study indicates that awareness of a legal duty to rescue does affect the way people perceive the legitimacy of the behavior in question.[36] When asked to evaluate the morality of the conduct of an individual who saw another person drowning and did nothing to help, a group of subjects who were told there was a legal requirement of assistance in such situations judged the inaction more severely than the group that was told there was no such legal obligation. The researchers considered that the observed tendency to see an illegal failure to act as more reprehensible than a legal one stemmed from a disposition to support legitimate authority and an inclination to infer that the law represented majority opinion.

In recent years, as uneasiness with the no–duty–to–rescue rule has grown, there have been a few tentative signs of movement in the common law position. Some courts have shown a willingness to expand the "special relationship" exception. Several states have enacted laws imposing reporting duties on motorists involved in traffic accidents, and, in some cases, on bystanders.[37] Largely at the instance of the medical profession, all American jurisdictions have removed one obstacle to rescues by enacting "Good Samaritan" laws granting immunity from civil liability to persons who inadvertently cause harm when they voluntarily come to the aid of an endangered person.[38] When the State of Vermont adopted one of these statutes in 1967, it tacked onto its version a penal section establishing a general duty to assist another in peril,[39] thus becoming—without any particular fanfare—the only American jurisdiction to take a European-style approach. Minnesota later followed suit.[40] The Vermont and Minnesota statutes indicate that there is nothing alien to American values in making the failure to come to the aid of an endangered person a criminal offense. But the traditional rule persists, and has moved from the backwaters of tort law, where it affected relatively few people, to the forefront of constitutional law where it has been deployed in an important legal-political debate about the obligations of all citizens to one another, and the kind of government we have.

THE (MISSING) DUTIES OF
GOVERNMENT

Unless we are Vermonters or Minnesotans, we may have to be reconciled to the fact that, if we collapse on the street, no mere passerby is obliged to help us, even by calling the police. But most of us assume that, in our advanced society, we have *collectively* taken on responsibility for our fellow citizens in distress by establishing and funding police and fire departments, public hospitals and clinics, social service agencies, and the like. If we were in grave peril and if a policeman came along, *he* would have to help us, wouldn't he? That is what the plaintiffs argued in the case of *Jackson v. City of Joliet.*[41]

On a November evening in 1980, a policeman chanced on the scene of a single-car accident which had occurred about two minutes before his arrival. The car was overturned and on fire. Although the car's lights were on, its motor running, and its wheels still spinning in the air, Officer Taylor made no effort to determine whether there was anyone inside, nor did he call an ambulance. He did summon the fire department, and then proceeded to direct traffic around the scene. The occupants of the car, Jerry Ross, 17, and Sandra Jackson, 16, burned to death.

Did Officer Taylor have a duty to look in the car, or to call an ambulance? It is safe to assume that the job description of a policeman includes the duty to come to the aid of citizens in distress and danger. In everyday life we observe police officers fulfilling that duty through countless instances of helpful, even heroic, behavior.[42] But what happens when they fall down on the job? It seems likely that a flagrant neglect of duty would subject a policeman to departmental discipline, ranging from being reprimanded to suspension or even discharge. But sometimes the question arises, as it did in *Jackson v. Joliet,* whether he or his department is obliged, in addition, to compensate the person or the family of the person he failed to assist.

In general, the courts in such cases have taken as their starting point the same general principle of tort law that was applied in *Yania v. Bigan*—that one does not have a duty to rescue a stranger in distress.[43] One might think that when the potential rescuer is a *police officer,* whose very job is to protect us, the principle might be different. But that notion was recently described by the California Supreme Court as a "widely held misconception concerning the duty owed by police to individual members of the general public."[44] The fact is that, in civil damage actions, most courts apply the same rules to police officers as to private citizens. The standard formula invoked is: "The duty to provide public services is owed to the public at large, and, absent a special relationship between the police and an individual, no special legal duty [to the individual] exists."[45]

The reasons why courts almost uniformly adhere to the rule barring private suits for negligent failures to perform police duties are mainly pragmatic. As the court explained the matter in a District of Columbia case where police failed to answer repeated calls for help:

> Establishment by the Court of a new, privately enforceable duty to use reasonable diligence in the performance of public functions would not likely improve services rendered to the public. The creation of direct, personal accountability between each government employee and every member of the community would effectively bring the business of government to a speedy halt, "would dampen the ardor of all but the most resolute, or the most irresponsible in the unflinching discharge of their duties," and dispatch a new generation of litigants to the courthouse over grievances real and imagined. An enormous amount of public time and money would be consumed in litigation of private claims rather than in bettering the inadequate service which draws the complaints. Unable to pass the risk of litigation costs on to their "clients," prudent public employees would choose to leave public service.[46]

These various factors—the need to provide citizens with redress for harms caused by public employees; the need to conserve limited public resources; the desirability of stimulating improved delivery of public services; the danger of undermining the morale of public servants—have been weighed and balanced by state legislatures across the nation. The details of the various statutory measures differ, but all states have established some system of accountability for acts performed by public employees, combined with some devices to protect the public purse from being drained by expensive litigation and large damage awards. Sometimes they accomplish the latter by establishing varying types of immunity from suit; sometimes by placing a dollar limit (a "cap") on the amount of damages that can be recovered.[47]

Apparently finding their prospects under Illinois law unpromising, the lawyers in *Jackson v. Joliet* turned to federal law, specifically to an 1871 civil rights act. That act permitted those citizens to sue for damages who have been deprived of federally guaranteed rights by persons acting "under color of" state law.[48] This Reconstruction era statute, rediscovered by civil rights plaintiffs' lawyers in the 1960s, was successfully used in damage actions against local law enforcement officers who had deprived black Americans of their constitutional rights. Litigators across the country were quick to realize that the statute might be deployed in a variety of other contexts. By the time of *Jackson v. Joliet,* a new era of what has come to be called constitutional tort litigation was in full swing. A wide variety of litigants had begun to seek remedies in the federal court system for an assortment of wrongs committed by state officials, but the precise scope of the statute was still unclear.

Jackson v. Joliet presented the question of whether a constitutional tort action could be based on a failure to act. The plaintiffs alleged that the accident victims, Jerry and Sandra, were deprived of a constitutional right—life—when Officer Taylor failed to rescue them while serving in his official capacity as a policeman. That theory was rejected in the appellate court's opinion by Judge Richard Posner, who, besides being an influential scholar and a federal judge, is a prominent theorist of the "law and economics" school. He began by noting that there is no general common law duty to rescue a "stranger," citing *Yania v. Bigan*.[49] Then, still relying on well-settled authority, Judge Posner pointed out that, "a mere failure to rescue [does not become actionable] just because the defendant is a public officer whose official duties include aiding people in distress."[50] And he observed that the theory advanced by the plaintiffs that the right to life secured by the Fourteenth Amendment to the Constitution includes the "right to receive the elementary protective services that the state routinely provides users of its highways" was based on a misconception about the constitutional duties of government:

> The problem with this argument is that the Constitution is a charter of negative rather than positive liberties. . . . The men who wrote the Bill of Rights were not concerned that government might do too little for the people, but that it might do too much to them. The Fourteenth Amendment, adopted in 1868 at the height of laissez-faire thinking, sought to protect Americans from oppression by state government, not to secure them basic governmental services. . . . The concern was that some states might provide those services to all but blacks, and the equal protection clause prevents that kind of discrimination.[51]

There was no remedy in federal court for the plaintiffs, then, because "the difference between harming and failing to help is just the difference . . . between negative liberty—being let alone by the state—and positive liberty—being helped by the state."[52]

Judge Posner was careful to emphasize that the absence of a *constitutional* right to be provided with police and fire protection, or other basic services, does not mean that citizens have no rights at all regarding these matters. Rather, he explained, it is up to the *states* in our federal system to provide their citizens with such services, and to establish appropriate remedies when and if these services are wrongfully withheld or negligently provided. If federal courts were to use the Fourteenth Amendment and the federal civil rights laws to prod states into providing services, he said, the judges would be changing the due process clause from "a protection against coercion by state government to a command that the state use its taxing power to coerce some of its citizens to provide services to others."[53] If citizens are not satisfied with the way their state deals with these matters, the political process is open to them:

> If local government does a bad job of providing police and fire protection, political retribution will come swift and sure. . . . We need not fear that unless the federal courts intervene the type of incompetence alleged in these complaints will flourish unchecked by state law.[54]

The civics teachings of *Jackson v. Joliet* received the emphatic approval of the United States Supreme Court in *DeShaney v. Winnebago County Department of Social Services.*[55] That 1989 landmark case also involved a failure to rescue and a vision of the kind of government we have. Little Joshua DeShaney, aged one at the time of his parents' divorce, was placed in the custody of his father, Randy, who moved from Wyoming to Wisconsin shortly thereafter. Joshua's mother remained in Wyoming. Child welfare authorities in Wisconsin first learned that Joshua might be at risk two years later when Randy's second wife notified the police that he was beating the boy. Later, evidence that Joshua was in grave danger mounted until it became overwhelming. Suspicious injuries were reported by hospital emergency room personnel, and numerous home visits by social workers disclosed many signs of repeated and serious abuse. Yet, except for one brief period during which Joshua was placed in the temporary custody of a hospital, the local department of social services failed to remove him from his hazardous environment. Finally, in March 1984, four-year-old Joshua was beaten so severely by his father that he fell into a life-threatening coma. The brain damage he suffered left him profoundly retarded.

The issue in *DeShaney v. Winnebago County Department of Social Services* was whether Joshua, now institutionalized, and his mother could recover damages from the social worker assigned to his case, and from the department of social services where she was employed. Apparently because Wisconsin law placed a $50,000 cap on recovery of damages for official misfeasance, they sued under the same federal statute invoked in the *Joliet* case. Their complaint characterized Joshua's interest in bodily integrity as a "liberty" interest and alleged that the defendants, by failing to intervene to protect Joshua against his father's violence, had deprived him of his constitutionally protected liberty while acting "under color of" state law. After losing in the lower courts (with the appellate court's opinion written by Judge Posner),[56] Joshua's lawyer appealed to the Supreme Court. The reasoning of Chief Justice Rehnquist's opinion (for a majority of six justices) upholding judgment for the defendants was similar to Judge Posner's in *Jackson v. Joliet*. The Due Process clause of the Fourteenth Amendment, the Chief Justice said, "is phrased as a limitation on the State's power to act, not as a guarantee of certain minimal levels of safety and security."[57] Citing a line of cases in which the Supreme Court had held that the Due Process clauses confer no affirmative rights to governmental provision of medical services, welfare, or housing, he concluded that "a State's failure to protect an individual against private violence simply does not constitute a violation of the Due Process Clause."[58]

There might have been a duty to protect Joshua, the Chief Justice went on, if a "special relationship" had existed between the child and the department of social services.[59] For example, if Joshua's abuse had occurred in a foster home where the state had placed him, his case might have come within the scope of precedents imposing duties on government officials to provide basic services to persons in prison or police custody, or to involuntarily committed patients in state mental institutions. But the six majority justices saw no such relationship here. It was on this point that Justice Brennan's dissent took issue with the majority. Conceding (reluctantly) that there may be no rights to basic governmental services under the Constitution as it is presently construed,[60] Justice Brennan regarded the *DeShaney* case as involving the state's failure to follow through competently on

a duty it had voluntarily assumed. Once Winnebago County established a program specifically designed to help neglected or abused
children, he reasoned, it invited and even directed citizens and other
state actors to depend on that program to protect battered children.
Thus *DeShaney* was not a simple case of failure to act, but a situation
where the state had set up a system encouraging concerned doctors,
nurses, neighbors, friends, teachers, and relatives to rely on the Department of Social Services to investigate and deal with reports of
suspected child abuse. On this analysis, Wisconsin's child-protection
program, by cutting the boy off from other potential sources of aid,
"effectively confined Joshua DeShaney within the walls of Randy
DeShaney's violent home. . . ."[61] In Justice Brennan's view the case
was thus analogous to the decisions involving "special relationships"
with prisoners and inmates of mental institutions.

The majority, however, held that Joshua's remedy, if any, must
come from state law, not federal constitutional law. Like Judge Posner, Chief Justice Rehnquist pointed out that the extent to which
states must protect citizens from one another is a matter that the
Framers "were content to leave . . . to the democratic political
processes."[62] He went on to make a statement, which, though legally correct, could easily be misunderstood by a layperson as endorsing a vision of government that is less responsive to citizens in
need than ours actually is:

> Consistent with these principles, our cases have recognized that the
> Due Process Clauses generally confer no affirmative right to govern-
> mental aid, even where such aid may be necessary to secure life,
> liberty, or property interests of which the government itself may not
> deprive the individual.[63]

In purely legal terms, the foregoing statement did not constitute
a startling innovation in constitutional law. But from the earliest
days of the republic, it has been the case that a certain gap exists
between popular understandings of the Constitution and the ways in
which that document is read by judges, lawyers, historians, and
other specialists.[64] Since the Constitution did not always occupy
such a central position in our system of cultural meanings as it does
today, such gaps in communication or interpretation were of interest
mainly to intellectual and social historians. Supreme Court decisions
these days, however, have a surprisingly wide readership among
nonlawyers. And—more important for present purposes—an even

wider public follows them through secondary sources. To such readers, the Chief Justice's statement in *DeShaney* could easily sound like an endorsement of an image of government that the United States decisively repudiated in the 1930s. Though we as a nation are committed in principle and in fact (if not to the same degree as other liberal democracies) to the education of the young, the protection of public health and safety, and assistance to the needy, the Court's language might suggest otherwise. The above passage all too readily lends itself to the interpretation that we are (in the Court's view) a nation of strangers—a nation that *in principle* leaves the helpless to their own devices. This potential for misunderstanding was compounded by the fact that Chief Justice Rehnquist described the events of the *DeShaney* case as having occurred in what he called the "free world": "While the State may have been aware of the dangers that Joshua faced in the free world, it played no part in their creation, nor did it do anything to render him any more vulnerable to them."[65] The Chief Justice seems to have meant no more than to emphasize here the distinction between a "public" realm of governmental regulation, and a "private" realm where individuals are left free of state coercion. But "free world" was a most unfortunate choice of words to designate the hell of pain and terror from which a helpless little boy had no escape.[66]

The United States long ago rejected a vision of the separation between public and private ordering that would leave the weak completely at the mercy of the strong. Like the shocking rescue cases in tort law, however, the *DeShaney* decision is apt to give the appearance of legitimating a failure to come to the aid of a fellow human being in distress. This aspect of the legal language that was used to refuse relief to Mr. Yania's widow, to the survivors of the Joliet accident victims, and to Joshua DeShaney, no doubt was unnoticed by the judges involved. Court opinions are, after all, primarily addressed to a specialized interpretive community, rather than to the litigants whose interests are directly affected, or to the broader public. Among lawyers, the denial of a civil damage remedy is regarded as neutral on the question of whether some obligation other than a legal one existed. Lawyers understand, too, that not every important problem can or should be "constitutionalized." Where the *DeShaney* opinion is to be faulted primarily is that it failed to take into consideration the increasing influence of legal discourse, especially the Supreme Court's constitutional discourse, on political discussion generally. Words that convey one sense to legally trained individuals may carry a very different meaning to the wider audience that now reads Supreme Court decisions, or, more often, newspaper digests of them.

In the absence of a conversion of the majority justices to the dissenters' point of view, how might the *DeShaney* opinion have avoided giving the appearance of promoting a misleading vision of the American political regime as one that leaves the most vulnerable citizens to fend for themselves? Or of suggesting that those who enjoy the benefits of living under our constitutional order have no corresponding obligations? If the opinion writer had taken the time to describe briefly the remedies potentially available under Wisconsin law—such as criminal prosecution of Randy DeShaney, disciplinary action against the social worker, and damages of up to $50,000 from the state[67]—the denial of a *constitutionally* based tort claim would have been better contextualized. He then could have gone on to make his point that, if the citizens of Wisconsin regard these remedies as insufficient, they can expand or refine them through the ordinary political process. It is true that these points are of little moment to the DeShaneys and their lawyers. But Supreme Court justices must keep in mind the potential implications of their decisions for the future development of the law, while attending to the primary business of deciding the case at hand.

Furthermore, in pointing out (correctly) that the *Constitution* does not establish affirmative government obligations to come to the aid of citizens, the majority opinion could have emphasized the extent to which our political regime, by statute, has long been one in which state and federal governments alike have committed themselves in principle and in practice to a vast array of affirmative governmental obligations. The great statutes of the American welfare state, in fact, are constitution-like in character, with strong preambles declaring programmatic rights, and substantive provisions establishing the principles, standards, programs, and agencies that are supposed to carry these rights into effect.[68] If the *DeShaney* opinion had accompanied its statement of what is not in the Constitution with a forceful reminder of the extent to which we as a nation nevertheless are committed by statute to positive rights, the reference to the regular political processes would have seemed less like a brush-off. Even a brief mention of the great social achievements that have been brought about in this country through ordinary politics, would have helped to place in a fuller context the opinion's admonition that the remedy for failures and weaknesses in the delivery of social services is not to be found in the Constitution.

By giving the impression that the United States Constitution somehow embodies a no-duty-to-rescue rule writ large, the opinion in the *DeShaney* case miseducates the public about the American version of the welfare state, and about the role of citizens in shaping and reshaping it. To be sure, the constitution-like statutes in which the welfare obligations of government are established do not commit us to guaranteeing the degree of security from cradle to grave that is the professed goal of some other nations, but they do promise that we, through our government, will lend a helping hand to those of our fellow citizens who cannot help themselves. In the veins, arteries, and capillaries of federal and state government, these basic commitments are transformed into the direct and indirect provision of a broad range of services and financial assistance—sometimes fairly well, as in the case of older people; often inadequately, as in the case of families with children. A characterization of American constitutional law by the nation's highest court that *appears* to put these statutory welfare commitments in tension with our basic constitutional values becomes part of the dynamics that will affect the future course of those commitments. If the Court had emphasized that our Constitution permits—though it does not require—a responsive, affirmatively acting, state, its contribution to political discourse would have been more constructive as well as technically correct. It would have helped to bring together the two halves of the divided American political soul—our insistence on limiting government, and our commitment to protecting the weak and helpless.

As with individual duties to rescue, then, the importance of these constitutional tort cases extends beyond their immediate facts. Where Supreme Court decisions are concerned, the message about responsibility that the law is communicating to public officials and citizens is just as significant as the outcome of the case. Questions regarding precisely what remedies should be available for public or private failures to rescue, and whether or not private damage actions should figure among them, are subsidiary. Law reformers who advocate the use of constitutional tort litigation in individual cases, as the primary means to stimulate provision or improvement of basic services in general, have grasped the wrong end of the stick. Like the critics of the no-duty-to-rescue rule who see our much-abused system of tort law as the principal framework for working out a new approach to the "Bad Samaritan" cases, they have put the individual right (and, perhaps, the prospect of lawyers' fees) ahead of the question of civic obligation.

Furthermore, it is far from clear that permitting individual tort remedies in cases like *DeShaney* would be an effective means of promoting more responsible action by government employees. That is certainly not the principal purpose of such actions. The main preoccupation of an advocate for an injured child cannot be the welfare of abused children in general or the setting of conditions to prevent child abuse in the long run (although these factors will play a certain role in the thinking of an ethical practitioner). The primary business of tort law and its practitioners is not preventive and general, but remedial and particular. If former Justice Brennan's (quite plausible) dissenting view had prevailed in *DeShaney,* and Joshua had recovered damages in excess of the $50,000 maximum allowed by Wisconsin law, this would certainly have benefited him and his mother. But would it have significantly improved the chances that Wisconsin social workers, and social workers elsewhere, would intervene in a timely manner in the future on behalf of other battered children? Or would the prospects for improving service overall have been impaired by the drain that defending such litigation imposes on the meager resources available to police departments, social service agencies, and the like? Unfortunately, we have very little empirical data to help us evaluate whether tort actions are likely to be helpful or counterproductive in promoting more responsive government.[69]

Ultimately, improved social welfare services require increased appropriations or more efficient use of existing resources, and more imaginative recourse to nongovernmental groups, as well as such intangibles as leadership, dedication to public service, good employee morale, and citizen cooperation. Chief Justice Rehnquist was surely correct in reminding us that participation in civic life and ordinary politics, time-consuming and frustrating as it may be, is the main road to change in these respects. What is regrettable is that the Chief Justice may have underestimated the extent to which the Court's rhetoric can make this difficult path more tortuous than it already is.

DOES LANGUAGE MATTER?

As in the case of individual duties to rescue, it is instructive to cast a glance at how other countries to which we commonly compare ourselves conceive of governmental obligations to come to the aid of the needy. One factor that distinguishes the American welfare state from many others is the absence of a *constitutional* commitment to affirmatively protect the well-being of citizens. In most nations of Western Europe, programs such as old-age pensions, national health insurance, and unemployment compensation enjoy constitutional protection on a par with that accorded to such individual rights as property and free speech. The comparative constitutional law scholar Gerhard Casper, commenting on Chief Justice Rehnquist's statement in *DeShaney* that the Due Process Clauses confer no affirmative rights to government aid even where necessary to secure life, liberty, or property, has written: "It is very difficult to imagine any European Court possessed of the power of judicial review [making] a stark statement of this kind."[70] The main reason this is so is that, when West European countries moved closer to the American concept of constitutionalism after World War II by adding Bills of Rights to their constitutions, they also carried forward their own prior notions of the affirmative responsibilities of the state.[71] Most of the newer European constitutions, unlike our eighteenth-century charter, expressly supplement "negative" rights (protections *against* government) with affirmative constitutional commitments to the protection of the health and welfare of citizens.[72] These "positive rights" reflect the view that the state has a duty not only to refrain from violating the rights of its citizens, but affirmatively to promote their welfare through intervention in the economy and through insuring a minimum level of well-being to all.

At first glance, then, the gulf might seem great between European-style constitutional commitments to a social welfare state and the American constitutional regime of negative liberties. Chief Justice Rehnquist's opinion in the *DeShaney* case does contrast sharply with, say, the West German Constitutional Court's recent dictum that the state is obliged not only to offer minimum subsistence to those citizens who need it, but to create social conditions enabling or empowering individuals to pursue a dignified life.[73] In practice, however, the opposition is less than the language used would suggest. For proclamations of social and economic rights in the constitutions of other nations do not give rise to directly enforceable rights of individuals. They are, rather, what European lawyers call "programmatic rights," statements of public goals and social aspirations whose implementation must await legislative or executive action, and budgetary appropriations.[74] The European welfare states, like our own, are composed of complex statutory networks of social services, networks constructed through ordinary legislative politics.

Though we in the United States lack even programmatic social and economic rights at the federal constitutional level, we do have comparable rights under the statutes that established our version of the welfare state in the 1930s, and the laws that expanded it in the "Great Society" years: the Social Security Act, the national housing and education legislation, Medicare, Medicaid; and in the legislation (and occasionally in the constitutions[75]) of the various states. The contrast with Europe diminishes further when one takes account of the fact that many statutory entitlements under these American programs have achieved (by court decision) a certain constitutional status. Thus, once certain statutory benefits (such as welfare) are granted, they cannot be withdrawn without due process of law, nor can they be distributed in a way that denies equal protection.[76] To be sure, the United States, more than most other developed countries, adheres to the principle that, once a basic social safety net is in place, the welfare of citizens is best served by guaranteeing them freedom from governmental coercion and leaving them to develop their own capacities in competition with one another. But the basic commitment is there.

The bottom-line question in all welfare democracies is the same: how well does the political process as a whole serve the needs of those who cannot help themselves? Here, though constitutional language is but one factor among many, it cannot be said to be irrelevant. For it has a powerful effect on how we imagine the role and the ends of government. In democratic regimes, highly visible acknowledgments of governmental obligations to come to the aid of citizens in need, and judicial reaffirmations of these obligations, can help to promote responsiveness and responsibility in the political process. West European constitutional commitments to economic and social protection are meant to, and probably do, guide legislative action, judicial interpretation, and public deliberation to some extent in the countries where they are present.[77]

The principal virtue of the European constitutional formulations, however, does not lie in what is most obvious—their relatively greater attentiveness to the economic and social responsibilities of the state. After all, a mere commitment to social assistance from cradle to grave can lead to relaxed vigilance concerning who is eligible for the cradle and who is ready for the grave. It is, rather, that they keep responsibilities—of citizens and the state alike—prominently in view, along with rights. The place accorded to responsibilities by American and continental legal systems, respectively, seems related importantly to the shape of the welfare state in each country—its basic commitments, the spirit in which it is administered, the degree of support and approval it receives from taxpayers, and the extent to which it disables or empowers those who depend on it.

This comparative excursus is not intended to suggest that our Constitution needs amendment, or that European social welfare states could or should serve as models for law reform here. That is far from my intent. The point, once again, is to suggest that language does matter, and that, under modern American circumstances, legal language matters more than ever. This being so, we need to consider the likelihood that old legal language and old legal silences may be acquiring new and unfortunate meanings in a society whose rights talk is filled with uprooted law talk.

THE SHIFTING SOUNDS OF SILENCE

The anomalous rescue rules vividly exemplify the traditional silence of American law regarding the duties of citizens, individually or collectively, to come actively to the aid of one another. What remains to be explored is the way in which the connotations of silence, like the meanings of words, can shift over time. The absence of a legal obligation to rescue or summon help for another person in peril was only to be expected when law itself was relatively undeveloped. Likewise, the fact that our eighteenth-century Constitution does not contain public undertakings of responsibility for poor relief seems unremarkable when we reflect on the deliberately limited size and tasks of the federal government it envisioned. Radical changes in context, however, have infused these silences with meanings that were unintended by jurists of long ago and that now are at variance with fundamental American understandings.

The principal changes that have produced this effect are the greatly increased power and pervasiveness of law and central governments, on the one hand, and the diminished authority and effectiveness of many customary, conventional, ethical, and religious norms (and the groups that generate them), on the other. Law, for better or worse, now penetrates deeply into every aspect of life. Government, whether pursuant to a constitutional obligation or not, plays an ever greater role in the lives of individuals as a source of support and security. Under these conditions, law becomes increasingly identified with legitimacy in the minds of citizens, whether it was meant to or not. Americans today, rightly or wrongly, regard many legal norms, especially those of criminal, family, and constitutional law, as expressions of minimal common values. They are disconcerted by legal norms that seem to be radically at odds with common understandings. In such circumstances, the silences of law can begin to speak. Now that law has assumed an increasingly prominent position in relation to other social norms, we need to be especially careful in our modern defenses or restatements of older positions.

Traditionally, it may have been a sufficient explanation of the no-duty-to-rescue rule that the approval or disapproval of the community could be counted on to see that most people did the right thing, most of the time. Contemporary uneasiness with the rescue rule, however, arises mainly in connection with situations where there is no "community"—members of a crowd witness an assault in a subway station; apartment dwellers hear screams at night in the street below; motorists speed by an accident scene on the highway. Rules devised in and for a society where family members, neighbors, ministers, and employers were very much involved in each others' lives, resonate differently in our more mobile urban age. In a society whose members are, more often than not, literally strangers, and where law is more pervasive than any other common bond, traditional legal ways of talking about responsibility are no longer surrounded and supplemented by other normative discourses.

As social norms become weaker, a kind of moral vacuum arises. We need, therefore, to be aware, when we restate traditional legal norms, that law has a tendency in our society to move into this vacuum. To a person who takes her *moral* bearings to some extent from law, a judge's statement that "strangers" have no *legal* duties to one another, except to avoid active harm, may convey a message quite different from what the judge intends. One way to deal with this state of affairs is for law-sayers to take special care to explain how narrow a meaning is intended. What does not seem to be possible, however regrettable this fact may be, is to eliminate the tendency on the part of many people in contemporary American society to regard certain types of law as carrying a moral charge.

Countries in the continental European legal tradition were able to negotiate these aspects of the difficult transition from *Gemeinschaft* to *Gesellschaft* with somewhat greater ease. This was due not only to their relatively greater homogeneity, but to the happenstance that a well-developed language of responsibility had found its way from a variety of sources into many of their foundational public documents at the dawn of the modern era.[78] Rudimentary principles capacious enough to encompass the basic responsibilities of citizens, for themselves as well as for one another, and minimal duties to participate in civic life, as well as an obligation on the part of government to secure the conditions necessary for a decent life, are prominent in the French revolutionary documents as well as in various eighteenth- and nineteenth-century European codes. Modern European constitutions carry forward this tradition, by establishing—along with political, civil, and social rights—responsibilities on the part of the state and its officers, of citizens in general, and often of property owners and parents in particular.

Our own tradition of the minimal "night-watchman" state— well-suited for a young nation endowed with vast natural resources and a vibrant civil society—has not generated much highly visible public language about responsibility. Blackstone's primer on rights, bred into the bone of American lawyers, postulated that the principal aim of society was to protect individuals in their absolute rights, but that "with regard to absolute duties, which man is bound to perform considered as mere individual, it is not to be expected that any human municipal law should at all attempt to explain or enforce them."[79] The Declaration of Independence proclaimed our inalienable rights to life, liberty, and the pursuit of happiness, but the only duty it mentioned was that of overthrowing an unjust government after a long train of abuses. Though many state constitutions mentioned a few civic duties, the federal Bill of Rights did not. This omission, unremarkable when state and local governments were relatively powerful, makes it difficult to construct a public rhetoric of responsibility now that the federal constitution has become a kind of national sacred text. So far as the duties of the state are concerned, the widely accepted European notion—that the very legitimacy of government depends in part on its direct attention to the material well-being of citizens—was very different from the American Founders' idea of securing "the general welfare." When the United States finally committed itself in the 1930s to a system in which the government guarantees certain minimal levels of economic security, this was not a delivery on a constitutional promise, and was in fact against the background of our traditional mistrust of government.

The point here is not to suggest that our Constitution should be amended to include a bill of civic duties, or to add what Franklin Delano Roosevelt called a "second bill of rights,"[80] which would accord constitutional status to those economic and social obligations that our government has in fact assumed. It is merely that lawmakers need to pay more careful attention to the new meanings that our traditional legal silences about responsibility are acquiring. Attending to these silences does not mean that they have to be filled up with law. The basic insight of the American Founders was sound: freedom requires many law-free spaces, where social life is left to the regulation of norms other than those of state-guaranteed law. Perhaps the law should not attempt to impose on everyone a general duty to rescue, but surely this cannot be because summoning aid to the scene of an accident is "above and beyond the call of duty." Perhaps the failures of government officials to assist persons in danger should not be the subject of constitutional tort actions, but surely this is not because we tolerate an idea of the "free world" that leaves the weak completely at the mercy of the strong.

Members of the legal profession may understand that a judge's emphatic denial of a legal duty to snatch my neighbor's child from the path of the oncoming threshing machine has no bearing whatsoever on my moral duty to do so. Lawyers likewise realize that the Supreme Court's refusal to recognize a constitutional duty for government officers to come to the aid of little Joshua DeShaney and other vulnerable individuals does not delegitimate duties arising from state law and constitution-like statutes. But when reported in the larger society, technically proper legal negations of responsibility can easily miseducate the public about what it means to be a citizen. Careless judicial pronouncements can harden the lines on a cultural grid which already seems to have decreasing room for a sense of public obligation.

At the very least, judges and legislators need to be more conscious of the radiating pedagogical effects of their activities in a law-saturated society. Lawmakers and law-sayers have more responsibility today than ever before to consider how their words will be understood—not only within a professional community schooled to distinguish between law and morality, but by a wider public that experiences these spheres as overlapping and interpenetrating. Willing or no, judges and legislators can no longer afford to ignore the way in which law, especially criminal, family, and constitutional law, is aspirational and educational, expressing something about what kind of people we are and what kind of society we are in the process of creating.

As matters now stand, the relative inconspicuousness, in American law, of individual and collective duties to come to the aid of others, cannot be said to be without consequences for the poor, the homeless, the unemployed, and those who, like Joshua DeShaney, are at especially high risk. Modern liberal polities, in order to live up to their own professed ideals, require not only a citizenry that is prepared to accept some responsibility for the less fortunate, but citizens who are willing, so far as is possible, to take responsibility for themselves and their dependents. Conservatives tend to lament deficiencies in the latter area; progressives, in the former. But neither finds in American public discourse a ready vocabulary to express these important (and inseparable) concerns.

Law, to be sure, will not by itself determine whether we will be able to develop a richer language, and ultimately, better attitudes and habits, of responsibility. But law and public policy are not entirely irrelevant to this task. As Martin Luther King, Jr., once wrote,

> Let us never succumb to the temptation of believing that legislation and judicial decrees play only minor roles. . . . The habits, if not the hearts, of people have been and are being altered every day by legislative acts, judicial decisions, and executive orders.[81]

Furthermore, there is reason to believe that public discourse, in neglecting responsibility, is doing less than it might to encourage fairly widespread American attitudes about duty and obligation. Though People for the American Way discovered an alarming indifference to *civic* duty among young people, another recent study reveals that *personal* responsibilities rank high among the professed values of a mixed-age group. In a survey commissioned by the Massachusetts Mutual Life Insurance Company, most respondents ranked "Being responsible for your actions," and "Being able to provide emotional support to your family," as their most important personal values.[82] At the very bottom of the list for most of them was "Being free of obligations so I can do whatever I want to do." If such replies represent the real convictions of the respondents, it is unfortunate that our official language does so little to affirm and support these attitudes. It is still more regrettable when the legal system inadvertently fosters irresponsible behavior, as has been the case with certain aspects of American family law.

All over the Western world, as divorce became relatively easily available on nonfault grounds in the 1970s and 1980s, legislatures began to rethink the principles on which laws regarding the economic consequences of divorce were based. Currently, the new postdivorce support law that has emerged in several Atlantic-European countries, displays three different types of approach to the problems of continuing dependency after divorce: a *continental* pattern; a *Nordic* pattern; and an *Anglo-American* pattern.[83] The differences among the patterns are primarily marked by the way they allocate responsibility for postdivorce support in cases where minor children are involved.

Continental countries such as France and West Germany place a strong emphasis on the financial obligations of former providers, supplemented where necessary by the state. In general, it can be said that the same legislation which permitted freer terminability of marriage in these countries also made it relatively difficult for either spouse to escape family economic responsibilities after divorce. Indeed, some French and German commentators have claimed it has become financially more difficult to terminate a marriage than it was before the "liberalizing" reforms.

A different approach was adopted in the Nordic welfare states. In these countries, there is much greater emphasis on spousal self-sufficiency, and child support is computed in such a way as to exact a substantial, but not extremely burdensome, contribution from the noncustodial parent. This system is made possible only because a relatively large part of the cost of marriage dissolution is absorbed by society as a whole through generous programs of public benefits. Divorce is treated, in a sense, like illness or unemployment, a personal calamity whose economic consequences are mitigated through social solidarity.

Against this background, what is striking about the way most American states now handle postdivorce finances is that they endorse in principle a Nordic-type commitment to spousal independence and self-sufficiency, but fail to establish the conditions necessary to realize this ideal in practice. Gradually, over the past twenty years, the federal government has moved to assist and to prod the states into more vigorous enforcement of child-support obligations, and considerable progress has been made in this area. At each step, however, reformers had to overcome vigorous opposition from civil libertarians concerned that employer wage-deduction, and federal help in tracing, violated the privacy rights of support debtors. Even with the stepped-up legal emphasis on child support in recent years, still widely lacking in the United States are the following features of the Nordic and many continental systems: careful judicial supervision of the spouses' agreements regarding financial arrangements for children; mechanisms to ensure that the amount of child support is fixed at an adequate level; highly efficient child support collection systems; "maintenance advance" systems in which the state not only collects unpaid child support, but partially absorbs the risk of nonpayment by advancing support up to a fixed amount in cases of default. Notably absent, too, from the American scene is the relatively generous package of public benefits and services for families that exists in Sweden, and, to a lesser degree, in France and West Germany. Alone among nations, we have moved not merely to no-fault divorce, but towards no-responsibility divorce.

The matter is of more than theoretical importance. Cross-national studies repeatedly show that the proportion of children in poverty in the United States is greater than in other countries with which we frequently compare ourselves.[84] In England and the United States, a typical unemployed female head of household lives on half of the net average production worker's wage, while her French, Swedish, or West German counterpart lives on 67 to 94 percent of what an average production worker earns in those countries.[85] In England, though, these low levels of public assistance are relatively generous in view of the size of that country's gross national product. Thus, it is the United States which has taken a most unusual and seemingly irrational stance—having embraced principles of free terminability of marriage and spousal self-sufficiency after divorce, it has failed to assure *either* public or private responsibility for the casualties. Yet, few Americans would endorse in principle the notion that we can divorce our children. And few would defend the idea that a nation can afford to be indifferent to the conditions under which its young citizens are being raised.

For a fuller understanding of these and other puzzling discrepancies between common moral intuitions and our public, official approaches to problems involving responsibility, we need not only to explore the surface of rights talk, but to probe some more of its buried assumptions. Thus far, in our investigation of American rights talk, we have observed a tendency to formulate important issues in terms of rights; a bent for stating rights claims in a stark, simple, and absolute fashion; an image of the rights-bearer as radically free, self-determining, and self-sufficient; and the absence of well-developed responsibility talk. These are the obvious characteristics that give our American rights dialect a cast of its own. Now, we must proceed a little further. In the deep structure of our language of rights, there is yet another trait that sets us apart: a neglect of the social dimension of personhood, and a consequent carelessness regarding the environments that human beings and societies require in order to flourish.

FIVE

The Missing Dimension of Sociality

In *The Republic* and in *The Laws,* Plato offered a vision of a unified society, where the needs of children are met not by parents but by the Government, and where no intermediate forms of association stand between the individual and the State. The vision is a brilliant one, but it is not our own.

—Justice William J. Brennan[1]

The American dialect of rights talk disserves public deliberation not only through affirmatively promoting an image of the rights-bearer as a radically autonomous individual, but through its corresponding neglect of the social dimensions of human personhood. In his studies of language and thought in simple societies, Claude Lévi-Strauss demonstrated how discourse and syntax can operate in countless ways to color and supplement a group's vocabulary.[2] Though the American rights dialect has little in common with the unwritten languages to which the great anthropologist devoted much of his attention, it is a case in point. Just as our stark rights vocabulary receives subtle amplification from its encoded image of the lone rights-bearer, our weak vocabulary of responsibility is rendered fainter still by our underdeveloped notion of human sociality. Neglect of the social dimension of personhood has made it extremely difficult for us to develop an adequate conceptual apparatus for taking into account the sorts of groups within which human character, competence, and capacity for citizenship are formed. In a society where the seedbeds of civic virtue—families, neighborhoods, religious associations, and other communities—can no longer be taken for granted, this is no trifling matter. For individual freedom and the general welfare alike depend on the condition of the fine texture of civil society—on a fragile ecology for which we have no name.

These deficiencies in the deep structure are not readily detectable when we listen to rights talk. It is always harder to discern what is absent than to hear what is present. One becomes aware, however, that something is missing from the underlying assumptions of public discourse, as well as from its basic vocabulary, in many situations where people have difficulty translating an important concern into political or legal language. The flag-burning dispute, to recur to a familiar example, elicited passionate defenses of freedom of expression on the one hand, and equally fervent protests against desecration of the national symbol on the other. The arguments for the former position were easy to make, fitting into familiar First Amendment grooves. They carried the day. The rebuttals tended to have a sputtering quality; they sounded more in emotion than in reason. The problem for the flag defenders, in part, was that the flag-burning controversy pitted individual rights against community standards. Accustomed as we are to the notion that a person's liberty should not be curtailed in the absence of direct and immediate harm to specified others, we can barely find the words to speak of indirect harms, cumulative injury, or damages that appear only long after the acts that precipitated them. The flag dispute was, in fact, a skirmish in what some have called a "culture struggle"—a contest over the fundamental understandings of what kind of society we are, and the role of common moral intuitions in contributing to those understandings.[3]

What was never fully brought to expression in the controversy was the underlying disagreement between those who equate all widely held standards with majoritarian oppression, and those who regard the extension of constitutional protection to, say, flag-burning, child pornography, or sadomasochistic art, as an assault on all the practices and procedures through which a society constantly defines and redefines itself. The maintenance of a vital democratic society, a society with a creative tension between individual freedom and the general welfare, requires that a continuing debate take place about just such matters. If political discourse all but closes out the voices on one side of the debate, liberalism itself is at risk. Yet that is precisely what our simple rights dialect regularly does.

Even more difficult than common moral standards to explain and defend in current political language are the interests of communities and their members in staving off threats to their very existence.

Communities are often caught in a pincer between individual rights on the one hand, and reasons of state on the other. Thus, when Detroit's Poletown residents mounted their campaign to prevent the taking and destruction of their neighborhood, they found that the most readily available vocabulary—that of individual property rights—enabled them to speak about only part of the problem. They could not find a way to communicate effectively with legislators, judges, or the press about other kinds of losses: a rich neighborhood life; shared memories and hopes; roots; a sense of place. When, as a last resort, they brought a lawsuit, they were, in effect, laughed out of court when they resorted to the only legal terms that even came close to enabling them to voice their deepest concerns—the analogy to environmental protection. Nor was Poletown an isolated tragedy. Urban "renewal" programs in the 1950s and 1960s carelessly wiped out many other neighborhoods and destroyed irreplaceable social networks in the name of a cramped (and frequently mistaken) vision of progress.

It has been difficult, similarly, for persons in areas affected by plant closings to air the full range of their concerns within the standard framework of legal and political discourse. When a Youngstown, Ohio, coalition of unions, religious groups, and community organizations went to court to try to delay, and explore alternatives to, the departure of the steel mills that had been the lifeblood of that city since the turn of the century, their arguments were as halting and awkward as the Poletown "environmental" claim. One theory advanced by the Youngstown plaintiffs was that a kind of "community property right" had arisen somehow from the lengthy relationship between the steel companies and the city, a right that gave rise to an obligation on the part of the companies not to leave the city in a state of devastation. The federal appellate judge who denied relief was sympathetic, agreeing that the mill closing was an "economic tragedy of major proportions" for Youngstown.[4] The judge pointed out, however, that American law recognizes no property rights in the "community." Dubbing their lawsuit a "cry for help," he advised the plaintiffs that their plea should be addressed to those bodies where public policy regarding plant closings is formulated—the federal and state legislatures.

But the Youngstown plaintiffs, like the Poletown residents, had already failed to make their case in the ordinary political arena. In Ohio, as in nearly all American states, efforts to draw legislative attention to problems related to plant-closings had been unsuccessful. Legislative discussions of the matter have been framed chiefly in terms of a clash between the need and right of businesses to adapt to new circumstances, on the one hand, and the merely economic interests of individual workers, or organized labor, on the other. It is impossible, of course, to know whether legislative outcomes would have been different if the terms of the discussion had been more capacious. But it is noteworthy that the United States is practically alone among the industrialized nations in lacking broad-gauged legislative programs addressed to the noneconomic as well as economic effects of factory closings on families, communities, and workers.[5]

Once again, from a comparative perspective, we are in the presence of a kind of puzzle. The dislocations caused by plant closings, partial shutdowns, relocations, and mass economic layoffs have given rise everywhere to broadly similar problems. Ripples go out through entire communities when work disappears and workers remain. In the nations of Western Europe, a wide variety of statutory schemes have long been in place to ease the transitions made necessary by obsolescence and competition. These statutes, at a minimum, require that substantial advance notice of proposed closings be given to affected workers and local governments; and that owners and managers consult with worker representatives and local government officials concerning the effects of the closing. Most of those countries, in addition, have established programs for the retraining and, if necessary, relocation of affected workers. Such legislation is not seen as especially "pro-labor," but rather as addressed to the long-term general interest in maintaining the conditions that promote family life, community life, and a productive work force.[6] In the United States, by contrast, a modest federal plant-closing bill that merely requires large companies to give 60 days notice of a proposed major layoff was adopted only in 1988, and even then only over then–President Reagan's veto.

A kind of blind spot seems to float across our political vision where the communal and social, as distinct from individual or strictly economic, dimensions of a problem are concerned. In a leading environmental-law decision, the Supreme Court held that the Sierra Club had no standing to argue for preservation of federal parkland as a *shared* natural resource. The only way the association could remain in court was to establish that particular *individuals* would be harmed by the recreational development proposal it was challenging. Justice Blackmun, in dissent, rhetorically posed the key question: "Must our law be so rigid and our procedural concepts so inflexible that we render ourselves helpless when the existing methods and the traditional concepts do not quite fit and do not prove to be entirely adequate for new issues?"[7] While this question awaits a negative answer, long-term interests are often held hostage to the short-run, and communities are often at a disadvantage when pitted against the state and a large corporation, as in Poletown, or against the market and corporate actors, as in Youngstown. The same is often true when individual rights are in conflict with the general interests of the community of which they are members—as witness a recent Supreme Court decision involving Indian lands. In the late nineteenth century, Congress (in an effort to promote the assimilation of Native Americans into the larger society) had divided some communal reservations of Indian tribes into modest individual land allotments. Over time, as successive generations of owners died, the original parcels were split up through inheritance into ever-smaller fractions. Eventually, some parcels had hundreds, and many had dozens, of co-owners. In such cases, the only way for the "owners" to profit from their holdings is to lease out the land and divide the rental income in proportion to their shares. Even then, an individual's share of the rent is often so small that it is less than the administrative cost of transferring it to him or her. By the 1980s, there was wide recognition that the allotment policy had been "disastrous for the Indians."[8]

To remedy the situation, Congress passed a statute in 1983 that would have begun gradually to reconsolidate the smallest and most unprofitable of these individually owned interests under tribal ownership. The statute provided that any share which constituted less than two percent of the tract to which it belonged, and which had earned less than $100 in the year preceding the death of the owner, would return to the tribe when its owner died, rather than passing by will or intestate succession. This consolidation scheme was challenged by certain heirs and devisees of three deceased members of the Oglala Sioux Tribe. The trial court in South Dakota, close to the situation, ruled against the plaintiffs. As a threshold matter, the trial court found that the plaintiffs had no standing to attack the statute. The deceased property owners may have been deprived of something (the right to pass the property in question on to their heirs), but this deprivation occurred at a time when the plaintiffs had no rights whatsoever in the property. For an heir or devisee has no rights in the property of his ancestor or testator until that person's death. In any event, the court went on, the statute was constitutional under a long line of cases recognizing that Congress has extensive power to alter the law of intestate succession and testamentary disposition.[9] The statute did not interfere with anyone's ownership rights so long as he or she lived; it merely removed one stick from the owner's bundle of rights—the power to transmit ownership upon death.

The United States Supreme Court agreed that the Congressional aim of encouraging consolidation in the hope "that future generations of Indians would be able to make more productive use of the Indians' ancestral lands" was "a public purpose of high order." The Court noted also that the current state of the law under the "takings" clauses of the Constitution gives legislators "considerable latitude in regulating property in ways that may adversely affect the owners." Furthermore, the Court agreed that the heirs or devisees of the deceased owners had no standing to complain in their own names, for no rights had ever vested in them. Nevertheless, the Court unanimously held that the statute could not stand.

Writing for the Court, Justice O'Connor found that Congress had crossed the line into unconstitutionality by removing one of the components of the ownership rights belonging to the *deceased* Indians. Congress' broad powers to restrict or even eliminate intestate or testamentary succession, she wrote, did not extend to completely extinguishing both kinds of succession, even where a small individual interest and a high public purpose were involved. As for standing, the heirs and devisees could be permitted to assert the rights of the deceased Indians in the same way that an administrator of a decedent's estate can prosecute the dead person's claims and collect his debts. Weighing but "weakly" on the other side, said Justice O'Connor, was the fact that the deceased individuals had belonged to the tribe, and that consolidation of Indian lands in the tribe would benefit the group of which they had been members. That consideration could not prevail against the right of an individual to pass on even a small, unprofitable, fractional share of property. The Indian lands case, together with the *Poletown* case, is revealing of the extreme vulnerability of communities to individual rights on the one hand, and to imperatives of the state on the other.

The catalog is lengthy of instances where the Supreme Court has had difficulty bringing into focus the social dimension of human personhood, and also the kinds of communities that nourish this aspect of an individual's personality. Except for corporations (which the Court has recognized as "persons" and endowed with rights), groups or associations that stand between the individual and the state all too often meet with judicial incomprehension. Even in labor law, though Congress firmly committed the nation in the 1930s to a policy of protecting employee organizational activity and promoting collective bargaining, the Court's decisions in recent years have increasingly permitted individual rights to erode that policy. One searches these opinions in vain for any significant affirmation of the basic idea of labor law: that the best and surest way to protect individual workers is through protecting their associational activity. The justices often seem to be at odds with the underlying assumption of our labor legislation, that an individual might willingly agree to subordinate her own interests to some extent by casting her lot together with fellow workers in pursuit of common ends which are frequently, but not exclusively, economic. Judicial adroitness at applying the constitutional principles of liberty and equality is rarely matched by a corresponding skill in implementing the congressionally endorsed principle of solidarity.[10]

The linguistic and conceptual deficiency in question here is not confined to the judiciary, as the Poletown and Youngstown situations demonstrate. American political discourse generally seems poorly equipped to take into account social "environments"—the crisscrossing networks of associations and relationships that constitute the fine grain of society. When associations do claim public attention, it is chiefly as "interest groups," that is, as collections of self-seeking individuals pursuing limited, parallel, aims. The connection between the health of the sorts of groups where character, competence, and values are formed, and the problem of maintaining our republican form of government, is generally kept out of sight, and therefore out of mind. An implicit anthropology—an encoded image of the human person as radically alone and as "naturally" at odds with his fellows—certainly contributes to this scotoma in our political and legal vision. Another factor, however, seems to be simply that favorable American circumstances have long fostered a sense of complacency about social environments.

In the beginning, that is, at the Founding, there was no particular reason for American statesmen to pay special attention to families, neighborhoods, or other small associations. These social systems were just there, seemingly "natural," like gravity on whose continued existence we rely to keep us grounded, steady, and attached to our surroundings. In all likelihood, the Founders just took for granted the dense texture of eighteenth-century American society, with its economically interdependent families and its tightknit communities. With most of the population clustered in self-governing towns and cities, the architects of our Constitution would have been hard put to conceive of the degree to which local and state government now has been displaced by federal authority. As for religion, whatever views men like Jefferson and Madison may have entertained personally, they probably supposed that churches deeply embedded in community life would always be around, too. How could they have foreseen that even families would lose much of their importance as determinants of individual social standing and economic security? Living in a country dotted with small farms and businesses, how could they have anticipated the rise and decay of great cities (so despised by Jefferson)? Or the eventual economic dependence of a large proportion of Americans on large, bureaucratic, public and private organizations? Or how much power these organizations would wield? Nor could they have imagined the rise and decline of broadly representative political parties; or the flourishing of public education, followed by its alarming deterioration.

This is not to say that the Founders underestimated the importance of the institutions whose durability they assumed. On the contrary, there is much evidence that they counted on families, custom, religion, and convention to preserve and promote the virtues required by our experiment in ordered liberty. Jefferson, Adams, and especially Madison, knew that the Constitution and laws, the institutionalized checks on power, the army, and the militia could not supply all the conditions required for the success of the new regime. They often explicitly acknowledged the dependence of the entire enterprise on the qualities of mind and character with which they believed the American population had been blessed. Madison, in *Federalist* No. 55, put it most plainly: "As there is a degree of depravity in mankind which requires a certain degree of circumspection and distrust, so there are other qualities in human nature which justify a certain portion of esteem and confidence. Republican government presupposes the existence of these qualities in a higher degree than any other form." Admitting that he could not foresee whether these qualities would endure as the country grew, Madison expressed great confidence that "the present genius" and "political character" of the American people were equal to the challenge.[11] With a variety of social institutions in place to nourish the "germ" (as Burke called it) of "public affections,"[12] the statesmen of our formative period concentrated their energies on the laws, and produced a remarkable design for government. The notion of civil society did not enter into the mainstream of American political and legal thought. The social environment, like the natural environment, was simply there. In both respects, we seemed endowed with inexhaustible riches.

On the European continent, by contrast, the French Revolutionaries inadvertently guaranteed that "society," as something quite distinct from the state, would become and remain a major subject of political and legal discourse. In imitation of the program of the Reformation to eliminate institutional intermediaries between man and God, the men of '89 set out to abolish the intermediate groups (*corps intermédiaires*) of the old regime that stood between citizen and state. Feudal statuses, the Church, guilds, and many aspects of family organization were targeted both as oppressive to individuals and as competitors with the state for the loyalty of citizens. In the Napoleonic era, the focus shifted. The revolutionary attack on family, religion, and craft associations lost much of its vigor, but communal and regional centers of power had to bow before the centralization of government. Part of the legacy of the period was an important political discussion that continued throughout the nineteenth century in continental Europe. Tocqueville, Durkheim, Hegel, Marx, Gierke, and others wrote at length about what the relations were or should be among individuals, the institutions of "civil society," and the state.

In France, where state and society first had been placed sharply in confrontation with one another, this theoretical speculation took the form of concern about what might ensue if social institutions became weaker as government became stronger. Examining the same historical developments that many of his contemporaries interpreted, with satisfaction, as effecting a continuous liberation of the free, self-determining individual from family and group ties, Tocqueville expressed some reservations. He pointed out that, with the growth of powerful centralized states, the very same groups that had once seemed to stifle individual development and to obstruct the consolidation of national power, could help to protect personal freedom and to provide useful checks on government. With his astonishing ability to see deeply into the long-term implications of developments that were just gathering momentum in his lifetime, Tocqueville anticipated that the loosening of group ties would present hazards, as well as opportunities, for the cause of human liberty. Like Burke, he insisted on the connection between rootedness and civic virtue:

> For in a community in which the ties of family, of caste, of class, and craft fraternities no longer exist, people are far too much disposed to think exclusively of their own interests, to become self-seekers practicing a narrow individualism and caring nothing for the public good.[13]

He was especially concerned that individualism ("a word unknown to our ancestors"), and excessive preoccupation with material comfort, would render people susceptible to new and insidious forms of tyranny. America, he thought, stood a good chance of forestalling such a fate through its many little associations that served as schools for citizenship. In the settings of townships, families, and other groups, citizens would accumulate "clear, practical ideas about the nature of their duties and the extent of their rights."[14] Each generation would learn anew to appreciate the benefits of, and sacrifices necessary for, a constitutional order. Tocqueville especially admired local governments like those he saw operating in New England, for he feared that destruction of regional and communal centers of power in France would take a heavy toll on democracy there.

> Local institutions are to liberty what primary schools are to science; they put it within the people's reach; they teach people to appreciate its peaceful enjoyment and accustom them to make use of it. Without local institutions a nation may give itself a free government, but it has not got the spirit of liberty.[15]

Another French social theorist, writing several decades later, warned of a different kind of loss. Emile Durkheim's concern was less for the political, than for the social and personal consequences of the decline of what he called "secondary groups."

> [C]ollective activity is always too complex to be able to be expressed through . . . the State. Moreover, the State is too remote from individuals; its relations with them too external and intermittent to penetrate deeply into individual consciences and socialize them within. Where the State is the only environment in which men can live communal lives, they inevitably lose contact, become detached, and thus society disintegrates. A nation can be maintained only if, between the State and the individual, there is intercalated a whole series of secondary groups near enough to the individuals to attract them strongly in

their sphere of action and drag them, in this way, into the general torrent of social life.[16]

It was only much later—with the rise of the powerful states and business corporations of the twentieth century—that Tocqueville's and Durkheim's insights could be fully appreciated. Just as certain works of great nineteenth-century mathematicians seemed useless until chaos science and the computer caught up with them,[17] so theories of civil society have only begun to come into their own as social conditions that were imagined a century ago become reality. To a great extent, urbanization, industrialization, bureaucracy, geographic mobility, mass culture, and centralization of political power have accomplished the project of the French revolutionaries, bringing citizens everywhere into ever more unmediated relationships with government. All over the industrialized world, "society" with its particularistic communities of memory and mutual aid, its relationships that cannot be captured in purely economic terms, appears to be in considerable disarray.

Many Eastern European thinkers have blamed the expansion of the state for the "withering away" of society. Thus Czeslaw Milosz has said:

> Quite contrary to the predictions of Marx, . . . instead of the withering away of the state, the state, like a [cancer], has eaten up all the substance of society. Destroying society, as a matter of fact.[18]

But observers in the West have pointed out that the market economy, too, can take a toll on society, including the family, by orienting human beings to means—especially money and power—rather than to ends.[19] Men and women in capitalist and socialist regimes alike may now glimpse their own reflections in Tocqueville's haunting passage on the loss of civic virtue:

> There are countries in Europe where the inhabitant feels like some sort of farm laborer indifferent to the fate of the place where he dwells. The greatest changes may take place in his country without his concurrence; he does not even know precisely what has happened; . . . Worse still, the condition of his village, the policing of his road, and the repair of his church and parsonage do not concern him; he thinks that all those things have nothing to do with him at all, but belong to a powerful stranger called the government. . . . Furthermore, this man

who has so completely sacrificed his freedom of will does not like obedience more than the next man. He submits, it is true, to the caprice of a clerk, but as soon as force is withdrawn, he will vaunt his triumph over the law as over a conquered foe. Thus he oscillates the whole time between servility and license.[20]

When nations reach this point, Tocqueville surmised, "either they must modify both laws and mores or they will perish, for the fount of public virtues has run dry; there are subjects still, but no citizens."[21]

Now that so much less "society" flourishes between the individual and the state, certain questions—long unasked in the United States—press for recognition: Where does a republic, depending on a citizenry capable of participating in democratic political processes, find men and women with a grasp of the skills of governing and the willingness to use them in the public service? Where does a welfare state find citizens with enough fellow feeling to reach out to others in need, yet with enough sense of personal responsibility to assume substantial control over their own lives? What, if anything, needs to be done to protect social environments—families, neighborhoods, workplace associations, and religious and other communities of obligation—that traditionally have provided us with our principal opportunities to observe, learn, and practice self-government as well as government of the self?

Though these questions are increasingly urgent, our current public discourse makes it difficult to talk about them. Our legal and political vocabularies deal handily with rights-bearing individuals, market actors, and the state, but they do not afford us a ready way of bringing into focus smaller groups and systems where the values and practices that sustain our republic are shaped, practiced, transformed, and transmitted from one generation to the next.[22] In short, we have a serious and largely overlooked ecological problem, yet our ability to address it lags even behind our halting progress on problems relating to natural environments.[23] Many naturalists have come to the realization that it borders on the bizarre to solemnly debate whether animals and trees have rights, at a time when all interdependent life on the planet is threatened by systematic degradation of the environment—a degradation that is often defended in the name of economic rights. In the human sciences, we have been slower to take a more global view. Consider what is missing from current debates about the smallest and most important of social environments—the family.

"THE WAR OVER THE FAMILY"

At first glance, it might seem that families are neglected neither in political nor legal discourse. "Family values" have long been a staple of American campaign rhetoric; family law is in a state of unprecedented ferment; and a lively discussion of "family policy" is currently taking place. On closer inspection, however, the politicians for the most part are confining themselves to empty platitudes; family law has become a battleground for a struggle between defenders of the "traditional" family and those who would deconstruct families into their individual component parts; and the family policy debate has degenerated into what Brigitte and Peter Berger have called "a vociferous war over the family."[24] Despite its sound and fury, the war over the family has an odd, remote, quality. Its principal partisans often seem more absorbed in their arguments with one another than with families themselves, or with the conditions that families might require in order to flourish. Many of the combatants seem to have achieved the peculiar mental state that the late Thomas Reed Powell associated with lawyers: the ability to think about something that is inextricably connected to something else without thinking about what it is connected to.

The war over the family is, to a great extent, a war of words, and about words. If a speaker consistently refers to "the family" rather than "families," or vice versa, this is often a signal that sides have been taken. (Here, since my intent is to challenge the terms of the debate, I will use these terms interchangeably, with the understanding that "the family" is a social institution—like "the firm" or "the law"—that can take many forms.)

There are four main positions in the conflict which can be briefly summarized as follows:

1. On the cultural right, we find the defenders of what in those circles is apt to be called the "traditional" family, imagined as a household founded on a marriage between a husband-breadwinner and a wife-homemaker. The family, in these quarters, is often said to be the "basic social unit."
2. On the cultural left, the "traditional" family is apt to be characterized as "patriarchal," the artifact of an oppressive male-dominated society, a social construct that both reflects and promotes the systematic subordination of women. Here, one tends to speak of "families" rather than "the family"; the individual is taken to be the basic unit of society; and there is particular solicitude for "nontraditional" family forms.

3. On the economic right, claiming that family poverty and related social ills have actually worsened over the period of greatest governmental attention to them, many conservatives advocate a laissez-faire family policy as a spur to self-reliance, and as the best protection in the long run for family life.
4. On the economic left, the same dismal statistics are widely believed to require redoubled public effort and expense, with the government taking over many of the tasks that family members no longer find it easy to perform.

Thus, one might say, with only a slight degree of caricature, we have the totem vs. the taboo on the culture front; and the heartless vs. the ham-handed on the economic front. Much of the frustration and discontent of American voters stems from having to make choices between these kinds of positions.

Until the 1960s it could be said that the American legal system embodied ideas about "the family" that corresponded fairly closely to those now held on the cultural right. The domestic relations law of the various states was organized around a marriage-centered conception of the family. Marriage was treated as an important support institution, and as a decisive determinant of the social status of spouses and children. The marital relationship was supposed to last until the death of a spouse and was not otherwise terminable, except for serious cause. Within the family, the law gave the husband-father the predominant role in decision making, and imposed on him primary responsibility for the material needs of the family. The wife-mother was to fulfill her role primarily by caring for the household and children. Family solidarity and the community of life between spouses were emphasized over the individual personalities and interests of family members. (Thus, for example, husbands, wives, and children, as a rule, could neither enforce contracts against one another, nor sue each other for personal injury damages.) Procreation and child rearing were assumed to be major purposes of marriage, and sexual relations within marriage were supposed to be exclusive, at least for the wife. Marriage, procreation, and divorce were supposed to take place within legal categories. Children born outside marriage had hardly any legal existence at all.

Obviously, these legal assumptions never corresponded perfectly to family behavior patterns in the United States. By the 1960s, several of them were quite noticeably at variance with the way many Americans were living. Over the past twenty-five years, American family law has been dramatically reshaped by statute and court decision, including constitutional rulings, to the point where it now embodies a set of assumptions closer to those of the cultural left. Divorce has become, in a sense, an individual right now that marriage has increasingly been made terminable on the request of either spouse. Explicitly gender-based legal distinctions have been eradicated from domestic relations law. Family members are, to some extent, able to tailor their relationships by contract, and to sue each other in tort. The legal differences between formal and informal marriage have been blurred, and nearly every vestige of legal discrimination against children born outside of marriage has been held unconstitutional. The old presumption that a husband's duty to support his wife would survive divorce has been replaced by the principles that ex-spouses should be self-sufficient, and that spousal support, if awarded, should be temporary.

In constitutional law, the image of marriage shifted suddenly from a community of life to an alliance of independent individuals. Striking down Connecticut's birth control law in 1965 as an unwarranted interference with the husband-wife relationship, the Supreme Court had waxed eloquent about marriage:

> Marriage is a coming together for better or for worse, hopefully enduring, and intimate to the degree of being sacred. It is an association that promotes a way of life, not causes; a harmony in living, not political faiths; a bilateral loyalty, not commercial or social projects.[25]

Seven years later, extending constitutional privacy protection to unmarried persons in another birth control case, the Court changed its tune. "[T]he married couple is not an independent entity with a mind and heart of its own, but an association of two individuals each with a separate intellectual and emotional make-up."[26] In a perceptive analysis of Supreme Court cases involving the parent-child relationship, Laurence Tribe has observed that, there too, upon close examination, "what at first may appear to be 'family rights' emerge as rights of individuals only."[27] In these and numerous other ways, the law began to treat families primarily as collections of individuals, bound loosely together with ties that were increasingly fluid, detachable, and interchangeable.

Now that the process of legally dissolving families into their component parts is well-advanced, it is only to be expected that we should see a flurry of disputes contesting the definition of "family" in various statutes and regulations. Confusion currently reigns as courts and legislatures try to figure out what is or should be considered a "family" for purposes of zoning, employee health and death benefits, succession to rent-controlled residential tenancies, and so on. If married couples, why not unmarried couples? If unmarried heterosexual couples, why not same-sex couples? If same-sex couples, why not friends without sexual relationships? Like "property," "family" has now become a pigeonhole into which lawyers try to fit all sorts of relationships even as the category itself is crumbling.

It is easy these days to see the defects in the idea that "the family" is isomorphic with the homemaker-breadwinner unit. Far from being "traditional," that type of family did not even become possible for large numbers of people until the early part of this century. Today, any discussion that takes sharp sex-role divisions in child raising and income production to be normative leaves most American families out of the picture. Women's educational and economic aspirations, steep increases in female-headed households, and the financial pressures that bear down on all child-raising households make it unlikely that the breadwinner-homemaker model will have a strong resurgence in the foreseeable future. What we do see, though, is the common use of that model—or a close variant of it—for a period of time when a couple's children are small. And this is a point of great importance, often neglected by the deconstructers of the family.

Some of the new legal images of family that are emerging, however, are as flawed as the traditional models had become. In the first place, the idea that existing gender-related differences in child-raising roles and income production can or should be disregarded is as unrealistic as the notion that they can be rigidly prescribed. The new economic interdependence between husbands and wives is highly asymmetrical, with women more vulnerable to divorce and to fluctuations in the labor market. Nowhere is this more evident than between parents of young children. In most such households, both spouses are employed, but the wife is bearing the primary responsibility for child raising, while her outside work yields lower pay, lower status, and less security than the husband's.

The notion that a "family" is whatever one wants it to be, moreover, is unhelpful in analyzing specific policy problems. The difficulty of arriving at an all-purpose definition of "family" need not doom the search for a sensible family policy, nor must it deprive the term of meaningful content in various contexts. Anthropologists and sociologists usefully remind us that, on the one hand, many family types coexist in every society; and, on the other, that family forms are not infinitely various. Generally, they have reserved the term family to designate groups containing more than one generation. The current legal disputes over the proper interpretation of the word in various contexts are attributable to several relatively recent developments: changes in behavior and attitudes regarding sexuality, procreation, and marriage; heightened awareness of and attention to American diversity; the desire of many persons involved in nontraditional living arrangements to win approval or at least legitimacy for these arrangements; and the efforts of single persons or informal cohabitants of various sorts to secure access to benefits or preferences currently dispensed on the basis of "family" membership. Courts, legislatures, city councils, and employers are in the process of adjusting to these developments. Eventually, it seems likely that "family," for legal purposes, will be defined in different ways, depending on the aims of the rules or programs involved. Many of the problems can and will be handled without using the word at all.

American political discourse permits many things to be said about the competing interests and ideals at stake in these disputes. But our individual rights–laden public language makes it surprisingly difficult to take account of the obvious fact that the public has a much greater interest in the conditions under which children are being raised than in the ways that adults generally choose to arrange their lives. European laws and policies, by contrast, routinely distinguish for many purposes (as sociologists do) between households that are engaged in child rearing and other types of living arrangements. But in the United States, which has never had an explicit national family policy, we are groping toward this useful distinction only slowly, and with more difficulty than seems necessary.

Thus, for example, when an area is zoned for single-family dwellings, it is hard to see any rationale for excluding a grandmother raising her two grandsons. Yet East Cleveland tried to do just that in the 1970s. The case had to go all the way to the United States Supreme Court for it to be settled that a municipality could not constitutionally limit the definition of family for zoning purposes to the so-called nuclear family.[28] American history and traditions, Justice Powell rightly observed, support "a larger conception of the family" in which many relatives and "especially grandparents shar[e] a household along with parents and children." It is doubtful, however, that Justice Powell would have approved expanding the concept of family to include a group of male college student housemates with four-month renewable leases, as the New Jersey Supreme Court did in 1990.[29] Dimly, one can discern in recent cases and statutes dealing with divorce,[30] unmarried cohabitation,[31] and zoning,[32] a growing sensitivity to the special circumstances of households that are, or have been, engaged in raising children. These developments are the first steps toward a sensible American family policy. Putting children at the center of our family policy does not belittle or degrade childless individuals, or stigmatize other types of living arrangements. It merely recognizes the high public interest in the nurture and education of citizens.

If we are eventually able to move beyond squabbles over what counts as a family, to the question of how best to aid and support child-raising families, we will find ourselves in the midst of other myopic disputes. There is now wide recognition that parents, especially single mothers, are under exceptional financial and personal stress. There is a consensus, too, across the political spectrum, on the necessity of improving and vigorously enforcing the child-support laws. Beyond this, however, there is little common ground. Many on the economic left advocate that government should come to the aid of families with massive public day-care, educational, housing, and assistance programs, while many on the economic right insist that such programs are not only ineffective, but counterproductive; that they foster dependency, rather than strengthening family life.

Though conservatives and liberals wrangle endlessly about the specifics of family policy, their usual explanations of why the matter is worth discussing are remarkably similar: healthy families enable individuals to reach their full potential; dysfunctional families breed delinquency and crime; families are the main source upon which we depend for the work force that funds our social security system and that sustains our competitive position in the world economy. Important as all these social and economic concerns undeniably are, it is nevertheless a striking feature of the current family policy debate that its participants rarely allude, even in passing, to the *political* implications of what appears to be a crisis in nurture and education. It is fair to say that most participants in the war over the family simply assume the existence of a free, democratic, and egalitarian regime as part of the background.

We do not hear very much about the relationship of nurture and education to the maintenance of such a regime. If history teaches us anything, however, it is that a liberal democracy is not just a given; that there seem to be conditions that are more, or less, favorable to its maintenance, and that these conditions importantly involve character—the character of individual citizens, and the character of those who serve the public in legislative, executive, judicial, or administrative capacities. Character, too, has conditions—residing to no small degree in nurture and education. Thus one can hardly escape from acknowledging the political importance of the family. Yet this is a subject on which family policy antagonists are strangely silent, giving their "war" at times the look of a game of blindman's buff.

Social historians of the future no doubt will be bemused by the fact that we late–twentieth-century Americans found it acceptable to discuss publicly in detail the most intimate aspects of personal life, while maintaining an almost prudish reserve concerning the political significance of family life. There are many plausible explanations for our reticence. One, no doubt, is the defect of our liberal virtues. Most of us aspire seriously to tolerance and broad-mindedness, with the consequence that it is hard to talk about certain matters that involve character. The word "judgmental" has become an epithet in some circles. A second factor that makes this kind of discussion difficult is that many of the changes that have adversely affected the caretaking and socializing capacities of families are associated with developments that few would care to call in question: improvements in the educational and economic position of women; the material benefits that a second family income provides; the ease with which one can terminate an unhappy marriage; and greater individual freedom generally—to realize one's own dreams, hopes, and ambitions, to overcome adversity, to make a fresh start. A third is the celebrated Pogo epiphany: "We have met the enemy and they is us." How many parents, if we are really honest, can say we have not passed the economic or emotional cost of some personal decision on to our children? All in all, it is easier not to talk about such matters.

It has become increasingly clear, however, that whatever can be said, for good or ill, about current patterns of family behavior, they are not optimal—economically or emotionally—for children. In 1990, a national commission on adolescent health reported that, for the first time in American history, a whole generation of American teenagers was "less healthy, less cared for, [and] less prepared for life than their parents were at the same age."[33] Scholarly and popular literature abounds with discussion and speculation concerning the relation between child-raising conditions and crime rates, national competitiveness, and the future of the social security system. Yet the first question that Tocqueville—or the Founders—would have been likely to ask is the very one we avoid: What are the implications of these conditions for sustaining the American experiment in ordered liberty?

On this score, the 1989 People for the American Way survey of the political attitudes of young Americans was disquieting. A key conclusion they reached was that a sense of the importance of civic participation was almost entirely lacking in "Democracy's Next Generation":

> Young people have learned only half of America's story. Consistent with the priority they place on personal happiness, young people reveal notions of America's unique character that emphasize freedom and license almost to the complete exclusion of service or participation. Although they clearly appreciate the democratic freedoms that, in their view, make theirs the 'best country in the world to live in,' they fail to perceive a need to reciprocate by exercising the duties and responsibilities of good citizenship.[34]

When asked to describe what makes a "good citizen," only 12 percent of the young people surveyed mentioned voting.[35] Fewer than a quarter said that they considered it important to help their community to be a better place.[36] Remarkably, when asked what makes America special, only seven percent mentioned that the United States was a democracy.[37] (One young person, though, replied, "Democracy and rock and roll.")[38] People for the American Way prefaced their report of these findings with the ominous statement: "[I]t is time to sound the alarm about the toll that the growing disconnectedness of America's young people will exact from our democracy."[39]

Though distressed enough to sound an alarm, People for the American Way offered no theory about *why* young people seemed so lacking in a sense of civic responsibility. In fact, one could read their findings and conclude that the attitudes revealed were simply a function of immaturity. The current generation might be no more or less self-centered or politically apathetic than their parents once were.

Doubt was cast on that semi-comforting interpretation, however, by a second study released in June 1990 by the Times Mirror Center.[40] The Times-Mirror study, too, reported a widespread indifference among young adults toward government, politics, public affairs,—and even to news about the outside world. Unlike People for the American Way, the Times-Mirror group searched back through 50 years of public opinion data to compare today's young people with Americans of the past. They concluded that the current cohort knows less, cares less, votes less, and is less critical of its leaders and institutions than young people have been at any time over the past five decades. Furthermore, although younger members of the public in the past "have been at least as well informed as older people," that is no longer the case with the current generation. Without purporting to provide an explanation of why this might be so, the Times-Mirror group did speculate off-handedly that the "decline of the family" might have played a role, along with "television" and the "lack of mobilizing issues."

The question of whether there is a connection between the civic apathy of many young people and current conditions of family life would seem at least to merit attention. Where do citizens acquire the capacity to care about the common good? Where do people learn to view others with respect and concern, rather than to regard them as objects, means, or obstacles? Where does a boy or girl develop the healthy independence of mind and self-confidence that enable men and women to participate effectively in government and to exercise responsible leadership? As Tocqueville cautioned, if democratic nations should fail in "imparting to all citizens those ideas and sentiments which first prepare them for freedom and then allow them to enjoy it, there will be no independence left for anybody, . . . neither for the poor nor for the rich, but only an equal tyranny for all."[41] Even under the best of conditions, he pointed out that the task would not be an easy one: "It is hard to make the people take a share in government; it is even harder to provide them with the experience and to inspire them with the feelings they need to govern well."[42]

Like many other high-minded nineteenth-century intellectuals, Tocqueville assumed that the family would be a dependable force in the service of these tasks. It was in the nation's homes where children would acquire the republican virtues of cooperation and self-restraint. It is strange, in a way, that he who had seen further than most of his contemporaries into the transformative effects of individualism and egalitarianism on traditional social arrangements, did not pursue the logic of his own analysis into the domain of family life. The reason, apparently, is that there seemed to him to be a self-evident distinction between bonds that were merely legal or social (like those between master and servant), and those he called "natural." He could thus write (and presumably believe) that, in general, "Democracy loosens social ties, but it tightens natural ones.

At the same time that it separates citizens, it brings kindred closer together."[43] That the great observer nodded here is now plain. But the aspects of current patterns of family organization that would have seemed admonitory to him are obscured for us by a nostalgic attachment to the "traditional" family on the one hand, and, on the other, by a relentless deconstruction of the family into collections of loosely affiliated individuals pursuing their own aims and interests.

ENVIRONMENTS WITHIN ENVIRONMENTS

To move from a verbal war over the family to sitting down and reasoning together about conditions of family life, it would be helpful to step back a few paces for a more comprehensive view of the problems. What is needed, in other words, is a shift from family *policy* to family *ecology*. Before we can frame "policy" for an institution that is inextricably connected to other institutions, we need to think more carefully than we have to date about connectedness. Family policy is not only a matter of responding to the present crisis, but of setting conditions and shifting probabilities for the future. Thus, as Urie Bronfenbrenner suggests in his important book on the ecology of human development, it is not enough to study a developing child alone, nor even to study a child within the setting of a family, for children and families are crucially affected by conditions in a host of interconnected environments.[44] Just as individual identity and well-being are influenced by conditions within families, families themselves are sensitive to conditions within surrounding networks of groups—neighborhoods, workplaces, churches, schools, and other associations. Public deliberation about family issues therefore needs to encompass such environments.

The importance of keeping these interacting social subsystems in view has been vividly illustrated by a path-breaking study of the effects of adversity in early childhood on human development.[45] In the early 1950s, an ambitious team of California researchers decided to begin following closely the development—from prenatal history to adulthood—of the entire group of children born in 1955 in a moderate-sized American community. The team selected the Hawaiian island of Kauai, with a population of about 45,000, as the location for the study. The island's multiracial population afforded the opportunity to take a variety of cultural differences in child-rearing practices into account, and its low geographic mobility was expected to and did facilitate follow-up. Health, educational, and social services on Kauai were comparable to those in communities of similar size on the mainland United States.

Sad to say, in this island paradise, nearly a third of the 698 children born in 1955 were classified at some point as in a "high risk" category; that is, they were exposed to four or more such drawbacks as physical disability, family discord, chronic poverty, and parents who were alcoholic, undereducated, or mentally disturbed. (Studies from the 1950s indicate that Kauai was similar in this respect to mainland communities.) As the years went by, the researchers were struck by the fact that many of the children they had identified as subject to severe disadvantages were able to lead personally satisfying and socially productive lives as adults. Remarkably, one out of three of these seriously disadvantaged children "went on to develop healthy personalities, stable careers and strong interpersonal relations."

The contribution of the Kauai project to social ecology is that, by closely monitoring the development of a large group at regular intervals from birth forward, the researchers were able to identify certain "protective factors" that can help children to survive and thrive *despite* early adverse conditions. These factors fall into three broad groups. The first, relating to the intelligence and other personal characteristics of the child, is largely beyond anyone's control. Some fortunate children apparently possess, even in infancy, engaging temperamental qualities that enable them to elicit positive responses from others. A second group of factors, not surprisingly, concerns the family setting. The Kauai investigators affirmed received wisdom that children, in general, benefit from having a stable, interactive, intact household; from having at least one caretaker (not necessarily a parent) with whom they can establish a close bond; and from having structure and rules in their milieu. The better the quality of the home environment, the more competence was displayed by the children.

Bearing in mind, however, that elements of the home environments of high-risk children are usually part of what places them at risk, it is the third group of protective factors identified in the study that is of potential importance to policy makers. This third group includes various support systems external to the family that may be affected to some extent, for better or worse, by governmental action or abstention. School, for example, played a crucial role in the lives of many of the survivor-children who saw it as a "home away from home, a refuge from a disordered household." Several youngsters also found role models, mentors, confidants, and opportunities for friendship in church groups, the YMCA or YWCA, 4-H groups, Boy and Girl Scouts, athletic groups, and the like. As Dr. Emmy Werner, the director of the project, put it, "With the help of these support networks, the resilient children developed a sense of meaning in their lives and a belief that they could control their fate." Active participation in a church (especially one providing intense activity, acceptance, and a sense of mission) was often a "critical turning point" in a child's life.[46] Interestingly, neither formal social service agencies nor mental health professionals were found to have played a significant role in enabling the children to cope with adversity.[47] In adulthood, too, most of the "survivor" individuals, in times of need, turned to informal sources of support and to other family members, rather than to the helping professions. This led Dr. Werner to suggest that, "In many situations it might make better sense and be less costly as well to strengthen such available informal ties to kin and community than it would to introduce additional layers of bureaucracy into delivery of services." Dr. Werner is careful to point out, however, that this does not mean that successful governmental programs like Headstart and the food plan for poor women and infant children (WIC) should be abandoned. What is needed, rather, is a more diversified family policy, fitting public and private initiatives together in creative ways.

The significance of the Kauai study was increased by a fortuitous accident of timing. The Kauai researchers tracked a group of children who, with hindsight, can be seen to have been pioneers in uncharted territory. For the 1955 cohort entered adolescence just at the beginning of a period of sudden demographic change that swept the entire industrialized world. The major shifts in birth rates, marriage rates, and divorce rates that began in the mid-1960s caught population experts everywhere by surprise. Looking back on a two-decade period, the French demographer Louis Roussel has written:

> What we have seen between 1965 and the present, among the billion or so people who inhabit the industrialized nations, is . . . a general upheaval across the whole set of demographic indicators, a phenomenon rare in the history of populations.
>
> In barely twenty years, the birth rate and the marriage rate have tumbled, while divorces and illegitimate births have increased rapidly. All these changes have been substantial, with increases or decreases of more than fifty percent. They have also been sudden, since the process

of change has only lasted about fifteen years. And they have been general, because all industrialized countries have been affected beginning around 1965.[48]

The children in the Kauai cohort were born just in time to experience the great demographic upheavals and the ambitious Great Society programs of the 1960s. When the winds of social change began to blow, the study reveals that families on Kauai experienced the same stresses as American families generally.

It was just in this period, too, that we witnessed "the breakdown of traditional ways of handling distress," ways that "are located in the family primarily, but also in the ethnic group, the neighborhood, the church."[49] The phenomena were not unrelated. As the writer of an unsigned essay in *The New Yorker* put it, we have experienced a "fraying of the net of connections between people at many critical intersections. . . ."

> Each fraying connection accelerates the others. A break in one connection, such as attachment to a stable community, puts pressure on other connections: marriage, the relationship between parents and children, religious affiliation, a feeling of connection with the past— even citizenship, that sense of membership in a large community which grows best when it is grounded in membership in a small one.[50]

In retrospect, it is apparent that many of the mutually reinforcing protective factors that had been found to promote the welfare of a significant minority of high-risk children in Kauai are far less securely in place now than they were for the 1955 cohort.

Indeed, all indications are that even more American children today are at "high risk," while less protection is available to them. In 1960, for example, fewer than 10 percent of American children lived in a single-parent home; by 1988, that figure had risen to nearly one-quarter,[51] and more than half of all children born in the 1980s are expected to spend at least part of the years before they reach 18 in a one-parent household.[52] The overwhelming majority of these homes, now as previously, are headed by women, and their economic circumstances are notoriously precarious. Nearly half of all female-headed families with children under six live in poverty.[53] Though rapid increases in women's labor force participation have been a positive development for families in many ways, they have profoundly affected the caretaking capacity of two- as well as one-

parent homes. While the proportion of American mothers with children under six who are in the labor force has increased from 30
percent in 1970 to 56 percent in 1988, adequate child care substitutes
have not increased correspondingly.[54]

Under the current circumstances, then, external support systems
like those identified in the Kauai study seem more necessary today
than ever—to help intact and functioning families to keep going, as
well as to assist members of families that are broken or faltering. The
problem, however, is that schools, churches, youth groups, and so
on, not only served as reinforcements for, but themselves depended
on, families, neighborhoods, and each other for personnel and reinforcement. They, too, are now under stress to a degree that would
have been hard to imagine in the mid-1950s. It is sobering to reflect
that the typical child-abuser is (as Randy DeShaney was) a loner, a
socially isolated individual without a support system.[55]

By demonstrating the importance, not only of well-known factors in the home environment to children, but of supportive external
communities to families and children alike, the Kauai study challenges us to reflect on the relative absence of public deliberation
concerning the state of the social structures within which we learn
the liberal virtues and practice the skills of government; the mediating institutions that stand as buffers between individuals and the
state; the diverse groups that share with families the task of nurtur-
ing, educating and inspiring the next generation.

Even if public discourse came to focus on such matters, however,
it must be acknowledged that it is difficult to imagine at this stage
what specific measures would flow from a more ecological approach
to family policy. What little we do know suggests that we should not
hold exaggerated expectations of what law and government can accomplish on their own. But there are a number of ways in which law
and government might do better for child-raising families. They
could at least endeavor to avoid undermining the social structures on
which families rely, and to surmount the present-mindedness that
characterizes so much of our public policy-making. Recognizing the
primitive state of our knowledge about the likely long-term effects of
changes in these areas, an ecological approach to family policy would
proceed modestly, encouraging local experiments, and avoiding the
court-imposed uniformity that would follow from excessive constitutionalization of family issues.

With these general principles in mind, one might begin by eliminating the appearance of public indifference created when we treat

child raising as though it were just one more "life-style" as to which the state must be "neutral." At the same time, we should endeavor to remove the appearance of sanctioning parental irresponsibility (as we did for so long in the area of child support), and as we do when we fail to respond to the Joshua DeShaneys brutalized by the very persons on whom they are dependent. Now that the two-earner child-raising family has become typical, government, employers, and unions must recognize that most employees, male and female, have family roles in addition to their work roles. Government must give more attention to the likely impact of tax, employment, zoning, and social assistance laws and policies on families. We urgently need to consider how government and employers can assist men and women to carry out the family responsibilities that most of them bear; how men can be persuaded to share with women more of the double burden of wage-work and homework; and how family members who perform caretaking roles can be protected from the risks entailed by their asymmetrical dependence on the principal family earner. At a minimum, we must be attentive to the ways in which governmental or employer policies may inadvertently be discouraging, impeding, or even penalizing those who are responsibly trying to carry out family roles.

We should not have to apologize for defining our society as one that relies heavily on families to socialize its young citizens, and that encourages, aids and rewards persons who perform family obligations. But an indispensable element of any such efforts to improve conditions for the nurture of citizens must be to attend more closely to the structures of civil society with which families are in a symbiotic relationship.

Admittedly, as in the case of natural ecological systems, the possibility exists that disintegration of family life, and the fraying of other social networks, has proceeded to the point where public deliberation, law, and government are powerless to help them. If American society already is producing too many individuals who are incapable of responsible parenthood, or of sustaining personal relationships, or of participating in civic life, it is rather late to worry about the state of our political discourse. In this connection, Nathan Glazer has written in a pessimistic vein:

> [There is much to be said both] for the insistence on a radical and egalitarian individualism, and for the defense of complex institutions and social bonds. . . . But if the first side wins out, as it is doing, the

hope that social policy will assist in creating more harmonious social relations, better working social institutions, broadly accepted as the decent and right way to order society, cannot be realized.[56]

But is it the case that "radical and egalitarian individualism" is "winning out"? Or is the individualism of our public discourse and our legal system more thoroughgoing than that which actually exists in our culture? It is true that Americans have a special history of what Michael Walzer has called the "four mobilities"—geographic, social, political, and marital.[57] Walzer has warned communitarians to face the fact that "there is no one out there" except Americans— "separated, rights-bearing, voluntarily associating, freely speaking, liberal" Americans.[58] Still, he adds:

> [C]ommunal feeling and belief seem considerably more stable than we once thought they would be, and the proliferation of secondary associations in liberal society is remarkable—even if many of them have short lives and transient memberships. One has the sense of people working together and trying to cope, and not . . . just getting by on their own, by themselves, one by one.[59]

What Walzer calls communal feeling might better be thought of as human sociality, the trait of individuals which still impels most Americans to seek to develop their own special qualities within various networks of relationships, beginning with emotionally and economically interdependent households, and fanning outward. Seemingly converging with the persistent efforts of Americans to perpetuate or form communities of memory and mutual aid, there are, on the political horizon, scattered traces of a groping search for civil society.

SEARCHING FOR CIVIL SOCIETY

The lack of a well-developed discourse about civil society has made it easy for Americans to overlook the costs exacted by the modern state and the market on the family and its surrounding communities of memory and mutual aid. Yet the evidence is mounting that we have been living for quite some time on inherited social capital, consuming our resources without replenishing them. It is symptomatic of the impoverishment of our political discourse that, as challengers to the individual-state-market mental grid have begun to appear, they have often turned instinctively to rights talk. Aside from heightening the cacophony of public discourse, however, "group rights" concepts are at least as problematic as our stripped-down, overly simple, versions of individual rights. Some forms of communitarianism, for example, would make majority rule normative as such, or would exalt groups and communities over the individual human beings who compose them.

Rights asserted on behalf of groups tend to pit group against individual, one group against another, and group against state. They thus raise spectres of individual oppression, of new tribalism, and of the old problem of faction. Endowing groups or communities with rights thus seems an unsatisfactory way to recognize the facts that human beings are social as well as self-determining, and that small social settings are conducive to human flourishing. Furthermore, to make families, neighborhoods, churches, unions, and so on, into group rights-bearers is to render them abstract and fungible. Yet these associations themselves are the varied and changing concrete manifestations of the efforts of men and women to order their lives in collaboration with one another. Like individuals and states, they too are subject to pathologies. Excessive preoccupation with one's immediate community can foster intolerance or indifference to the general welfare, as witness the proliferation of NIMBY (not-in-my-backyard) movements when new locations for prisons, group homes for the mentally retarded, and other public works are proposed. Undue deference to family autonomy can leave abused or neglected children at the mercy of their tormentors.

What we need therefore is not a new portfolio of "group rights," but a fuller concept of human personhood and a more ecological way of thinking about social policy. Groups are important, not for their own sake, but for their roles in setting the conditions under which individuals can flourish and order their lives together. Because individuals are partly constituted in and through their relationships with others, a liberal politics dedicated to full and free human development cannot afford to ignore the settings that are most conducive to the fulfillment of that ideal. In so doing, liberal politics neglects the conditions for its own maintenance. For the institutions of civil society help to sustain a democratic order, by relativizing the power of both the market and the state, and by helping to counter both consumerist and totalitarian tendencies.[60] The myriad associations that generate social norms are the invisible supports of, and the *sine qua non* for, a regime in which individuals have rights. Neither the older political and civil rights, nor the newer economic and social rights, can be secure in the absence of social arrangements that induce those who are disadvantaged by the rights of others to accept the restrictions and interferences that such rights entail.[61] When individual rights are permitted to undermine the communities that are the sources of such practices, they thus destroy their own surest underpinning. The paradox of liberalism seems to be that the strong state, the free market, and a vital civil society are all potential threats to individual citizens and to each other, yet a serious weakness in any one of them puts the entire democratic enterprise in jeopardy.

The relations among these three spheres may be characterized by creative tension or they may degenerate into mutual destruction. Thus, when the structures of one sector are becoming weak in relation to the others, the problem for statecraft becomes one of determining whether and how law and policy might help to revitalize, or to refrain from harming, the endangered one. Unfortunately, we do not know very much about how to support, or reinforce, or even how to avoid damage to the ongoing, mutually conditioning systems of civil society. The problems of protecting social environments are in many ways comparable to those of safeguarding natural environments. If democratic states need individual citizens with an array of qualities that—so far as we know—can best be nurtured within reasonably stable families; if families, in order to function effectively, need to be composed of individuals capable of commitment, and supported by communities of various sorts; and if communities in turn require certain kinds of individuals and families, public deliberation must make room for an ecological perspective.

Fortunately, there are a few signs of a shift to such a perspective on the part of public officials in both parties and in all branches of government, with the most encouraging of them occurring in the much-maligned legislative process. The 1990 child care legislation is a heartening example of a new way of thinking about social problems. Since the government has remained largely aloof from the problem of providing day care for the 55 percent of preschool children whose mothers work outside the home,[62] we have a pretty good idea of what is yielded by the hands-off approach favored by many conservatives: too much day care is being provided by poorly qualified persons for whom it is just a minimum-wage job, and too many children are simply left alone while their parent or parents work. Yet, conditions in the public schools have given rise to reasonable fears about direct governmental provision of day-care services, even if funds were to be made available for such a purpose.

In 1990, Congress came up with a bipartisan approach that was a credit to democratic politics. Described by *The New York Times* as "a monumental triumph,"[63] the child welfare legislation adopted that year took a diversified approach to the problem of day care. One important feature of the act was to bolster an existing and successful program, Headstart, so as to make it possible to enroll every eligible child by 1994. Its principal innovation, however, was to authorize federal funding for state-subsidized child care for working parents regardless of income (though with a recommendation that preference be given to low-income families). Congress gave the states discretion either to distribute money directly to day-care centers, or to issue vouchers that permit parents to choose their own day-care providers, including church-run centers that may take religious affiliation into consideration in their hiring practices.

This sensible legislation recognizes that nongovernmental community-based groups often can deliver services such as education and child care better and more efficiently than the state can.[64] This shift was long in coming, due to traditional hostility to social welfare spending in some quarters, and to reflexive opposition to voucher plans involving religious groups in others. Yet it seems plain that community-based day care will serve a double ecological purpose by aiding child-raising families, while helping to promote the vitality of the communities upon which many families depend. Day care can provide meaningful work for members of the community (especially older people), while responding to one of the most pressing needs of young parents. Government, in acting as a supporter of the provision of day care by persons well qualified and highly motivated to furnish it, thus can move simultaneously on a number of levels to set conditions and shift probabilities relating to the welfare of children. The years of struggle that preceded the adoption of these modest child-welfare measures in the United States (decades after more far-reaching legislation was in place in most other liberal democracies) illustrate our difficulties in moving beyond the impasse between those who oppose social spending, and those who favor direct governmental provision of services. These difficulties were intensified by our lack of a political language of human sociality and civil society.

The kind of debate that formed around Congressional attempts to develop new approaches to the problems of adolescent pregnancy is another case in point. In the late 1960s, the federal government had experimented with introducing important roles for citizen participation, non-governmental organizations, and local governments in social programs.[65] In 1981, taking the ideas behind these "community action" programs somewhat further, Congress adopted the Adolescent Family Life Act (AFLA), authorizing a series of grants to nonprofit private organizations, as well as to public bodies, for the development of programs to provide assistance to pregnant teenagers and adolescent parents.[66] In addition to providing funds for specific services, the act commissioned research directed to the discovery of fundamental causes and remedial measures. Congress identified the following long-range purposes: to promote "self-discipline and other prudent approaches to the problem of adolescent premarital sexual relations;" to promote adoption as an alternative for adolescent parents; to develop new approaches to the delivery of care to pregnant teenage girls; and to support research and demonstration projects "concerning the societal causes and consequences of adolescent premarital sexual relations, contraceptive use, pregnancy, and child rearing."[67]

This legislation quickly attracted wide attention and discussion, but not because of its innovative extension of participatory and community-based approaches to a serious and seemingly intractable social problem. Rather, supporters and opponents alike focused on a single provision of the act, specifying that grants may not be authorized for programs or projects that provide abortions or abortion counselling, or that actively promote abortion, nor for family planning services, unless such services are not otherwise available in the community.[68] Participants on both sides of the rights-based abortion debate immediately set the tone for the treatment of the adolescent pregnancy statute in the press. As a result, hardly any notice was taken of what is potentially the most important feature of the act: express Congressional endorsement of the view that it is desirable for government to support the efforts of nongovernmental and nonmarket groups to address a major social problem.

Whether or not it was wise to exclude funding for abortion and birth control, the Adolescent Family Life Act is an encouraging sign for social ecology. Like the national labor relations legislation of the 1930s, the statute represents a significant Congressional effort to address a social ill by trying to strengthen the resistance of the body social. The Senate Committee Report was refreshingly frank in acknowledging "the limitations of Government in dealing with a problem that has complex moral and social dimensions. . . ."[69] Unlike the superficially similar "community-based" programs of the 1960s and 70s, the AFLA does not set out to "organize" communities. Rather, it contemplates implementation by community groups that are already (if precariously) in place. Specifically, the act affirmatively sets out to "emphasize" the roles of family members, as well as those of religious, charitable and other voluntary associations.[70] Grant applicants are required to describe how families and "religious and charitable organizations, voluntary associations, and other groups in the private sector as well as services provided by publicly sponsored initiatives" will be included in their proposed activities.[71] AFLA, in other words, tries to work from the bottom up, not the top down. Its express inclusion of religious organizations and families suggests that the protection of neighborhood organizations, churches, families, and other such small-scale communities, is, if not a direct aim of the statute, at least a likely by-product.

The explicit reference by Congress to religious associations, however, provided the occasion for several advocacy groups to attack the act on constitutional grounds. Funding under the AFLA went, as Congress intended, to a wide variety of recipients— including state and local health agencies, private hospitals, community health associations, privately operated health care centers, and community and charitable organizations, many of them with ties to religious denominations. In due course, a lawsuit challenging the constitutionality of the AFLA was brought on the ground that the Establishment Clause of the First Amendment was violated by the inclusion of religious organizations among the participants.

In a decision that is an encouraging indicator of the Court's receptiveness to Congressional efforts to transcend the state-market framework, the Supreme Court held (5–4) in *Bowen v. Kendrick* that the AFLA is constitutional.[72] By holding that the statute, at least on its face,[73] did not foster "excessive entanglement" between church and state,[74] the Court has sent a signal to the elected branches that more creative uses of the structures of civil society may now be permissible in the American welfare state. According to Chief Justice Rehnquist, Congress's 1981 decision to augment the role of religious and other organizations in tackling the social and economic problems associated with teenage pregnancy, sexuality, and parenthood reflected "the entirely appropriate aim of increasing broad-based community involvement. . . ."[75] He went on to say, with respect to religious organizations in particular,

> Nothing in our previous cases prevents Congress from . . . recogniz-
> ing the important part that religion or religious organizations may
> play in resolving certain secular problems. Particularly when, as Con-
> gress found, 'prevention of adolescent sexual activity and adolescent
> pregnancy depends primarily upon developing strong family values
> and close family ties' . . . , it seems quite sensible for Congress to
> recognize that religious organizations can influence values and can
> have some influence on family life, including parents' relations with
> their adolescent children.[76]

Reviewing the Court's checkered pattern of church-state decisions over the past 40 years, the Chief Justice was able to pick out a
few strands of common sense and practical reason. He pointed to the
"long history of cooperation and interdependency between governments and charitable or religious organizations," and to the fact that
social services have long been furnished through religiously affiliated
charitable groups without controversy and with community
support.[77] He noted that "this Court has never held that religious
institutions are disabled by the First Amendment from participating
in publicly sponsored social welfare programs."[78]

Former Justice Brennan, though he joined the dissenters in the
Kendrick case, has been eloquent on various occasions, too, in recognizing the importance of families and their supporting communities to the maintenance of a liberal society. The American social
vision, as he wrote in the epigraph to this chapter, is not that "of a
unified society, where the needs of children are met . . . by the
Government, and where no intermediate forms of association stand
between the individual and the State."[79] Indeed, Justice Brennan
often emphasized in his opinions that the law sometimes must attend
to the conditions that communities require in order to flourish. He
pointed out the paradoxical dependence of individual freedom on
groups where such freedom may not be the primary value in a decision upholding the right of a Mormon religious institution to favor
its own members in making employment decisions: "Solicitude for
a church's ability to [maintain its own definition of itself] reflects the
idea that furtherance of the autonomy of religious organizations often furthers individual religious freedom as well."[80]

It is thus apparent that, even on an ideologically diverse Supreme
Court, there are glimpses of a growing appreciation of the importance of the structures and institutions of civil society. Meanwhile, a
surge of "communitarian" and "republican" scholarship in the nation's law schools likewise seems to be seeking for some way to

temper radical individualism and to tend the seedbeds of civic virtue. These efforts, however, remain countercurrents to the prevailing judicial and academic tendency to cling to the familiar individual-state-market grid. Just as mainstream contemporary moral philosophy has little conceptual place for a notion of the good,[81] contemporary law and politics still have little room for consideration of the sorts of institutions where notions of the good are generated, regenerated, and transmitted.

This is not to say that law and government alone could reinvigorate the seedbeds of civic virtue. Some years ago, on the eve of the rights revolution, a respected American judge warned new American citizens against treating the legal system as the ultimate bulwark of freedom:

> I often wonder whether we do not rest our hopes too much on constitutions, upon laws and upon courts. These are false hopes; believe me, these are false hopes. Liberty lies in the hearts of men and women; when it dies there, no constitution, no law, no court can save it; no constitution, no law, no court can even do much to help it. While it lies there it needs no constitution, no law, no court to save it.[82]

Judge Learned Hand's reminder of the limits of law needs to be tempered, however, with the recognition that constitutions, laws, and courts do have a modest bearing on habits and attitudes. And nowhere are these legal influences more a factor to be reckoned with than in the legalistic society of the United States.

The inadequate attention to human sociality and civil society in mainstream American law and political theory have practical consequences. The lack of public discourse regarding responsibility, sociality, and civil society, leaves us to work out our own vision of the kind of people we are and the kind of society we want to become, mainly in terms of the individual, the state, and the market. Our overblown rights rhetoric and our vision of the rights-bearer as an autonomous individual channel our thoughts away from what we have in common and focus them on what separates us. They draw us away from participation in public life and point us toward the maximization of private satisfactions. They incline us to shift the costs and risks of current policies regarding natural resources, pollution, public indebtedness, social security, and public health onto our children and future generations.[83] In these respects, the American rights dialect poorly serves our historic commitment to representative government, our post–New Deal acceptance of a form of welfare state, and our constitutional aspiration to "secure the blessings of liberty to ourselves and our posterity."

Our ability to escape this mental prison, by imagining a regime of rights where freedom, responsibility, privacy, and sociality could coexist in fruitful dialogue is diminished by another distinctive feature of our rights discourse: its insularity. Ironically, many other countries have been able to refine their rhetoric of rights and to enrich their public discourse by reflecting on American constitutionalism. We, for the most part, have remained resolutely turned inward. Yet, the experience of other liberal democracies suggests that forceful rights talk need not exclude a well-developed language of responsibility; that rights need not be formulated in absolute terms to be effective and strong; and that the rights-bearer can be imagined as both social and self-determining.

SIX

Rights Insularity

A living civilization must be able not only to give but
to receive and to borrow. Borrowing is more difficult
than it seems; it is not every man who can borrow
wisely, and put an adopted implement to as good use
as its original master. . . .

But a great civilization can also be recognized by its
refusal to borrow, by its resistance to certain
alignments, by its resolute selection among the foreign
influences offered to it and which would no doubt be
forced upon it if they were not met by vigilance or,
more simply by incompatibility of temper and appetite.
—Fernand Braudel[1]

In 1989 the National Geographic Society announced the
results of a cross-national survey in which several thousand participants from ten countries were asked to identify sixteen places on a
world map.[2] Compared to people from other leading nations, Americans and Soviets performed poorly in this simple exercise. Young
Americans (ages 18–24) did worst of all, coming in last among the
participants in their age group. In general, as compared to Swedes,
West Germans, Japanese, French, and Canadians, citizens of the two
superpowers were not adept at finding such out-of-the-way spots as
the Pacific Ocean, Central America, or Italy. Americans and Soviets
alike displayed what the National Geographic Society termed "an
astonishing lack of awareness of the world around them."

This relative unconcern with the rest of the world pervades
American legal culture as well. Except for Joseph Story, who died in
1845, no American Supreme Court justice has shown as much interest in the law of other nations as many foreign judges now do in
ours. Except for a brief flicker of attention to English criminal pro-

145

cedure in the 1970s, the United States Supreme Court in recent years has exhibited little curiosity about the jurisprudence developed elsewhere regarding the great legal issues of our times. This is so even though most of our judges and commentators readily acknowledge that we ourselves haven't got it quite right in many areas. American jurists know, better than anyone else, how much of our constitutional law represents a *pis aller*—the best we could do for the time being in the face of seemingly insoluble problems of bigness, federalism, heterogeneity, racial tension, lack of consensus, and so on. Our Court's history is one in which accident and drift have, at times, played roles at least as great as reason, deliberation, and choice.

Thus, it is remarkable that we are so little inclined to give ourselves the benefit of considering how other liberal pluralistic democracies approach the many vexing legal problems that we have in common. American lawyers admire Louis D. Brandeis for his memorable description of our federal system as providing the nation with many "laboratories," where the effects of legal innovation and experiments can be observed.[3] Yet at a time when jurists in many other nations are taking the whole world as their theatre of observation, most of their American brothers and sisters remain resolutely turned inward. As political boundaries lose much of their former significance in the current international economic order, there are numerous indications that a new transnational legal culture is developing.[4] Ironically, it is a culture to which the United States has substantially contributed, but in which at present it barely participates. In the realm of rights, this curious combination of American influence and insularity is well-exemplified by the different ways in which the American Supreme Court and the European Court of Human Rights have analyzed the privacy rights of homosexuals.

A TALE OF TWO CITIES: BELFAST AND ATLANTA

On January 21, 1976, police visited the Belfast home of Jeffrey Dudgeon, a 30-year-old shipping clerk, in order to execute a warrant issued under the Misuse of Drugs Act. Their search revealed, in addition to a quantity of marijuana, certain personal papers of Mr. Dudgeon in which homosexual activities were described. At the time, the Belfast police were investigating the disappearance of a young boy who was believed to be in the company of homosexuals.

Officers asked Mr. Dudgeon (and he agreed) to accompany them to the station, where they questioned him at some length about his sexual life before releasing him. They then turned over his file to the public prosecutor who decided that it would not be in the public interest to charge Mr. Dudgeon under two nineteenth-century statutes that provided criminal penalties for certain homosexual acts.

The matter did not end there, however. Mr. Dudgeon lodged a formal complaint against the United Kingdom of Great Britain and Northern Ireland with the European Commission of Human Rights in Strasbourg. In due course, that body ruled that Northern Ireland's legal prohibition of sexual acts committed in private between consenting adult males violated Mr. Dudgeon's rights under Article 8 of the European Convention on Human Rights. In that Convention, a right of privacy is explicitly recognized, but, characteristically, a strong statement of the right is followed by recognition of circumstances under which the right might be limited:[5]

ARTICLE 8.

1. Everyone has the right to respect for his private life and family life, his home and his correspondence.

2. There shall be no interference by a public authority with the exercise of this right except such as is in accordance with the law and is necessary in a democratic society in the interests of national security, public safety or the economic well-being of the country, for the prevention of disorder or crime, for the protection of health or morals, or for the protection of the rights and freedoms of others.[6]

The United Kingdom appealed to the European Court of Human Rights which affirmed the Commission's decision in 1981.[7]

In August, 1982, on our side of the Atlantic, a remarkably similar series of events was set in motion when police went to the apartment of Michael Hardwick, an Atlanta, Georgia, bartender, to serve a warrant on him for having carried an open container of alcohol in public. The officers were directed by a house guest to the bedroom where they found Mr. Hardwick and another man *in flagrante delicto*. Mr. Hardwick was charged with violating a long-unenforced Georgia sodomy statute, but the District Attorney, like his Northern Irish counterpart, declined to prosecute. Mr. Hardwick, like Mr. Dudgeon, decided to pursue the matter. He brought an action in Federal District Court asserting that the Georgia statute, by placing him under imminent danger of arrest, violated his constitutional right to privacy. A Federal Court of Appeals agreed with him, and reversed the dismissal of his complaint.[8] In 1986, however, the United States Supreme Court upheld the Georgia statute, ruling that the privacy rights recognized in the Court's prior decisions did not protect homosexual activity.[9]

The line of American contraception and abortion decisions that our Supreme Court found inapplicable in *Bowers v. Hardwick* had been brought to the attention of the European Court by counsel in *Dudgeon,* and obviously figured in the way some of the European judges saw the issues.[10] Yet the *Dudgeon* case was ignored by lawyers for both of the principal parties in *Bowers,* and by the majority and dissenting justices alike.[11] What is one to make of the differences in result and in range of inquiry in these two cases? What, if anything, does American rights discourse lose through its insularity? A closer look at *Dudgeon* and *Bowers* sheds some light on these questions.

Dudgeon v. The United Kingdom

Not so long ago, the suggestion that a supranational tribunal in Strasbourg could decide that a criminal statute of a sovereign nation violates the human rights of one of that nation's own citizens would have seemed preposterous, and the supposition that the nation concerned would modify its law to conform to such a judgment, far-fetched. In recent years, however, the European Convention on Human Rights has brought just such a situation into being. The United Kingdom subjected itself to international standards when, along with the other members of the Council of Europe, it ratified the Convention and accepted the jurisdiction of the European Court.[12] Thus, an individual citizen of the United Kingdom, Jeffrey Dudgeon, could request a tribunal in Strasbourg to review legislation of his own government[13] for conformity to norms of "higher" law.

It was by no means a foregone conclusion, however, that Mr. Dudgeon's attack on the Northern Irish statutes relating to homosexual behavior would be successful. Since he had not been involuntarily detained and was never prosecuted, a threshold question was whether his grievance merited judicial attention at all. The majority of the European Court resolved this initial point in his favor, saying that the "very existence of this legislation continuously and directly affects his private life," and that the police interrogation demonstrated that "the threat hanging over him was real."[14] Having found that Northern Irish law thus did infringe Mr. Dudgeon's "right to respect for . . . private life" protected under paragraph 1 of Article 8 of the Convention, the Court proceeded to determine whether the statutes in question could nevertheless be justified under paragraph 2 as "necessary in a democratic society . . . for the protection of health or morals, or for the protection of the rights and freedoms of others."

Here, again, the *Dudgeon* case was not free of difficulty. Even in the view of the majority judges, *some* degree of regulation of private sexual conduct, both homosexual and heterosexual, could be justified as "necessary in a democratic society," not only where the protection of minors is concerned, but also to protect "the moral ethos of society as a whole."[15] Furthermore, it had been settled in prior decisions that the Court would not hastily second-guess a member state's judgment on what is "necessary," especially where customs and attitudes relating to sexual behavior were concerned. Over the years, the Court had developed three broad guidelines for determining whether a particular law relating to health and morals could be justified under paragraph 2:

1. "Necessary" should not be equated with "reasonable" or "useful"; but rather should be understood to imply the existence of a "pressing social need."
2. Since what is "necessary" for the protection of health or morals varies from time to time and place to place, it should be left up to the national authorities of the country in question to make the initial assessment of "pressing social need," and they should be accorded a certain margin of discretion in making that judgment.
3. Since two "hallmarks" of a "democratic society" are "tolerance and broadmindedness," any restriction on a Convention right must be "proportionate" to the legitimate aims pursued by the national authorities.[16]

Applying the first of these principles to the *Dudgeon* case, the Court accorded considerable weight to the fact that a large majority of the member states of the Council of Europe (including the rest of the United Kingdom) had already abolished criminal penalties for homosexual acts between consenting adults. Northern Ireland's laws on the subject, moreover, had long been unenforced. Noting the absence of evidence that nonenforcement had injured moral standards in Northern Ireland, or that there was a public clamor for enforcement there, the Court concluded that the Government had failed to demonstrate a "pressing social need." Nevertheless, in accordance with the second guideline, the Court accepted the Government's bare representation that the legislation was "necessary," that its mere existence served to protect the "moral ethos." It then proceeded to take up the question of proportionality under guideline three. Here, the majority found that, even assuming the existence of a substantial body of opinion in Northern Ireland to the effect that a change in the laws in question would be harmful to the moral fabric of society, such a consensus would not outweigh the detrimental effects of the threat these laws posed to the private lives of adults with a homosexual orientation. The Court therefore concluded, by fifteen votes (including the judge from the United Kingdom) to four, that the Northern Irish law, so far as it related to acts committed in private by consenting adults, was in violation of the right of private life protected by Article 8 of the European Convention.

The dissents in the *Dudgeon* case were mainly concerned with Mr. Dudgeon's lack of clear victim status, the degree of deference that ought to be accorded to majoritarian values, and the proper role of a transnational Court in dealing with delicate questions of the relation of national law to morality. The dissenting judge from the Irish Republic, Brian Walsh, in a learned opinion ranging from the Warren-Brandeis privacy article to debates among contemporary philosophers on law and morality, pointed out that serious legal-philosophical questions were involved in the *Dudgeon* case. Does an individual's right to private life concern himself alone or does it have "inseparable social dimensions"?[17] Is morality of no concern to the law or does the law have a legitimate role in shaping or maintaining "the institutions and the community of ideas, political and moral, without which people cannot live together"?[18] Who is to determine whether individual or social interests should prevail in a particular situation? How can one tell whether the law in question does more good than harm, or vice versa?

The very difficulty of these questions suggested to Judge Walsh that it would be unwise to establish a single "Euro-norm" concerning homosexual practices for a diverse group of countries extending from Turkey to Iceland.[19] Even the United States, he noted, had not applied its burgeoning privacy doctrine to protect the activities of homosexuals. The European Court's majority had gone too far, he thought, in limiting the margin of discretion that ought to be accorded to member nations in determining the necessity of a law relating to morals. By interpreting necessity as requiring a "pressing social need," the Court had made it virtually impossible for governments to legislate with a view toward setting long-term social conditions.

Bowers v. Hardwick

In comparison to *Dudgeon,* what is most remarkable about *Bowers v. Hardwick* is not its opposite result, nor even the American court's lack of curiosity about whether and how the privacy interests of homosexuals are recognized elsewhere, but the relative lack of depth and seriousness of the analysis contained in its majority and dissenting opinions. Justice White's succinct opinion for the majority reviewed the privacy doctrine developed in earlier cases and characterized it as protecting family relationships, marriage, and procreative liberty. He could see no basis for extending the doctrine to cover all types of sexual conduct between consenting adults. It certainly did not, he said, establish "a fundamental right to engage in homosexual sodomy."[20] Pointing out that twenty-four states and the District of Columbia still maintained criminal penalties on their statute books for certain sexual acts performed in private, he concluded that it would be inappropriate for the Court to supersede the legislative judgments of nearly half the states in the absence of clear authority "in the language or design of the Constitution."[21]

The principal dissenting opinion by Justice Blackmun (joined by Justices Brennan, Marshall, and Stevens) was similarly concise. Justice Blackmun took issue with the majority's characterization of the interest at stake in *Bowers* as a right to engage in homosexual sodomy. What the case really involved, he said, was " 'the most comprehensive of rights and the right most valued by civilized men', namely, 'the right to be let alone.' "[22] Then, apparently on the theory that two clichés are better than one, he observed that "a man's home is his castle," and concluded: "the right of an individual to conduct intimate relationships in the intimacy of his or her own home seems to me to be the heart of the Constitution's protection of privacy."[23]

Justices White and Blackmun both assumed that if a right were involved it must be a "fundamental" one; that is, that virtually no state interest could overcome it. Neither judge therefore thought it worthwhile to inquire into whether there was a rational basis for the Georgia statute, whether the privacy interests of homosexuals were outweighed by the interests of other citizens in officially maintaining certain traditional norms of sexual morality, or whether the means chosen by the Georgia legislature were reasonably related to legitimate ends they might have had in view.

Only Justice Powell, in a separate concurring opinion, tried to break out of the rigid categories employed by the other justices. Though agreeing with the majority that no fundamental right had been violated, he raised what the European Court would have treated as a problem of proportionality, suggesting that a hefty prison sentence for a single act of sodomy committed in a private home might well pose a serious issue under the Eighth Amendment's prohibition of cruel and unusual punishment.[24] In other words, he seemed to be searching for a position that would acknowledge the legitimacy of expressing a widely shared moral view in the criminal law, while avoiding disproportionate harms to those whose activity was thus disapproved. *The Washington Post* reported at the time that Justice Powell had originally agreed to join the group of justices who favored striking down the Georgia law, but that because he could not accept Justice Blackmun's reasoning, he switched his vote a few days later, giving a majority to the group that held the law constitutional.[25]

Regardless of how one views the outcome of *Bowers v. Hardwick,* it is hard to avoid a sense that the opinion writers in that case did not do justice to the gravity and complexity of the matter before them. This is not to insist that the result in *Bowers* was "wrong," and certainly not that *Dudgeon* was "authority" that American judges should have followed. The Supreme Court justices, however, and perhaps more especially plaintiff's counsel, did ignore a valuable (and readily available) resource.[26] Crosslighting from other cultural and political contexts cannot "solve" American problems, but it can illuminate them, in much the same way that the backlighting provided by history can clarify a contemporary dilemma. The six *Dudgeon* opinions, issued by some of the world's leading jurists, contained ideas and information that could have focussed issues, enlarged perspectives, improved the quality of reasoning, and ultimately helped to place our Court's decision—whichever way it went—on a sounder and more persuasive footing. Our rights jurisprudence in general could only benefit if American judges and lawyers in difficult and novel cases followed the practice (now routine in many other nations) of examining important decisions of leading courts elsewhere. This is such an obvious claim that one might be embarrassed to belabor it, were it not for the fact that it has not commended itself to any American Supreme Court justice since Story, who sat on the Court over a century and a half ago.

Some American resistance to the idea of consulting foreign law seems to be based on the notion that the only reason to look at another country's law is to decide whether or not to slavishly follow it. Thus, on one of the rare occasions when our Supreme Court alluded briefly to "the views of the international community," Mr. Justice Scalia objected vigorously in his dissent, as follows:

> We must never forget that it is a Constitution for the United States of America that we are expounding. The practices of other nations, particularly other democracies, can be relevant to determining whether a practice among our people is . . . so 'implicit in the concept of ordered liberty' that it occupies a place not merely in our mores but, text permitting, in our Constitution as well [citation omitted]. But where there is not first a settled consensus among our own people, the views of other nations, however enlightened the Justices of this Court may think them to be, cannot be imposed upon Americans through the Constitution.[27]

It is hard to see how anyone could disagree with the sentiments expressed by Justice Scalia. Imposing "the views of other nations" in the guise of constitutional interpretation would be as inappropriate as imposing a judge's own personal views in such a way. As Montesquieu observed long ago, differences among cultures and regimes are such that it would be "a great chance if [the laws] of one nation suit another."[28] Circumstances in the United States are sufficiently different from those in Europe to make it far from clear that the type of analysis employed in *Dudgeon* would or should have yielded the same result here. For one thing, the legislatures of the great majority of European nations had decriminalized adult homosexual activity, whereas only half the American states have done so. Furthermore, the role of the European Court under an international convention is not the same as that of the United States Supreme Court under our federal Constitution.

Nevertheless, the writers of all the *Bowers* opinions could have benefited if they had taken a look at the way the European judges struggled with the issues in *Dudgeon*. In the first place, they would have been forced to confront the tragic dimension of the case: the fact that a decision either way was bound to be felt as a real affront to the deeply held beliefs of many people. In *Bowers v. Hardwick,* both the majority opinion by Justice White and the Blackmun dissent ignore this dimension and, in so doing, slight the importance of the positions they reject. Thus, even a person who approves of the result in

Bowers v. Hardwick, may regret that Justice White's opinion (no doubt unintentionally) gives the appearance of a callous indifference toward the interests and feelings of an unpopular minority. The tone of the White opinion must have been perceived by members of an already stigmatized group as legitimating, if not promoting, a climate of intolerance. Even if the interests of members of this class of individuals did not rise to the level of "fundamental rights," those interests were not so insubstantial as the majority opinion made them seem. Similarly, even if one shares Justice Blackmun's view that Mr. Hardwick's individual rights should have prevailed, one may lament that judge's disdainful brush-off of a community's interests in establishing and maintaining a cultural environment conducive to traditional moral standards. Even if the intangible benefits to the putative majority of Georgia citizens in maintaining some kind of official moral code did not outweigh the more immediate harms to the homosexual minority, this did not mean those benefits were negligible. It is only a slight exaggeration to say that the two main opinions in *Bowers. v. Hardwick* make the case look like a battle between Yahoos and perverts.

If Justices White and Blackmun had examined the *Dudgeon* opinions, they might not have changed their minds, but they would have been reminded that a court can decide between competing positions without creating the impression that the view denied priority is entitled to little respect. Nearly all constitutional cases that reach the Supreme Court are hard cases: they almost always involve choices between positions that are well supported by weighty moral as well as legal arguments. More often than not, high courts are required to make choices that, either way, will entail substantial individual or social cost. In the justificatory reasoning of American Supreme Court judges, however, these aspects of decision-making are too often denied or suppressed.[29] The Court's ruling is made to appear almost inevitable: the winner's position entirely vindicated, the loser's thoroughly discredited. The matter is neatly tied up and the loose ends are snipped off. Moral and political issues of moment cannot, however, be so easily laid to rest. *Bowers v. Hardwick,* like *Roe v. Wade,*[30] and the *DeShaney* case,[31] is troubling in this respect. Though the authors of these decisions surely never meant to do so, they give the appearance of leaving developing fetuses, battered children, and persons with a homosexual orientation outside the community for which we Americans have a common concern.

The more searching and tentative style of the European Court, its open wrestling with the weaknesses as well as the strengths of the positions it eventually took in *Dudgeon,* gives winners fewer grounds for gloating and leaves the losers less reason to feel angry and alienated. The result in *Dudgeon* certainly must have aggrieved many Northern Irish citizens who saw it as contributing to the erosion of society's moral fabric. (Ironically, this was a point on which both Protestants and Catholics in that troubled country tended to agree.) But at least those who were disappointed could see that their point of view had been considered carefully. To criticize our current Court in this respect is not to call for more handwringing (or crocodile tears) before the judges lower the boom on the losing party. By showing that it has taken serious arguments seriously, a court bolsters the authority of its decision. Just as one can feel respect for the author of an opinion with which one disagrees, one can experience regret at the way in which what one considers to be the "right" outcome is justified. At stake in *Bowers,* as in every Supreme Court decision of importance, was not only the immediate dispute, but also the authority of the "least dangerous" branch of government.

Now that Supreme Court opinions (especially as they are excerpted, translated, and transmitted through the media) have a relatively wide readership, certain judicial virtues become more important than ever before. The way the Court decides hard cases inevitably affects the way the parties, their causes, and the future development of the issues are perceived by a large public that, for better or worse, increasingly regards the Supreme Court as a moral arbiter. As it happens, a long tradition of great American judicial writing has followed the practice of exposing the reader to the actual grounds of the decision and to the judge's reasoning process, including his or her doubts and uncertainties.[32] The most eloquent advocate for this sort of judicial authenticity, James Boyd White, explains:

> [T]he art of law is not that of linear reasoning to a secure conclusion, but an art, fundamentally literary and rhetorical in kind, of comprehension and integration: the art of creating a text—a mind and a community—which can comprise two things at once, and two things pulling in different directions. In speaking for one side as a lawyer, or for one result as a judge, that is, the legal mind should recognize (implicitly in the lawyer's case, explicitly in the judge's) what can be said for the other, thus by an art of integration creating a world in which differences can coexist.[33]

When the Court gives the impression that the losers, their points of view, and their way of life are being read right out of society, we all lose.

A further benefit that might have accrued to the opinion writers in *Bowers* relates to the problem of interpreting abstract, open-ended, formulations of rights. The cryptic *Bowers* opinions give few signs of an effort to develop the general notion of privacy through reasoned elaboration of whatever principles undergird that notion. In fact, they are so short on justificatory reasoning that the result in *Bowers* looks more like the mere product of majority vote than the outcome of collegial deliberation. The majority opinion simply pronounces that the Court's earlier privacy decisions do not apply. It does not explain how homosexual activity between consenting adults is less "private" than the clinic abortion of a well-developed fetus that was permitted in its previous cases. Nor is it clear why the majority balked at setting aside the obsolescent sodomy laws of half the states, when earlier privacy decisions had struck down even quite modern abortion laws in virtually all of them.

The European Court's decision-making techniques, by contrast, were reminiscent of the American tradition of judicial candor and craftsmanship as practiced by great judges like Robert Jackson, John Marshall Harlan, Henry Friendly, and Learned Hand. The majority opinion explained how its holding grew out of the guidelines developed in prior decisions. By prudently limiting the scope of its decision, the Court left related issues open for similar careful consideration in the future. While according priority to the privacy rights of adult homosexuals in *Dudgeon,* the Court made it clear that it was not endorsing a notion of private life that would exclude *any* consideration of the social implications of sexual activity. By confining its holding to the narrow proposition that the need for the criminal statute in question had not been shown to be so pressing as to justify a menacing legal posture toward the private lives of adult homosexuals, the Court avoided suggesting either that the practices in question amounted to fundamental human rights, or that all legal distinctions between homosexuals and heterosexuals were now invalid. The *Dudgeon* decision thus does not seem to prefigure uniform "Euro-norms" regarding homosexuals in employment, housing, adoption, family benefits, and so on. At present, there is a great deal of variation among the European legal systems with respect to these matters, and the Court's approach in *Dudgeon* suggests that the margin of appreciation to be left to the member states in these areas will be considerable.

In sum, *Dudgeon* not only helps us to see the defects in *Bowers v. Hardwick,* but in American privacy jurisprudence in general. The fact that the principal opinion writers on both sides in *Bowers* resorted more to bald assertion than principled justification is symptomatic of a pervasive difficulty in the privacy decisions of the Court. As we have seen, the failure of our Court adequately to conceptualize the privacy right in the first place has led to great difficulty in developing any principled limitations upon it. In *Bowers,* every one of the opinion writers assumed that, if a right were involved, there was virtually no state interest that could prevail against it. Dealing with what they considered to be a nearly absolute right, the majority could not see their way to extending it to cover homosexual activity. Paradoxically, the European Court, dealing with a strong, but not unbounded, concept of privacy, was able to give the principle of protecting private life more generous scope.

The main reason the European Court has been able to develop a more coherent body of privacy law is not that Article 8 of the European Convention contains a less open-ended norm than our judge-made right of privacy. It is rather, ironically, that the European judges have become proficient at the principled, modest, collegial, flexible, pragmatic techniques of judicial decision-making that were once the pride of the American common law. Like many great judges in the common-law tradition, the members of the European Court have realized that there can be no watertight separation between law and morality, or between public and private. The style and tone of the Court in this respect are reminiscent of the moral seriousness of Benjamin Cardozo and the hard intelligence of John Marshall Harlan. All the judges currently sitting on the European Court would probably endorse Harlan's dictum that "to attempt a line between public behavior and that which is purely consensual or solitary would be to withdraw from community concern a range of subjects with which every society in civilized times has found it necessary to deal."[34]

Ironically, then, if the American Justices in the *Bowers* case had read the *Dudgeon* opinions, they would have experienced a shock of recognition. In investigating foreign territory, they would have been beckoned back home. Some of them might then have been inspired to rediscover and to develop the vast potential of our own tradition of judicial decision-making. It is a tradition that could assist the current Court in avoiding both the unprincipled development of rights exhibited in the privacy cases and the equally unprincipled "balancing" of rights and interests that it has indulged in many search-and-seizure cases.[35]

THE ONE-WAY "OVERSEAS TRADE" IN RIGHTS

The *Bowers* and *Dudgeon* cases exemplify a growing disparity between the American Supreme Court and several foreign high courts in the range of inquiry they deem appropriate when confronted with novel and important problems. The phenomenon is not confined to the judiciary. In the current brisk international traffic in ideas about rights, Americans avail themselves less than they should, and less than many other peoples do, of opportunities to reflect on their own controversies in the light of the experiences of others. Courts and legal scholars in many other liberal democracies are quite knowledgeable and sophisticated in their use of American and other legal materials. The same cannot be said about their counterparts in the United States, who all too often maintain a posture of indifference, disdainful as it is ignorant, towards the approaches of other nations to our shared economic, social, and environmental dilemmas. As a British legal observer recently put it:

> With U.S. law being argued to Strasbourg institutions, and the House of Lords referring to both U.S. and Strasbourg law, perhaps it is now the Americans who have assumed the attitude once ascribed . . . to the British: when told how things are done in another country they simply say: "How funny."[36]

The European Court, of course, is entitled to no special credit for its comparative approach in *Dudgeon,* since that Court's very composition—one judge from each of the member countries of the Council of Europe[37]—guarantees that the collective wisdom of a wide variety of legal systems will be brought to bear on any issue that comes before it. In Europe generally, however, and in Australia, Canada, and New Zealand, national law is increasingly caught up in a process of cross-fertilization among legal systems.[38] Even France and England, traditionally bastions of legal aloofness, have begun to look outward as European economic integration progresses, and as transnational institutions extend their influence. Where rights are concerned, lawyers and judges the world over frequently consult American sources. A prominent English human-rights lawyer, Anthony Lester, recently wrote, "When life or liberty is at stake, the landmark judgments of the Supreme Court of the United States, giving fresh meaning to the principles of the Bill of Rights, are studied with as much attention in New Delhi or Strasbourg as they are in Washington, D.C., or the State of Washington, or Springfield, Illinois."[39]

Meanwhile, the United States resolutely steers its own course, looking neither to the East nor West, North nor South. Apart from the Universal Declaration of Human Rights and the Helsinki Final Act, the United States has shown a remarkable degree of reserve concerning the protection of rights at the transnational level, as evidenced by our nonratification of a number of human rights instruments to which all the other liberal democracies have subscribed.[40] To some degree, our reticence on this front seems to be due to a prudent unwillingness to render ourselves vulnerable to institutions heavily staffed by critics of American policies. In part, however, it is a reflection of arrogance (other people need supranational rights protection, but we don't) and willful ignorance (we have nothing to learn from other countries concerning human rights). So far as the American judiciary is concerned, *Bowers v. Hardwick* is but one instance where the United States Supreme Court not only ignored how other high courts had dealt with the same vexing issues it faced, but did not even seem to be aware of the way its own precedents had been used elsewhere. This unconscious insularity is pervasive in the judiciary, the legal profession, and the law schools.[41] It was certainly a sign of changing times when Robert Badinter, the President of the French Constitutional Council, told an audience of American constitutional scholars in 1989 that the United States legal system now appears "a little provincial" from a French point of view.[42] Criticizing Americans' relative lack of interest in the rights ideas of other nations, Anthony Lester has predicted that the once-great American legal influence abroad will gradually diminish unless we relinquish our isolationist stance.

On closer examination, however, those American ideas about rights that have had the greatest influence abroad are not those which are currently prominent in our rights talk. In fact, many other nations are constructing their own rights traditions through what Braudel in the epigraph to this chapter calls "resolute selection"—often

focussing on features of the American tradition that our current rights
dialect tends to neglect. This is apparent whether one considers the
influence of our Constitution itself, judicial interpretations of constitutional rights over the years, or the rights ideas elaborated in
American scholarly writing.

Chauvinism often leads us to exaggerate the extent, and to mis-
understand the kind, of influence the American Constitution has had
on constitution-making around the world. In a special bicentennial
issue, *Time* magazine called our Constitution "a gift to all nations,"
and boasted that of the 170 countries that exist today, some 160 have
written charters modeled directly or indirectly on ours.[43] Comparative lawyers would have to express some reservations about the
extent to which our Constitution really has served as a model, however. There are about 160 countries with single-document constitutions in the world today.[44] Thus, if basic laws contained in a single
document are a sign of the influence of our 200-year-old example,
the American model can be said to have decisively prevailed over the
model of constitutions that have grown by accretion over time—like
those of the United Kingdom, Israel, Libya, Oman, Saudi Arabia,
and New Zealand.[45] Beyond this, however, "influence" is more
difficult to trace or demonstrate. Andrzej Rapaczynski of Columbia
University has pointed out how many shades of meaning are contained in the idea of legal influence: reliance on common sources,
cross-fertilization, borrowing disguised as innovation, innovation
disguised as borrowing, and even "negative influence" (where a foreign model is known and rejected).[46]

It is undoubtedly the case that our eighteenth-century design for
government continues to hold a certain fascination for constitution-
makers the world over.[47] In large part, this is a tribute to its demonstrated ability to withstand two centuries marked by industrial and
technological revolutions, a civil war, major and minor depressions,
two world wars, and the battering of ordinary politics. Yet, widespread admiration and interest have not led to uncritical imitation. So
far as the very structure of government is concerned, other countries
have overwhelmingly opted for parliamentary forms over our presidential system. In the active period of constitution-making that followed World War II (over half of all existing constitutions were
adopted since the mid-1970s), the features of American constitutionalism that have attracted the most interest are the enumeration of
rights and the establishment of an independent judiciary empowered
to back them up. But even here it is the general idea of constitutional

rights and judicial review, rather than the specifics of our model, that has served as an inspiration.

There are major divergences from the American model, as we have seen, both in the catalogs of rights and in the terms in which specific rights have been formulated in modern constitutions and international declarations. Notably, the values given constitutional status by most nations in the post–World War II period include social as well as individual rights. As summarized by a leading European legal historian, the "basic inventory" includes "human dignity, personal freedom, and protection against arbitrariness, active political rights, especially freedom of voting, equality before the law, and society's responsibility for the social and economic conditions of its members."[48]

The legal formulations of these rights, as we have seen, tend to be more nuanced than those we find in the Declaration of Independence, the Bill of Rights, and the Fourteenth Amendment to the U.S. Constitution. The rights declarations of the United Nations, and of various European states, gather the past into the present, carrying forward into modern social democracy certain older notions concerning reciprocal obligations of protection and loyalty, as well as elements of classical and Biblical views of man, society, and law.[49] The large proportion of the world's legal systems that are based on the Romano-Germanic tradition imagine the human person as a free, self-determining individual, but also as a being defined in part through relationships with others. Many rights are viewed as inseparable from corresponding responsibilities; and liberty and equality are often seen as coordinate with solidarity, or what used to be called fraternity. Personal values are regarded as higher than social values, but also as being rooted in them.

Equally striking are the differences in mechanisms for enforcing rights. Although judicial review has spread widely since the late 1940s, most liberal democracies have not embraced the American system of permitting ordinary courts to rule on constitutional questions. Most countries have tended to prefer variants of a system developed in Austria in the 1920s, where such matters are referred to a tribunal that deals only or mainly with constitutional issues.[50] Judges on these special constitutional courts, especially in countries with long traditions of parliamentary government and legislative supremacy, often have more modest conceptions of their roles than many American Supreme Court justices began to display in the 1960s.[51] Current American practices of judicial review, it is well to remember, have evolved under very specific historical circumstances. Much judicial activism in recent years, as well as the approval it has received from academics, and such popular acceptance as it has found, was attributable to a lack of confidence in our state legislatures. This American attitude, grounded to some extent in our troubled history of race relations, has no real counterpart in most other liberal democracies.

In sum, the influence of the American Constitution on constitution-making elsewhere can be asserted only in a very general sense. What seems to have been most inspiring to other countries is the impressive example of a design for limited government that has proved flexible enough to withstand two hundred years of testing social change.

No consideration of the influence of American rights ideas today, however, can fail to include the interpretations and applications that the courts have given them, especially in the years since the Supreme Court moved personal liberties to the foreground of constitutional law. It is these United States Supreme Court decisions that are now most carefully studied all over the world. In countries that only relatively recently have given their courts the power to review executive, administrative, and legislative action in the light of constitutional norms, or that have established new courts for that purpose, judges have often looked abroad for guidance. And what better place to look than to the major decisions of a Court that had had longer experience with judicial review?

A Canadian Supreme Court judge, in an early decision under the 1982 Canadian Charter of Rights and Freedoms, expressed a view that seems to be widely held, especially in countries whose legal systems, like ours, are based on the English common law:

> The courts in the United States have had almost two hundred years experience at this task and it is of more than passing interest to those concerned with these new developments in Canada to study the experience of the United States courts.[52]

Irish Supreme Court judges and constitutional scholars, too, frequently say they have consulted the decisions of the United States Supreme Court in the years since 1937 when Ireland adopted a constitution with guarantees of political and civil rights.[53] Nor is the phenomenon confined to anglophones. Recently, a Vice-President of the European Commission on Human Rights expressed the hope that the Commission and the Court would develop a system of European human rights law that would be "something similar to this great jurisprudence . . . developed by the United States Supreme Court, on the basis of the Bill of Rights."[54] Plainly, if one is on the trail of the influence of American rights ideas, the scent picks up when we move from constitution-making to constitutional interpretation.

It is not clear, however, whether all the foreign jurists who profess to be impressed by our Court's "200 years of experience" realize that, apart from *Marbury v. Madison* where the Court first claimed the power of judicial review in 1803,[55] and the *Dred Scott* case where it was disastrously exercised in 1857,[56] the power to declare statutes unconstitutional was little used until the late nineteenth and early twentieth centuries. Nor is it certain that all foreign admirers of American rights ideas know the story of how our courts, in their first sustained venture into "activism," used the idea of economic rights to strike down early social and protective legislation.[57] The truth is, that where rights pertaining to fair criminal procedure, equal legal treatment, free expression, or privacy are concerned, the United States Supreme Court has only a slightly longer experience than a great number of other nations. For us, too, the great expansion of personal liberties and civil rights began in the post–World War II period.

Comparative research suggests that the influence of the United States Supreme Court's decisions since that time, while significant, has been more modest than many American jurists suppose. Most foreign judges are far from naive or uncritical in their use of legal materials from systems other than their own. Their widespread interest in, and familiarity with, American Supreme Court decisions seems to be combined, for the most part, with a high degree of sophistication. The judges who refer on occasion to American law not only seem to be fairly knowledgeable about the American legal system, but attentive to differences between our political, social, and legal context and their own. They tend to use American cases as sources of information rather than as authority, and as aids to, but not substitutes for, their own reasoning processes. In some countries—Ireland and Israel, for example—interest and expertise in American constitutional law coexists comfortably with attention to the law of the European civil-law countries and international bodies.

There is no better example of the combination of interest and caution that many anglophone judges manifest toward American rights ideas than the Canadian Supreme Court's 1988 decision in *Regina v. Morgentaler*.[58] This case, like *Roe v. Wade,* was a landmark in both abortion law and judicial review. In 1982, when the Canadian Constitution was "patriated" from the United Kingdom to Canada, it was amended to include a judicially enforceable Charter of Rights and Freedoms. The judges on the Canadian Supreme Court had barely begun to get their sea legs in the new system when they had to rule on the politically sensitive abortion question.

The issue in *Regina v. Morgentaler* was whether the sections of the 1969 Canadian criminal code pertaining to abortion violated rights protected by the 1982 Charter. The statute in question made abortion a criminal offense except when a therapeutic abortion committee of three doctors in an approved hospital had certified that continuation of the pregnancy would be likely to endanger the life or health of the pregnant woman. Considerable variations in access to abortions under this system were said to exist in different parts of Canada, with problems in access reported especially in remote regions. The arguments of the abortion clinic operators who challenged the statute were based "largely on American constitutional theories and authorities."[59]

The majority on the Canadian Supreme Court determined that the procedural prerequisites of the statute violated a pregnant woman's right to "security of the person" guaranteed by Section 7 of the Charter, which provides: "Everyone has the right to life, liberty and security of the person and the right not to be deprived thereof except in accordance with the principles of fundamental justice."[60] That did not dispose of the case, however, because, under Section 1 of the Charter, all rights are potentially subject to certain "reasonable limits." A statute violating a Charter right may still be upheld if the limits it imposes comply with the standard in Section 1: "The Canadian Charter of Rights and Freedoms guarantees the rights and freedoms set out in it subject only to such reasonable limits prescribed by law as can be demonstrably justified in a free and democratic society."

The majority decided that the abortion statute could not be saved under Section 1 because the means the legislature had chosen to effect the objective of protecting unborn human life were often arbitrary and unfair in operation. Like the European Court in *Dudgeon,* the Canadian Chief Justice's opinion looked for "proportionality" between means and end. He found that the Canadian system of abortion regulation, which made no distinction between early and late pregnancy, impaired the Section 7 rights of women more than was necessary, and had effects in many cases "out of proportion to the objective sought to be achieved."[61]

The resemblance to *Roe v. Wade* was confined to the bare result— striking down the statute. For the Canadian Court scrupulously rested its holding on narrow grounds, leaving the legislature with wide latitude to fashion a new system of abortion regulation. As an American commentator has astutely observed, the Canadian Court's decision was "a 'provisional' ruling, a ruling that invited Parliament to reconsider the question of abortion, perhaps with a more informed and thoughtful understanding of the relevant competing interests."[62] (As of this writing in 1990, Canadian legislators had not enacted a new abortion statute.)

The four separate opinions in the *Morgentaler* case afford an excellent opportunity to observe the variety of ways in which judges on an important modern court employ foreign legal sources in general, and American sources in particular. The fewest references to the law of other countries were made in the principal majority opinion, where Chief Justice Brian Dickson seemed mainly preoccupied with charting a wise and prudent course for judicial review. He began by citing cases from the United States, West Germany, and the European Court of Human Rights, not for their content, but merely to underscore the point that the issue was a difficult one and that "Courts and legislatures in other democratic societies have reached completely contradictory decisions. . . ."[63] Noting that the arguments against the statute relied on American sources, he quoted with approval the statement in an earlier Canadian case that "we . . . do our own Constitution a disservice to simply allow the American debate to define the issue for us. . . ."[64] He stated that it was "neither necessary nor wise" to explore whether the Canadian Charter provided a basis for broad-ranging American-style rights of privacy and individual autonomy.[65]

From that point on, the Chief Justice made no more direct references to American (or any other foreign country's) constitutional law. Yet, indirectly, he made it clear that he did not want to be perceived as tracing the footsteps or repeating the stumbles of the United States Supreme Court in the area of individual liberties. He labored to make it plain that although the court and legislature since 1982 were in a new ball game, they would not be playing by American rules; and that whatever form the new rules might take, the Court did not intend to displace Parliament as the chief policy-maker of the country. "[I]t remains true," he observed, "that this Court cannot presume to resolve all of the competing claims advanced in vigorous and healthy public debate."[66] Welcoming the opportunity to decide the case in such a way as to leave maximum leeway to legislative decision-making, he emphasized that "courts are not the appropriate forum for articulating complex and controversial pro-grammes of public policy."[67]

A second majority opinion, that of Justice Beetz, drew on the law of other countries to make the point (apparently for the benefit of Parliament) that many nations regulate abortion more strictly in the later stages of pregnancy than in the early weeks.[68] In the same vein, he pointed out that many countries require an independent medical opinion on the reasons for abortion; among them, the United King-dom, various Australian states, the Federal Republic of Germany, New Zealand and Switzerland.[69] Though Justice Beetz made several references to the laws of foreign countries, he did not accord any special emphasis to that of the United States.

The only one of the five majority justices to rely heavily on American cases was also the only judge on the Court who seemed impatient to begin instructing the legislature on the limits of its authority. Justice Wilson's opinion drew on several United States Supreme Court decisions (as well as the writings of a selection of academics) to support the propositions that the right to "liberty" in Section 7 of the Charter should be broadly construed to encompass a woman's right to decide matters relating to her private life, and that whether to have an abortion is such a matter. Justice Wilson claimed (with justification) that her highly individualistic interpretation of liberty was "consistent with the American jurisprudence on the subject."[70] With rather less justification, she asserted that reliance on American authorities was appropriate because the American version of individual personal decision-making "informs" the Canadian Charter.[71]

The dissenting opinion by Justice McIntyre adopted a deferential position on judicial review quite similar, in principle, to that ex-pressed by the Chief Justice. In support of this position it marshalled some of the famous United States Supreme Court dissenting opin-ions of Justices Holmes and Harlan criticizing our Court for blocking (in the name of property and contract rights) social and economic policies established by the elected branches of government.

Superficially, the *Morgentaler* case might be called an example of American legal influence. Certainly all the opinions manifest a high degree of awareness of American experience. History, proximity, accessibility, economic interdependence, and constant interchange (plus the fact that England has so little relevant precedent to offer on constitutional questions) made some sort of American legal influence almost inevitable in the post-1982 phase of Canadian constitutionalism. Still, with its links via Quebec to the French legal tradition, Canada is also well-poised to benefit from civil-law perspectives. (Three of the nine seats on the Supreme Court are reserved for judges with civil-law training.) When we look closely at *Morgentaler,* we see that most of the members of the Court consulted a variety of foreign legal sources, but did so in a cautious and critical fashion. The prevailing view in the Canadian legal academy, too, seems to be that while American analogies can be enlightening, "Canadian solutions must suit Canadian circumstances."[72]

Those "circumstances," of course, include cultural as well as legal conditions.[73] If, as Seymour Lipset claims, Canadian society is "more elitist, communitarian, statist, and particularistic (group oriented) than that of the United States,"[74] American constitutional law cannot provide the last word, though it may often prove a fertile source of ideas. Nor are the two neighboring legal systems congruent, despite their common ancestry. The Charter, as noted, diverges in both letter and spirit from its American counterpart in important respects. Like most postwar constitutions, the Charter has avoided hard-edged, American-style proclamations of individual rights. The rights it protects are subject to a variety of express limitations, and some are subject to legislative override.[75] They specifically include certain associational or group rights, but not property rights.[76] A special section on interpretation provides that the Charter is to be construed in a manner "consistent with the preservation and enhancement of the multicultural heritage of Canadians."[77] The drafters recognized that "most controversies about rights involve subtle choices or balances between individual and community interests."[78]

The year after the *Morgentaler* case was decided, the United States Supreme Court had occasion to reconsider its approach to the abortion question. With the five majority justices unable to agree on much besides the specific result (upholding viability testing and certain other provisions of a Missouri statute), the *Webster* case left *Roe v. Wade* technically in place and the community at large in substantial confusion.[79] Though our Court's attention was invited to foreign decisions in some of the briefs, the opinions of the Justices showed no evidence that any of them had attended to the wealth of information that is now available on how the courts and legislatures of other countries have dealt with this controversial and complex issue.

Yet, just as the United States Supreme Court in *Bowers* might have benefited from the Strasbourg judges' analyses in *Dudgeon,* so in the abortion cases it might have been aided by reflecting on the efforts of the Canadian judges in *Morgentaler.* At the very least, American judges could have seen how a liberal, democratic court can give strong protection to the interests of pregnant women in personal security without radically devaluing unborn human life at all stages of pregnancy, and how such a court can safeguard individual liberties without drastically curtailing legislative decision-making.

So far as constitution-making and judicial interpretation of rights are concerned, then, there is little evidence that, thus far, oversimplified rights ideas in the current American dialect are displacing nuanced and complex interpretations more suited to conditions elsewhere. The potential for such mischief, however, is not negligible, especially in view of the tendency of many judges and scholars abroad to rely more heavily on the works of academics than on primary sources. Foreign jurists, especially those whose native language is not English, are apt to feel overwhelmed by the complexity of our federal system and by the sheer volume of two centuries' worth of statutes, regulations, and court decisions. They feel especially daunted if they have not been trained in the common law, and are not conversant with its special technical terms and concepts. The impulse to turn directly to secondary sources must be almost irresistible where (as in all of continental Europe) judges by tradition accord great weight to scholarly writing.

There are several grounds for a certain uneasiness about the idea of foreign lawyers and judges acquiring their information about the American law of individual rights through scholarly treatises and articles. In the first place, many contemporary American specialists in constitutional law are among the foremost purveyors of excessively prodigal and absolutist rights talk. In their writing, they are often engaged in advocacy, trying to move the courts as well as to form opinion in the legal community. Most of them tend, moreover, to reduce the whole subject of limited government to Supreme Court decisions, ignoring the structure of government, the lively business of constitutionalism at the state level, the constitutional jurisprudence of the lower federal courts, and the internal constraints that are evidenced by the innumerable bills that are never passed or reported out of committee because most Congressmen believe them to be unconstitutional and by the large number of proposed amendments that have been defeated for similar reasons.[80]

Furthermore, not even the most learned treatise can do justice to the fertility, variety, and ambiguity of the case law, its surprising ability to put out new shoots, or to turn an old theme to a fresh purpose. American judges at their best have been virtuosos of practical reason, weaving skillfully back and forth between facts and law, the case at hand and the long-run, keeping stability and predictability in dynamic tension with flexibility and growth. The academics who summarize and systematize selected court decisions tend, by temperament or training, to be masters of abstraction. They perform an indispensable service, but reading their work can never substitute for immersion in a line of cases. Always at a certain distance from the practice, American academic writing has increasingly little in common with the everyday work of the profession. As Professor Andrew Kaufman has observed, "Never in the history of constitutional law scholarship in this country have the views from academia, almost all of them, been so different from the practice of judges" as they are at present.[81]

Lawyers trained in European universities, where significant consensus still exists concerning the classification of legal phenomena and the responsibilities of legal scholars, are apt to regard American scholarly works as more complete and authoritative than their authors mean them to be. The authors of our treatises typically do not exhibit the same mania for thoroughness of coverage, or striving for balanced evaluation, that characterizes European books bearing similar titles. They tend to be more imaginative than their continental counterparts, but also more idiosyncratic. Thus, even excellent works on American constitutional law risk being misunderstood by readers who have been schooled to regard a treatise as a comprehensive treatment of a subject by an author striving to be objective. Similarly, foreign readers accustomed to academic journals where the articles are refereed by experts and edited by professors, may mistake the material published in American student-run law magazines as more complete, accurate, and authoritative than it often is.

Fortunately, the most frequent references to American sources are made in English-speaking countries, where judges and lawyers tend to be relatively sophisticated in their use of American materials, and appropriately cautious about the suitability of American rights ideas for their own cultural, legal, and political contexts. Within other foreign interpretive communities, the influence of American rights ideas is moderated by, among other things, the fact that legal sources always acquire a somewhat different array of meanings in translation.[82]

All in all, then, the American influence in the "one-way trade" in rights ideas, whether in constitution-making or constitutional interpretation, seems to have been less extensive and direct than might at first appear. The chief effect of regular consultation of American experience abroad seems to have been precisely what Americans could expect to gain if the traffic in ideas flowed in both directions— assistance in working out distinctively national solutions to national problems.

The favorable trade balance that the United States appears to enjoy in the great diffusion of rights ideas that is taking place in the world today is less hefty than many Americans suppose. More important, however, from an American point of view, is the fact that, in this sort of commerce, to be an exporter without being a judicious importer is to be at a disadvantage. Our own rights tradition, and our struggles to make that inheritance real for all Americans, have inspired others around the world. In closing our own eyes and ears to the development of rights ideas elsewhere, our most grievous loss is not the influence of our legal ideas, but rather the kind of assistance in the never-ending project of revitalizing and renewing our own rights tradition that can be gained from observing the successes and failures of others.

In the famous opening paragraph of *Federalist* No. 1, Alexander Hamilton wrote, "it seems to have been reserved to the people of this country, by their conduct and example, to decide the important question, whether societies of men are really capable or not of establishing good government from reflection and choice, or whether they are forever destined to depend for their political constitutions on accident and force."[83] After two hundred years, the time seems overdue for Americans to acknowledge that the "conduct and example" of other republics are also relevant to this fateful question. Ironically, what we have missed through our insularity is the opportunity for rediscovery of our own tradition, with its tremendous potential for self-renewal and for creative adaptation to new and challenging circumstances.

SEVEN

Refining the Rhetoric of Rights

> Those who won our independence believed that the
> final end of the state was to make men free to develop
> their faculties; and that in its government the
> deliberative forces should prevail over the
> arbitrary. . . . They believed that . . . the greatest
> menace to freedom is an inert people; that public
> discussion is a political duty; and that this should be a
> fundamental principle of the American government.
> —Justice Louis D. Brandeis[1]

The strident rights rhetoric that currently dominates American political discourse poorly serves the strong tradition of protection for individual freedom for which the United States is justly renowned. Our stark, simple rights dialect puts a damper on the processes of public justification, communication, and deliberation upon which the continuing vitality of a democratic regime depends. It contributes to the erosion of the habits, practices, and attitudes of respect for others that are the ultimate and surest guarantors of human rights. It impedes creative long-range thinking about our most pressing social problems. Our rights-laden public discourse easily accommodates the economic, the immediate, and the personal dimensions of a problem, while it regularly neglects the moral, the long-term, and the social implications.

Rights talk in its current form has been the thin end of a wedge that is turning American political discourse into a parody of itself and challenging the very notion that politics can be conducted through reasoned discussion and compromise. For the new rhetoric of rights is less about human dignity and freedom than about insistent, unending desires. Its legitimation of individual and group egoism is in flat opposition to the great purposes set forth in the Preamble to the

171

Constitution: "to form a more perfect Union, establish Justice, promote the general Welfare, and secure the Blessings of Liberty to
ourselves and our Posterity."

Merely refining the rhetoric of rights—if such a thing could be
done—would hardly remedy all the ills that currently beset American culture and politics. Yet language, with its powerful channeling
effects on thought, is centrally implicated in our dilemma and in our
prospects for surmounting it. Political language will be an important
determinant of our success or failure in preserving and developing
the democratic idea under social and economic conditions that could
not have been imagined by the Founders. Unfortunately, American
political discourse has become vacuous, hard-edged, and inflexible
just when it is called upon to encompass economic, social, and environmental problems of unparalleled difficulty and complexity. To
make matters worse, the possibility must be reckoned with that our
shallow rights talk is a faithful reflection of what our culture has
become. Thus a critique of our current rights talk must at least
address some difficult questions whose answers are far from clear. Is
our distinctive rights dialect, for better or worse, a mirror of contemporary American society? If not, what indigenous materials, if
any, are at hand from which to fashion a more capacious public
language? If such materials exist, is there any reason to believe that
Americans could or would employ them to change the way we
debate public issues?

Even one who wishes to believe that our current political discourse does not do justice to the richness and variety of American
moral sentiments must acknowledge that it does grow out of, and
reflect, our culture and aspirations in certain unmistakable ways. Our
political speech has become as lifeless and cliché-ridden as the generic, popular speech that we use to communicate across most ethnic, economic, and other differences in the course of an average day.
Like the basic patter we routinely deploy in dealing with strangers,
political speech has to be intelligible to a wide assortment of individuals who increasingly share few referents in the form of common
customs, literature, religion, or history. Under these circumstances,
it is not surprising that contemporary public figures borrow heavily
from a language that takes the individual as the basic social unit, that
treats all individuals as presumptively strangers to one another, and
that distances itself from moral judgment. The hallmark of legal
discourse, whose very symbol from ancient times has been the blind-

fold, is to deliberately disregard the particular traits that make one human being different from another.

Our anemic political discourse does help to solve a communications problem arising out of our diversity. But abandoning the effort to inform, explain, justify, and translate has higher costs in the realm of politics than in popular speech. It deprives citizens of the information and reasoned argument they need to hear in order to make intelligent choices among candidates, and to responsibly assess the long- and short-term costs and benefits of proposed programs and policies. When political actors resort to slogans and images rather than information and explanations, they hinder the exercise of citizenship. Leaving so much unsaid, they create a discrepancy between what we officially proclaim and what we need in order to make sense of our lives.[2] The result for many people is a generalized frustration with politics that observers often misdiagnose as civic apathy.

Our careless rights talk is of a piece with another troubling aspect of contemporary American culture. It is a specific instance of the tendency of middle-class Americans, observed by Robert Bellah and his colleagues, to use a "first language" of individualism in speaking of what is most important to them.[3] Bellah's *Habits of the Heart* study suggests, moreover, that the sort of individualism that now pervades American speech and society is different in kind from the older individualisms of the frontier, of early capitalism, and of traditional Protestantism.[4] The current strain is characterized by self-expression and the pursuit of self-gratification, rather than by self-reliance and the cultivation of self-discipline. Rights in the current American dialect are the expression of desires the drafters of the Bill of Rights viewed with suspicion—to be completely free, to possess things totally, to be treated justly without being asked to act justly. Christopher Lasch, in his sombre works of social criticism, makes it seem plausible that our current rights talk tells the whole story. He claims that America has lost its basic stock of patriotic, biblical, and folkloric legends that once provided young people with ideals toward which they might aspire, and with frameworks for endowing their lives with meaning. Without that background, he says,

> the foreground fills the whole picture—an insistent "I want." Wants themselves become formless and unspecifiable. To the question, "What *do* they want, then?" there is only one answer in the case of people whose desires are unformed by the experience of participating in a culture larger than themselves: "Everything."[5]

The surveys of the political attitudes of young Americans to which I have referred from time to time contain much to support Lasch's pronouncement that "the moral bottom has dropped out of [American] culture."[6] A collective portrait emerges from them of a population of young adults that is indifferent to public affairs and that places its highest value on self-fulfillment.[7]

There is much evidence, however, that cooperative, relational, patterns of living survive in the United States to a greater degree than our individualistic public rhetoric would suggest. Most Americans still live, work, and find meaning within a variety of overlapping small groups that generate, as well as depend on, trust, fairness, and sharing. Around the kitchen table, in the neighborhood, the workplace, in religious groups, and in various other communities of memory and mutual aid, men and women maintain ongoing dialogues about freedom and responsibility, individual and community, present and future. The commonest and most particularistic of these discourses is household table talk with its familiar shorthand expressions born of shared family and, often, ethnic history. To be sure, the language of rights has invaded American homes, but there it is often held in check by recollection and retelling of the family's concrete experiences, and by the household's fund of stories about relationships, obligations, and the long-term consequences of present acts and decisions. Some of every family's talk is intelligible only to its own members, but much is also part of a more widely dispersed American conversation.[8]

Traditionally, it has been women who have taken primary responsibility for the transmission of family lore and for the moral education of children. As mothers and teachers, they have nourished a sense of connectedness between individuals, and an awareness of the linkage among present, past, and future generations. Hence the important role accorded by many feminists to the values of care, relationship, nurture, and contextuality, along with the insistence on rights that the women's movement in general has embraced. Women are still predominant among the country's caretakers and educators, and many are carrying insights gained from these experiences into public life in ways that are potentially transformative. Their vocabularies of caretaking are important sources of correctives to the disdain for dependency and the indifference to social bonds that characterize much of our political speech.

Another indigenous discourse that contains helpful antidotes for some of the extremes of rights talk is one that itself has been a major contributor to those excesses. It is ironic that Americans have saturated their political language with what is only a secondary language of the law. The predilection for exaggeration and absoluteness that all of us often indulge when speaking of rights seems recognizably related to the strategic use of language by courtroom performers, hardball negotiators, takeover artists, and other zealous advocates ready to go to almost any lengths on behalf of a client or a cause. The majority of lawyers in the United States, however, spend most of their working hours engaged in the legal equivalent of preventive medicine.

The rank and file of the legal profession help their clients to plan and maintain relationships that depend on regular and reliable fulfillment of responsibilities. They know that the assertion of rights is usually a sign of breakdown in a relationship. They endeavor to prepare agreements, leases, estate plans, charters, and bylaws, so as to minimize occasions for friction. They are careful—often to a fault—in their use of language. When discord arises, they assist in negotiation and adjustment. Only when something goes drastically wrong is the matter turned over to the litigator, and even then, her initial efforts normally will be directed toward settlement. Most lawyers (like most other people) understand that, over time, selective exaggeration and omission undermine relationships as well as credibility. They, too, tell their children the cautionary tales of Chicken Little and the little boy who cried "Wolf." Abraham Lincoln's exhortation to lawyers to be "peacemakers" still reflects the commonsense ideals, and the way of life, of lawyers engaged in what is still the main business of the profession—helping citizens to live decently together.

> Discourage litigation. Persuade your neighbors to compromise whenever you can. Point out to them how the nominal winner is often a real loser—in fees, expenses, and waste of time. As a peacemaker the lawyer has a superior opportunity of being a good man. There will still be business enough.[9]

Similarly, the uncelebrated majority of American judges are engaged in a kind of work that is characterized by careful distinction and discerning accommodation. Practical reason, not abstract theorizing, dominates the day-to-day activity of the typical American judge. Year in and year out, she weaves back and forth between facts and law, the parts and the whole, the situation at hand and similar situations that have arisen in the past or are likely to arise in the future. She attends carefully to context, she explores analogies and distinctions, the scope and the limits of generalizing principles. She recognizes that neither side has a monopoly on truth and justice. She is neither a mere technician nor a tyrant, but something between an artist and an artisan, practicing what the Romans called the "art of the good and equitable."

Within the legal academy, too, the tolerance for complexity and the sense of proportion that are often lacking in the rights fraternity are still the criteria of scholarship in the less glamorous areas of law—taxation, antitrust, contracts, torts, property, and so on. All in all, the dominant ethos of the legal profession is still one where civility and adequately complex speech are the order of the day, and where nuance and subtlety are expected to the degree required by the subject under discussion.

There is further untapped potential for renewal of political discourse within immigrant groups, in ethnic enclaves, and within religious and other associations. American thinking about the favored subject of property rights, for example, has been decisively shaped by an increasingly problematic belief that man can master and subdue the natural world. We have much to learn from native Americans who have long known that there is a way in which the land owns us, even as we pretend to own the land, and that we ignore that fact at our own peril. Many conservationists are coming to recognize that, where environmental issues are concerned, the biblical language of stewardship may be more appropriate than endowing trees with rights, and more conducive to responsible use of resources than vague promises that everyone has a "right" to a healthy environment.

The greatest hope for renewal, perhaps, lies in the American political tradition itself, in its time-honored ideals of tolerance, respect for others, public deliberation, individual freedom and responsibility, and the mandate for self-restraint implicit in the rule of law. In a spirited defense of liberalism "properly understood" against its communitarian critics, Stephen Macedo has argued that the "moral core" of our public order is a commitment to public justification, that is, to an ongoing process of demanding, offering, and testing public moral arguments and reasons.[10] Such a commitment, it must be acknowledged, assumes that men and women are capable of giving and accepting the kinds of reasons which are not mere references to narrow interests, but which can survive critical examination and be widely seen to be good.[11] But it does not require us to pin all our hopes on the rational faculties of human beings, or to underestimate the degree of intractable discord in a large and diverse society. When we are left with important matters upon which agreement seems, for the time being, unobtainable, the liberal virtue of moderation suggests that often the best thing to do will be "to moderate our claims in the face of the reasonable claims of others, to balance, and split at least some of our differences."[12]

The United States (more than many other less diverse and more secularized countries) thus seems endowed with a wide array of cultural resources that could help to temper some of the extravagances and remedy some of the deficiencies of our rights talk. We do not lack materials for refining our deliberations concerning such matters as whether a particular issue is best conceptualized as involving a right; the relation a given right should have to other rights and interests; the responsibilities, if any, that should be correlative with a given right; the social costs of rights; and what effects a given right can be expected to have on the setting of conditions for the durable protection of freedom and human dignity. The very heterogeneity that drives us to seek an excessively abstract common language may indeed be one of our most promising resources for enriching it.

But how might this latent cultural energy be released? Could some latter-day Abraham Lincoln find a way to draw on our rich but highly diverse cultural heritage in order to speak to "the better angels of our nature"? Might some new Martin Luther King, Jr., call on the teachings of the world's great religions to reunite our love of individual freedom with our sense of a community for which we accept a common responsibility? A host of daunting obstacles make it increasingly difficult for ideas and arguments possessing any degree of complexity to break into a public conversation that is kept simple by habit and technology. Rights language not only seems to filter out other discourses; it simultaneously infiltrates them. (What parent has not heard about children's rights in the midst of an argument over mittens, manners, or spinach?)

Moreover, the men and women who wield the most influence in our society, and enjoy the greatest access to the public forum, are often the most remote from alternative American discourses and the sources from which they spring. To members of the knowledge class that now predominates in government, political parties, corporations, universities, and the mass media, strong ties to persons and places, religious beliefs, or attachment to traditions are frequently

relatively unimportant, or even counterproductive.[13] Geographically
mobile, and deriving prestige, power, and satisfaction from their
work, American movers and shakers are often at best indifferent to
the "delicate communities on which others depend for practical and
emotional support."[14] Their common attitude that the educated are
better equipped to govern than the masses finds its institutional expression in a disdain for ordinary politics and the legislative process,
and a preference for extending the authority of courts, the branch of
government to which they have the easiest access.[15]

Over a century ago, John Stuart Mill warned that a soft form of
tyranny was being exercised by untutored majorities and by a vulgar
press whose members were "much like" their "mediocre" readers:
"the opinions of masses of merely average men are everywhere become or becoming the dominant power."[16] The emerging mass media, he thought, were especially threatening to "exceptional" men
and women, intellectuals, and creative persons. In the midst of the
rights revolution, however, a new form of soft tyranny has been
building. Hyperindividualistic values and language have become pervasive in the education and information industries. Journalism has
become one of the professions, leaving what Mill referred to pejo-
ratively as "average" men and women with few spokespersons or
outlets for their concerns. A press more preoccupied with celebrities
than with the world of work, and often more disposed to entertain
than to inform, inevitably loses touch with the daily lives of most
Americans. A striking instance of this trend is the virtual disappearance of the once respected "labor beat" from American newspapers,
and the scanty coverage accorded by the media generally to workers'
issues.[17] A study of labor and the media showed that in 1989 the
three network evening news programs devoted only about two percent of their time to all American workplace issues, including child
care, the minimum wage, and occupational safety and health. These
developments are all the more remarkable when one reflects on the
sharp rise in women's labor force participation since the 1960s, and
on the steadily increasing importance of paid employment as a determinant of standing and security in American society.[18] Speculat-
ing on the reasons for the decline in media attention to issues of vital
interest to the 100 million men and women who compose the American labor force, the director of the study, Jonathan Tasini, observed:
"There is a growing gap between the experiences of working people
in the United States and the individuals who are supposed to report
on their lives."

What, then, are the prospects for the sorts of broad-based, free-ranging, reasoned processes of deliberation that our constitutional order both invites and requires? In a landmark free-speech case, from which the epigraph to this chapter is taken, Justice Brandeis asserted that public discussion is indispensable to a regime that purports to be concerned with the free development of the human person. Deliberation, he said, is our best defense against arbitrary rule, and an "inert people" the principal menace to freedom. What Justice Brandeis left out (and what American political actors generally ignore), however, is that supporters of a system that relies so heavily on public deliberation cannot afford to neglect the effective conditions for deliberation. The greatest obstacle to political renewal under present circumstances may not be an "inert people" so much as the failure of persons in positions of leadership to provide models by personal example and to work actively to create opportunities for discussion.

At the most basic level, deliberation requires time, information, and forums where facts, interests, and ideas can be exchanged and debated.[19] It requires vigorous political parties with the ability to articulate programs and attract participation. If deliberation is not to take the form of a mere clash of unyielding interests, and to end in seemingly irreconcilable conflicts, these simple necessary conditions are not sufficient. It is becoming plain that our liberal regime of equality and personal freedom depends, more than most theorists of liberalism have been willing to admit, on the existence and support of certain social assumptions and practices: the belief that each and every human being possesses great and inherent value, the willingness to respect the rights of others even at the cost of some disadvantages to one's self, the ability to defer some immediate benefits for the sake of long-range goals, and a regard for reason-giving and civility in public discourse. It took a Tocqueville—with his peculiar combination of sympathy, curiosity, and ironic distance—to see how essential, and yet how difficult, it would be for democratic regimes to nourish the habits and beliefs on which their ambitious enterprises depend. If participation and deliberation are not to be merely the means of advancing short-term individual and group interests, if they are also to serve as aids to transcending these narrow concerns, political leaders must attend to the social structures where cultural value systems are transmitted, and where civic skills are acquired.

In his 1990 New Year's address, Czechoslovak President Vaclav Havel rhetorically asked a question that is pertinent to our own circumstances: How did a people that to all appearances was beaten down, atomized, cynical, and apathetic find the strength to embark on a great project of social and political renewal?

> [W]e ask where the young people, in particular, who have never known any other system, find the source of their aspirations for truth, freedom of thought, civic courage, and civic foresight? How is it that their parents, the generation which was considered lost, also joined in with them?[20]

Havel's first comment on his own question was that "man is never merely a product of the world around him, he is always capable of striving for something higher."[21] A second factor that helped to regenerate a seemingly moribund political life, according to Havel, was the recovery of the "humanistic and democratic traditions" that "lay dormant somewhere in the subconscious of our nations and national minorities, and were passed on from one generation to the next in order for each [of] us to discover them within us when the time was right."[22] The main carriers of these dormant traditions were the associations of civil society—communities of mutual aid like Solidarity in Poland, and many communities of memory, both ethnic and religious. The slogans that stirred them and that spread like brushfire from country to country were not only about rights. They were about the courage to be honest; about men and women "living in truth"; and about calling "good and evil by name."[23]

With hindsight, it seems that no small part of the great transformations that have taken place in East Central Europe have been powered by the same kinds of forces that still silently support our mature, and relatively complacent, democracies in the West. The East European freedom movements can be and often are described in abstract political language as campaigns for "human rights." But they were also (like the American civil rights movement of the 1950s and 1960s) nourished through their dark days and nights by inspiring religious leaders. Participants in these historic struggles found strength and solace in communities of shared experience and recollection, as well as in their common quest for political and civil liberties.

Here at home, where humanistic and democratic traditions are far from dormant, political life, in theory, should be easier to revive, and its prospects less uncertain. On the political horizon, there are scattered signs that may well favor a revision in the location, terms, and content of political debate, bringing it closer to potential sources of renewal. The Supreme Court seems to be relaxing its hold on some of the issues that it had removed from legislative and local control with little mandate from the design, text, or tradition of the Constitution. This more deferential judicial posture leaves wider scope for democratic processes of bargaining, education, and persuasion to operate. It gives state and local governments more leeway to be "laboratories" where a variety of innovative approaches to vexing social problems (open-air drug markets, child care, drunk driving) can be tested on a limited basis, and their successes or failures assessed. Like muscles long unused, atrophied political processes will move awkwardly at first; they will need exercise before they become healthy and strong. Meanwhile, slowly but irreversibly, African-Americans, Asian-Americans, Hispanics, women, and others who have been underrepresented in politics, are assuming their rightful roles in public life. To what extent their presence will have a transformative effect on the terms and content of public discussion is an open question (transformation works both ways), but some will bring new insights and modes of discourse into the public square.

At the grassroots level, men and women of widely varying beliefs and backgrounds are increasingly manifesting their discontent with what had come to seem an unwritten law that morally or religiously grounded viewpoints are out of bounds in public dialogue.[24] Whether or not this unrest amounts to a full-blown "culture struggle," as some say, it is bringing still more new players onto the political scene. Many of them, like Dr. King, are adept at articulating their perspectives in such a way as to make them accessible to all men and women of good will. Long years of interfaith discussions, begun in an effort to improve relations between Christians and Jews, and among Christian sects, have produced secular side effects as substantial as they were unexpected. In learning, slowly and with great difficulty, to communicate across painful memories and profound differences, members of America's religious groups have made important discoveries. They learned that they could enter into dialogue, find some common ground, and, where common ground did not seem to exist, achieve mutual understanding—all without losing their own religious distinctiveness. Fear, suspicion, divisiveness, and intolerance were lessened, not aggravated, through open exchange. In resolutely seeking out ways to "translate" particular discourses, without sacrificing subtlety and complexity; in finding areas of agreement; and in learning to disagree without losing mutual respect, America's religions have helped to model ways of entering into dialogue across deep differences. They have provided challenging and inspiring examples of coexistence in pluralism.

Many devotees of rights talk will find these bits of evidence, scattered examples, and suggestive developments unconvincing. Those who hold that only power can check power will be unmoved by a case that pins so many hopes on cogent argument, persuasion, negotiation, and self-restraint. Those who believe that, in many cases, there is no basis whatsoever for communication or mutual understanding between political antagonists will prefer rights in their starker forms, untempered by limits or obligations. Those who count on science to take care of environmental problems, and on economic growth to provide for posterity, will be untroubled by the present-mindedness of rights talk. Those who consider that families, churches, labor unions, and the like are more apt to oppress than to empower individuals, will be content to continue to work out our collective destiny on the individual-state-market grid. Those who have given up on ordinary politics and the legislative process will not be unduly distressed if most important controversies are entrusted to the courts for decision.

Unhappily, there are all too many reasons to give naked force its due, to despair of mediating group conflict, to live for the moment, and to be cynical about politics. Spousal and child abuse in some households, periodic religious scandals, and corrupt leaders in some unions have soured many on the potential of the nation's families, churches, and workers' groups to serve as seedbeds of civic virtue or as buffers between the individual and large organizations. It is an illusion, however, to believe that the "parchment barriers" of legal rights alone can shelter citizens from the arbitrary exercise of public or private power. There should be no mistaking the fact that a conversation carried on in our current American rights dialect is a dialogue of despair, an admission that we have lost the historic wager in *Federalist* No. 1 that our political order need not be determined by force and accident, but can be established through "reflection and choice."

Only time will tell whether the public square can be effectively regained for an ongoing broad-based conversation about the means and ends of government, about what kind of society we are, and about what kind of future we hope to create for our children and for posterity. The very features that have made us different from other

advanced welfare democracies may turn out to be the most conducive to the renewal of political discourse: the variety of our racial and
ethnic groups, the opportunities for innovation and experimentation
inherent in our sort of federalism, our neighborliness, our stubborn
religiosity, and even, within bounds, our attachment to a gambling,
risk-taking, profit-making economy. There is reason to believe that
a significant constituency exists in the United States for candor,
moderation, and complexity adequate to the matter at hand. What is
less clear is whether Americans in positions of leadership have the
will, ability, courage, and imagination necessary to respond to and
mobilize such a constituency.

Refining the rhetoric of rights would be but one element in a
project of transformative politics. Yet even quite small shifts in circumstances can produce remarkable distant effects in complex
systems.[25] The American experiment in ordered liberty has been
brought to its present state by a long series of great and small events.
Luck and misfortune have played their role, and so have the sheer
exertion of force and power. What is of more interest, however, are
the shaping effects of the experience, the intelligence, the imagination, the decisions, the sacrifices, and the personal examples of the
men and women who have preceded us. Which of these ingredients
will predominate in the period of our own stewardship is not within
anyone's power to predict. If the ancient practice of politics is in any
sense a science, its subject matter is the elusive one of shifting probabilities. Still, politics, as Havel has reminded the world, is not only
the art of the possible: "It can also be the art of the impossible, that
is, the art of making both ourselves and the world better."[26] While
the current state of the art does not exactly provide grounds for
optimism, it does leave room for the more sober, responsible, attitude that prophets have called hope.

Notes

Editor's note: As matters of style in this book, ellipses at the ends of quoted passages have been omitted, and displayed quotations have been made to start at a uniform margin.

PREFACE

1. Michael Oreskes, "Study Finds 'Astonishing' Indifference to Elections," *New York Times,* 6 May 1990, 32.
2. Stephen Knack, "Why We Don't Vote—Or Say 'Thank you,'" *Wall Street Journal,* 31 December 1990, 11.
3. Kiku Adatto's study of presidential campaign news coverage in 1968 and 1988 revealed the alarming fact that "the average 'sound bite,' or bloc of uninterrupted speech, fell from 42.3 seconds for presidential candidates in 1968 to only 9.8 seconds in 1988." *Sound Bite Democracy: Network Evening News Presidential Campaign Coverage, 1968 and 1988* (Research Paper R-2) (Cambridge: John F. Kennedy School of Government, Harvard University, 1990), 4.
4. Charles Taylor, *Sources of the Self: The Making of the Modern Identity* (Cambridge: Harvard University Press, 1989), 91.

ONE The Land of Rights

1. Plato, "The Republic," in *The Dialogues of Plato,* Benjamin Jowett trans. (Chicago: Encyclopaedia Britannica, 1952), Book VIII, 409.
2. Alexis de Tocqueville, *Democracy in America,* trans. George Lawrence, ed. J. P. Mayer (Garden City, New York: Doubleday Anchor, 1969), I, 270.
3. E.g., Franz Wieacker, "Foundations of European Legal Culture," 37 *American Journal of Comparative Law* 1, 6 (1990).
4. Some historians have remarked on the legalistic character of American society even in the early colonial days when lawyers were scarce and citizens were supposed to be visible saints. See Daniel R. Coquillette, "Introduction: The 'Countenance of Authoritie'," in *Law in Colonial Massachusetts* (Boston: Colonial Society of Massachusetts, 1984), xxi.
5. Jean-Jacques Rousseau, "The Social Contract," in *The Social Contract and Discourses,* trans. G. D. H. Cole (London: Dent Dutton, 1973), 206. Cf. Tocqueville, *Democracy in America,* I, 305, 307.
6. Rousseau, *The Social Contract,* 207.
7. Tocqueville, *Democracy in America,* I, 270.
8. Lawrence M. Friedman, "Law, Lawyers, and Popular Culture," 98 *Yale Law Journal* 1579, 1598 (1989).

9. Gerald Gunther, *Individual Rights in Constitutional Law,* 4th ed. (Mineola, N.Y.: Foundation Press, 1986), 95; Laurence H. Tribe, *American Constitutional Law,* 2d ed. (Mineola, N.Y.: Foundation Press, 1988), 772–73, 776.

10. Lawrence Baum, *The Supreme Court,* 2d ed. (Washington: Congressional Quarterly, 1985), 160, 162, 166.

11. State court activism in this area was urged (and perhaps stimulated) by Justice William Brennan in "State Constitutions and the Protection of Individual Rights," 90 *Harvard Law Review* 489 (1977).

12. *Brown v. Board of Education of Topeka,* 347 U.S. 483 (1954).

13. *Reynolds v. Sims,* 377 U.S. 533 (1964), foreshadowed in *Baker v. Carr,* 369 U.S. 186 (1962).

14. The United Nations Universal Declaration of Human Rights was adopted by the General Assembly on December 10, 1948. U.N.-sponsored international covenants on Economic, Social and Cultural Rights and on Civil and Political Rights were ready for signature in December 1966 and came into force a decade later. Most of the major powers, but not, so far, the United States, have ratified these covenants. The United States did, however, sign the Declaration and the Helsinki Final Act of 1975 which calls for a nonbinding commitment to stated international norms of human rights. We have also ratified a small number of human rights treaties addressed to particular topics: slavery, forced labor, political rights of women, the status of refugees, genocide, and torture.

15. *Texas v. Johnson,* 109 S. Ct. 2533 (1989), reaffirmed in *United States v. Eichman,* 110 S. Ct. 2404 (1990).

16. People for the American Way, *Democracy's Next Generation* (Washington: People for the American Way, 1989), 14.

17. Ibid., 67–69.

18. Plato, *The Republic,* 409.

19. *Palko v. Connecticut,* 302 U.S. 319, 325 (1937).

20. There is a vast literature on the history and theory of rights and natural right. Works that I have found of particular interest are: Ronald Dworkin, *Taking Rights Seriously* (Cambridge: Harvard University Press, 1977); Richard E. Flathman, *The Practice of Rights* (Cambridge: Cambridge University Press, 1976); John Finnis, *Natural Law and Natural Rights* (Oxford: Clarendon Press, 1986); Charles Fried, *Right and Wrong* (Cambridge: Harvard University Press, 1978); Morton Horwitz, "Rights," 23 *Harvard Civil Rights–Civil Liberties Review* 393 (1988); Michael J. Sandel, *Liberalism and the Limits of Justice* (Cambridge: Cambridge University Press, 1982); Leo Strauss, *Natural Right and History* (Chicago: University of Chicago Press, 1953); Michel Villey, *Le Droit et les Droits de l'Homme* (Paris: Presses Universitaires de France, 1983).

21. See, generally, Louis Henkin, *The Age of Rights* (New York: Columbia University Press, 1990); Morton Keller, "Powers and Rights: Two Centuries of American Constitutionalism," 74 *Journal of American History* 675 (1987).

22. "Declaration of the Rights of Man and of the Citizen" in *Constitutions et documents politiques,* 10th ed., ed. Maurice Duverger (Paris: Presses Universitaires de France, 1986), 17.

23. Clifford Geertz, *The Interpretation of Cultures* (New York: Basic Books, 1973). See also James Boyd White, *When Words Lose Their Meaning* (Chicago: University of Chicago Press, 1984).

24. Vaclav Havel, "Words on Words," *The New York Review of Books,* January 18, 1990. (Speech on receiving the Peace Prize of the German Booksellers Association.)
25. U.S. Department of Justice, Immigration and Naturalization Service, *A Welcome to U.S.A. Citizenship* (Washington: U.S. Government Printing Office, 1977), 3.
26. *Trop v. Dulles,* 356 U.S. 86, 102 (1958) (Warren, C. J.).
27. Participation in community and political life is the single most strongly emphasized theme in the official booklet distributed to prospective Canadian citizens. Department of the Secretary of State of Canada, *The Canadian Citizen* (Ottawa: Department of the Secretary of State, 1985).
28. United Nations Universal Declaration of Human Rights, Article 29.
29. See, especially, Martin P. Golding, "The Primacy of Welfare Rights," 1 *Social Philosophy and Policy* 119 (1984); Richard E. Morgan, *Disabling America: The "Rights Industry" in Our Time* (New York: Basic Books, 1984); Michael Sandel, *Liberalism and the Limits of Justice* (Cambridge: Cambridge University Press, 1982); Richard Stith, "Living without Rights—In Manners, Religion, and Law," in *Law and the Ordering of Our Life Together,* ed. Richard J. Neuhaus (Grand Rapids: Eerdmans, 1989), 54; Michel Villey, *Le Droit et les Droits de l'Homme* (Paris: Presses Universitaires de France, 1983); Tom Campbell, *The Left and Rights* (London: Routledge & Kegan Paul, 1983).
30. Edmund Burke, *Reflections on the Revolution in France,* ed. J. G. A. Pocock (Indianapolis: Hackett Publishing, 1987). Burke contrasted the abstract rights of liberty and equality with "the *real* rights of men" (his emphasis) which he described as a patrimony from our forefathers, the product of practical reason and the experience of men in civil society, rather than sterile theorizing about "natural" or "universal" man. Among these "real" rights (the rights of Englishmen) Burke listed several, beginning with the right to live under law:

> They have a right to the fruits of their industry and to the means of making their industry fruitful. They have a right to the acquisitions of their parents, to the nourishment and improvement of their offspring, to instruction in life, and to consolation in death. Whatever each man can separately do, without trespassing upon others, he has a right to do for himself; and he has a right to a fair portion of all which society, with all its combinations of skill and force, can do in his favour. In this partnership all men have equal rights, but not to equal things. (p. 51).

31. Marx was as scornful as Burke of the "so-called *rights of man,*" and even more emphatic in condemning their failure to take into account human sociality. In his view, the "liberty" of the French Declaration was merely the liberty "of man regarded as an isolated monad, withdrawn into himself." It was "founded . . . upon the separation of man from man"; indeed, it was the very "right of such separation." As for equality, it did not go beyond the idea of man as "an individual separated from the community." It was but the right to be equally treated "as a self-sufficient monad." Karl Marx, "On the Jewish Question," in *The Marx-Engels Reader,* ed. Robert C. Tucker (New York: Norton, 1972), 24, 40, 41.
32. Robert Wright, "Are Animals People Too?" *New Republic,* 12 March 1990, 20, 27.
33. Thomas Jefferson, "Inaugural Address," in *The Life and Selected Writings of Thomas Jefferson* (New York: Modern Library, 1944), 323.

TWO The Illusion of Absoluteness

1. William Blackstone, *Commentaries on the Laws of England*, Book I, *138.
2. *Louisiana Leasing Co. v. Sokolow*, 48 Misc. 2d 1014, 266 N.Y.S. 2d 447 (N.Y. Civ. Ct., Queens County, 1966).
3. John Locke, "The Second Treatise of Government" in *Two Treatises of Government*, ed. Peter Laslett (Cambridge: Cambridge University Press, 1963), Chapter Five ("On Property").
4. M.-T. Meulders-Klein, "The Right Over One's Own Body: Its Scope and Limits in Comparative Law," 6 *Boston College International and Comparative Law Review* 29, 78 (1983).
5. Locke, *Second Treatise*, 395.
6. Ibid. (Locke's emphasis).
7. Jean-Jacques Rousseau, "A Discourse on the Origin of Inequality," in *The Social Contract and Discourses*, trans. G. D. H. Cole (London: Dent Dutton, 1973), 59.
8. William Blackstone, *Commentaries on the Laws of England*, Book II, *3.
9. Ibid., *4.
10. Ibid., *8.
11. Ibid., *2.
12. Daniel J. Boorstin, *The Mysterious Science of the Law* (Cambridge: Harvard University Press, 1941), 3.
13. Letter from Thomas Jefferson to Bernard Moore (1765), *The Writings of Thomas Jefferson*, vol. 9 (New York: Putnam, 1898), 480–85.
14. "Letter from Lincoln to John M. Brockman of September 25, 1860," Abraham Lincoln, *Speeches and Writings 1859–1865* (New York: Library of America, 1989), 180.
15. John B. Minor, "Notes," 3 *Southern Law Review* 197 (1874).
16. Robert A. Ferguson, *Law and Letters in American Culture* (Cambridge: Harvard University Press, 1984), 11.
17. For a penetrating scholarly analysis of the role that protection of private property played in the formation of American constitutional government, see Jennifer Nedelsky, *Private Property and the Limits of American Constitutionalism: The Madisonian Framework and its Legacy* (Chicago: University of Chicago Press, 1991).
18. Ibid.
19. William T. Fisher, *The Law of the Land: An Intellectual History of American Real Property Doctrine* (Oxford: Oxford University Press, forthcoming).
20. J. G. A. Pocock, *Politics, Language, and Time* (New York: Atheneum Press, 1971), 91.
21. *Charles River Bridge v. Warren Bridge*, 36 U.S. (11 Pet.) 420, 548 (1837).
22. *Dred Scott v. Sandford*, 60 U.S. (19 How.) 393 (1857).
23. E.g., *Lochner v. New York*, 198 U.S. 45 (1905) (New York statute establishing 60-hour limit on bakery employees' work week held unconstitutional).
24. *Hammer v. Dagenhart*, 247 U.S. 251 (1918) (Federal statute prohibiting interstate commerce in the products of child labor held unconstitutional).
25. *Coppage v. Kansas*, 236 U.S. 1 (1915) (Kansas statute outlawing "yellow dog" anti-union employment agreements held unconstitutional).
26. Ibid., 14.
27. Ibid.
28. Ibid. (emphasis added).

29. Comment, "The Right to Privacy in Nineteenth Century America," 94 *Harvard Law Review* 1892 (1981).

30. Ibid., 1898.

31. Aviam Soifer, "Reviewing Legal Fictions," 20 *Georgia Law Review* 871, 891 (1986).

32. *Village of Euclid v. Ambler Realty Co.*, 272 U.S. 365 (1926).

33. *Nebbia v. New York*, 291 U.S. 502, 523 (1934).

34. *National Labor Relations Board v. Jones & Laughlin Steel Corp.*, 301 U.S. 1 (1937) [overruling *Coppage v. Kansas*, 236 U.S. 1 (1915)]; *West Coast Hotel v. Parrish*, 300 U.S. 379 (1937).

35. *Calder v. Bull*, 3 U.S. (3 Dall.) 386, 388 (1798).

36. *Berman v. Parker*, 348 U.S. 26 (1954).

37. *Hawaii Housing Authority v. Midkiff*, 467 U.S. 229 (1984).

38. Ibid., 241. It should not be assumed that the *Hawaii Housing* decision was necessarily a victory for have-nots. The single largest landowner was a trust whose beneficiaries were aboriginal Hawaiians, whereas many of the "tenants" were affluent mainlanders who had migrated to Hawaii. The property right, like other rights, is a two-edged sword and one edge is often sharper than the other.

39. Ibid., 242.

40. Letter from Holmes to Harold Laski of October 22, 1922, *Holmes-Laski Letters*, ed. Mark DeWolfe Howe (Cambridge: Harvard University Press, 1953), 457.

41. *Poletown Neighborhood Council v. City of Detroit*, 410 Mich. 616, 304 N. W. 2d 455 (1981).

42. Jeannie Wylie, *Poletown: Community Betrayed* (Urbana, Ill.: University of Illinois Press, 1989), 52.

43. *Buckley v. Valeo*, 424 U.S. 1 (1976); *First National Bank of Boston v. Bellotti*, 435 U.S. 765 (1978).

44. Locke, *Second Treatise*, 328–29.

45. Thurman W. Arnold, *The Folklore of Capitalism* (New Haven: Yale University Press, 1937), 121–22; Charles A. Reich, "The New Property," 73 *Yale Law Journal* 733 (1964).

46. See Charles Reich, "Individual Rights and Social Welfare: The Emerging Legal Issues," 74 *Yale Law Journal* 1245 (1965).

47. See, generally, on the right-to-hearing cases, Laurence H. Tribe, *American Constitutional Law*, 2d ed. (Mineola, N.Y.: Foundation Press, 1988), 685–706.

48. See generally, for this point of view, Richard A. Epstein, *Takings: Private Property and the Power of Eminent Domain* (Cambridge: Harvard University Press, 1985).

49. Rousseau, "Discourse on Inequality," 76.

50. Blackstone, *Commentaries on the Laws of England*, II, *2.

51. Ibid., *7.

52. Ibid., *15.

53. Rousseau, *The Social Contract*, 178–81.

54. Aristotle, *Nicomachean Ethics*, I.8. 1099.

55. Deuteronomy 24:19–21.

56. As James Miller reminds us, Rousseau's predecessors and peers, by his own account, were not his contemporaries, "but the republicans of the past and the classical authors who had first defined the vocabulary of political thought."

Rousseau: Dreamer of Democracy (New Haven: Yale University Press, 1984), 110.

57. Ibid., 6.
58. William H. McNeill, *History of Western Civilization* (Chicago: University of Chicago Press, 1969), 518.
59. See Mary Ann Glendon, Michael Gordon, and Christopher Osakwe, *Comparative Legal Traditions* (St. Paul: West, 1985), 49–50.
60. French Civil Code, article 544.
61. See generally James Q. Whitman, *The Legacy of Roman Law in the German Romantic Era: Historical Vision and Legal Change* (Princeton: Princeton University Press, 1990); Michael John, *Politics and the Law in Late Nineteenth Century Germany: The Origins of the Civil Code* (Oxford: Clarendon Press, 1989).
62. Karl Marx, *Writings of the Young Marx on Philosophy and Society,* ed. and trans. L. Easton and K. Guddat (Garden City, N.Y.: Doubleday, 1967), 40, 46.
63. F. von Savigny, *System des heutigen Römischen Rechts,* Vol. 1, (Berlin: Veit, 1840), 367.
64. German Civil Code, article 903.
65. *Allgemeines Landrecht für die Preussischen Staaten von 1794* (Frankfurt: Metzner, 1970), Part 2, Title 13.
66. Alexis de Tocqueville, *The Old Regime and the French Revolution,* trans. Stuart Gilbert (New York: Doubleday Anchor, 1955), 226–27.
67. See Bertrand de Jouvenel, *Sovereignty: An Inquiry into the Political Good,* trans. J. F. Huntington (Chicago: University of Chicago Press, 1957).
68. W. McNeill, *History of Western Civilization,* 559.
69. William Pfaff, *Barbarian Sentiments: How the American Century Ends* (New York: Hill and Wang, 1989), 25.
70. The Canadian Charter of Rights and Freedoms is the official name for the first 34 sections of the Constitution Act of 1982. Canada Act 1982, Can. Rev. Stat. Appendix II, No. 44 (1985).
71. *Basic Law of the Federal Republic of Germany* (Bonn: Press and Information Office, 1981), 20.
72. See the discussion of the West German constitutional law of property in Donald P. Kommers, *The Constitutional Jurisprudence of the Federal Republic of Germany* (Durham: Duke University Press, 1989), 247–71.
73. Ronald Dworkin, *Taking Rights Seriously* (Cambridge: Harvard University Press, 1977), 269.
74. A fundamental right is distinguished by the fact that it can be restricted by law only when the state meets the burden of proving that a "compelling government interest" is involved. Other rights may be abridged whenever that is part of a rational scheme to achieve some legitimate governmental purpose. Since the Supreme Court rarely finds a reason "compelling," the classification of a right as fundamental puts it largely beyond legislative control.
75. Alexis de Tocqueville, *Democracy in America,* trans. George Lawrence, ed. J. P. Mayer (Garden City, N.Y.: Doubleday Anchor, 1969), II, 488.
76. See Mathias W. Reimann, "Prurient Interest and Human Dignity: Pornography Regulation in West Germany and the United States," 21 *University of Michigan Journal of Law Reform* 201 (1987). Compare the decision of the European Commission on Human Rights that the dissemination of ideas encouraging racial discrimination in violation of the rights and freedoms of others was not pro-

tected by the right to free expression guaranteed by Article 10 of the European Convention on Human Rights [*Glimmerveen and Hagenbeek v. The Netherlands,* 4 European Human Rights Reports 260 (1979)], with the decision of the American courts that the First Amendment protected from prior restraint a planned march by a group of neo-Nazis through a community where a number of Holocaust survivors resided, *Collin v. Smith,* 578 F.2d 1197 (7th Cir. 1978), *cert. denied,* 439 U.S. 916 (1978).

77. Quoted in Charles L. Black, Jr., "Mr. Justice Black, The Supreme Court, and the Bill of Rights," *Harper's Magazine,* February 1961, 63.

78. Ibid. Professor Black argues that the cases in which speech can be legitimately regulated are so few that it is more accurate, as well as strategically preferable, to speak of the right to free speech as absolute rather than as almost absolute.

79. Ibid., 68.

80. See David L. Shapiro, "In Defense of Judicial Candor," 100 *Harvard Law Review* 731, 744 (1987).

81. Laurence H. Tribe, *American Constitutional Law,* 2d ed. (Mineola, N.Y.: Foundation Press, 1988), 785.

82. United States Constitution, Amendment V. See also Amendment XIV.

83. Blackstone, *Commentaries on the Laws of England,* Book I, *125.

84. Ibid.

85. Ibid., *129 (Blackstone's emphasis).

86. Ibid., *124.

87. As John Langbein has explained, significant consequences follow from the fact that American lawyers are "fact adversaries" as well as "law adversaries," "The German Advantage in Civil Procedure," 52 *University of Chicago Law Review* 108 (1985).

88. John Updike, "The Virtues of Playing Cricket on the Village Green," *New Yorker,* 30 July 1990, 85, 86.

THREE The Lone Rights-Bearer

1. Samuel D. Warren and Louis D. Brandeis, "The Right to Privacy," 4 *Harvard Law Review* 193 (1890).

2. Karl Marx, "On the Jewish Question," in *The Marx-Engels Reader,* ed. Robert C. Tucker (New York: Norton, 1972), 40.

3. Ibid.

4. In writing this chapter, I have benefited from Michael Sandel's discussions of how American constitutional law, and liberal theory generally, has neglected what he calls the "situated" or "encumbered" self. Sandel maintains that persons are always "situated" or "embedded" in a social context, and that everyone is more or less "encumbered" by social ties. See, e.g., Michael J. Sandel, *Liberalism and the Limits of Justice* (Cambridge: Cambridge University Press, 1982), 179–83.

5. William Blackstone, *Commentaries on the Laws of England,* Book 1, *124.

6. John Stuart Mill, "On Liberty," in *Utilitarianism, Liberty, and Representative Government* (New York: E. P. Dutton, 1951), 94.

7. Quoted in Dennis O'Brien, "The Right of Privacy," 2 *Columbia Law Review* 437 (1902).

8. B. S. Markesinis, *A Comparative Introduction to the German Law of Tort,* 2d ed. (Oxford: Clarendon Press, 1990), 37–38.

9. *Roberson v. Rochester Folding Box Co.,* 171 N.Y. 538 (N.Y.C.A. 1902).

10. Judge Richard Posner has observed, regarding privacy claims, "Very few people want to be let alone. They want to manipulate the world around them by selective disclosure of facts about themselves." "The Right of Privacy," 12 *Georgia Law Review* 393, 400 (1978).

11. Warren and Brandeis, *The Right to Privacy,* 196.

12. Ibid., 213.

13. Ibid., 214.

14. Ibid., 193. The famous phrase "the right to be let alone" was attributed by the authors to Judge Cooley, the author of a leading treatise on torts, published two years previously. Ibid., 195. Cooley, however, appears to have had in mind a right not to be physically assaulted, rather than a general right to personality. See James H. Barron, "Warren and Brandeis, 'The Right to Privacy,' 4 Harvard Law Review 193 (1890): Demystifying a Landmark Citation," 13 *Suffolk University Law Review* 875, 878 (1979). For a survey of earlier nineteenth-century invocations of privacy interests, see Comment, "The Right to Privacy in Nineteenth Century America," 94 *Harvard Law Review* 1892 (1981).

15. Ibid., 220.

16. J. S. Mill, "On Liberty," 81, 85.

17. Ibid., 96.

18. Ibid.

19. Ibid., 164–65 (Mill's emphasis).

20. Ibid., 165–66.

21. Ibid.

22. Ibid., 166.

23. Ibid., 175.

24. Quoted in James Barron, "Demystifying a Landmark Citation," 912.

25. Ibid.

26. *Olmstead v. United States,* 277 U.S. 438 (1928).

27. Ibid., 478 (Brandeis J., dissenting). For a searching critique-cum-defense of the Brandeis dissent, see Aviam Soifer, "Reviewing Legal Fictions," 20 *Georgia Law Review* 871, 898–911 (1986).

28. See Edward H. Levi, *An Introduction to Legal Reasoning* (Chicago: University of Chicago Press, 1948), 5–6.

29. E.g., *Public Utilities Commission v. Pollak,* 343 U.S. 451 (1952); *Frank v. Maryland,* 359 U.S. 360 (1959); *Mapp v. Ohio,* 367 U.S. 643 (1961).

30. Erwin Griswold, "The Right to be Let Alone," 55 *Northwestern Law Review* 216, 217, 224 (1960).

31. *Griswold v. Connecticut,* 381 U.S. 479, 527 (1965).

32. E.g., *Pierce v. Society of Sisters,* 268 U.S. 510 (1925) (parents' right to provide religious schooling); *Meyer v. Nebraska,* 262 U.S. 390, 402 (1923) (right to have children taught in their native language overrides "desire of legislature to foster homogeneous people with American ideals. . . ."); *Prince v. Massachusetts,* 321 U.S. 158, 166 (1944) (respect for "the private realm of family life which the state cannot enter").

33. *Skinner v. Oklahoma,* 316 U.S. 535, 541 (1942).

34. *Griswold v. Connecticut,* 381 U.S. 479, 499, 502 (1965) (opinions of Harlan, J., and White, J.)

35. Ibid., 482, 484, 486.

36. Ibid., 486, 487.

37. Ibid., 486, 487, 495, 497.

38. Ibid., 495, quoting from *Poe v. Ullman,* 367 U.S. 497, 551, 552 (1961) (Harlan, J., dissenting).

39. *Eisenstadt v. Baird,* 405 U.S. 438, 453 (1972).

40. Michael J. Sandel, "Moral Argument and Liberal Toleration: Abortion and Homosexuality," 77 *California Law Review* 521, 527–28 (1989).

41. Kenneth B. Noble, "Key Abortion Plaintiff Now Denies She Was Raped," *New York Times,* 9 September 1987, A23.

42. *Roe v. Wade,* 410 U.S. 113, 153 (1973).

43. *Doe v. Bolton,* 410 U.S. 179 (1973).

44. Lisa Belkin, "Woman Behind the Symbols in Abortion Debate," *New York Times,* 9 May 1989, A18.

45. The European statutes are described in detail in Mary Ann Glendon, *Abortion and Divorce in Western Law* (Cambridge: Harvard University Press, 1987), 10–42.

46. *Doe v. Bolton,* 410 U.S. 179, 192 (1973): "[T]he medical judgment may be exercised in the light of all factors—physical, emotional, psychological, familial, and the woman's age—relevant to the well-being of the patient. All these factors may relate to health."

47. Laurence H. Tribe, "The Abortion Funding Conundrum: Inalienable Rights, Affirmative Duties, and the Dilemma of Dependence," 99 *Harvard Law Review* 330, 342 (1985).

48. Ibid. (Tribe's emphasis).

49. *Roe v. Wade,* 153–54: "[Some] argue that the woman's right is absolute and that she is entitled to terminate her pregnancy at whatever time, in whatever way, and for whatever reason, she alone chooses. With this we do not agree. . . . [A] state may properly assert important interests in safeguarding health, in maintaining medical standards, and in protecting potential life."

50. *Roe v. Wade,* at 158.

51. See especially, *Colautti v. Franklin,* 439 U.S. 379 (1979) (limitations on a doctor's choice of abortion techniques so as to provide the best opportunity for the fetus to be born alive held unconstitutional); *Thornburgh v. American College of Obstetricians and Gynecologists,* 476 U.S. 747 (1986) (mandatory information about risks of abortion, possible availability of medical assistance and child support, and availability of printed matter concerning characteristics of fetus and organizations to assist with alternatives to abortions held unconstitutional; provisions regulating postviability abortions also struck down).

52. *Roe v. Wade,* at 159.

53. *Harris v. McRae,* 448 U.S. 297 (1980) (upholding the "Hyde Amendment" to Title XIX of the Social Security Act, excluding abortions from Medicaid coverage); and *Maher v. Roe,* 432 U.S. 464 (1977); *Poelker v. Doe,* 432 U.S. 519 (1977), and *Beal v. Doe,* 432 U.S. 438 (1977) (all upholding state denial of medical expenses or hospital facilities for nontherapeutic abortions sought by indigent women).

54. *City of Akron v. Akron Center for Reproductive Health Inc.,* 462 U.S. 416 (1983) (holding unconstitutional a city ordinance requiring physician to inform pregnant woman, before her consent to abortion, of state of development of fetus,

risks of abortion, and availability of assistance from agencies, and imposing a twenty-four-hour waiting period after consent); and *Thornburgh v. American College of Obstetricians and Gynecologists*, 476 U.S. 747 (1986).

55. *Bellotti v. Baird* (Bellotti I), 428 U.S. 132 (1976); *Bellotti v. Baird* (Bellotti II), 443 U.S. 622 (1979); *H.L. v. Matheson*, 450 U.S. 398 (1981); *Hodgson v. Minnesota*, 110 S. Ct. 2926 (1990) and *Ohio v. Akron Center for Reproductive Health*, 110 S. Ct. 2972 (1990).

56. *Bowers v. Hardwick*, 478 U.S. 186 (1986).

57. *Webster v. Reproductive Health Services, Inc.*, 109 S. Ct. 3040 (1989).

58. Jean Badinter, "Le droit au respect de la vie privée," 1968, *Juris-Classeur Périodique* I. 2136.

59. Markesinis, *German Law of Tort*, 38.

60. The Basic Law of the Federal Republic of Germany (*Grundgesetz*) Article 2(1). Here and throughout I use the official translation published by the Press and Information Office of the Federal Government (Bonn, 1987).

61. *Bundesgerichtshof Decision of April 2, 1957*, 24 BGHZ 72, 80.

62. In France, from the late nineteenth century to 1970, the courts worked out protection in tort law for what they began to call *la vie privée* or, sometimes, "the intimacy of private life." Finally, bowing to the insistence of nearly all French legal scholars that the right of privacy needed to be placed on a statutory basis, the National Assembly amended the Civil Code in 1970 to "consecrate" the case law and to provide a principled basis for its further development. In England, even today the invasion of privacy as such is not recognized as a tort. See Basil S. Markesinis, "Our Patchy Law of Privacy—Time to Do Something About It," 53 *Modern Law Review* 802 (1990).

63. *Bundesgerichtshof Decision of 25 May 1954*, 13 BGHZ 334.

64. See, especially, *Bundesgerichtshof Decisions of 26 November 1954*, 15 BGHZ 249; *2 April 1957*, 24 BGHZ 72; *14 February 1958*, 26 BGHZ 349; and *18 March 1959*, 30 BGHZ 7.

65. *Bundesgerichtshof Decision of 14 February 1958*, 26 BGHZ 349, 354.

66. *Bundesgerichtshof Decision of 18 March 1959*, 30 BGHZ 7, 11–12.

67. See Markesinis, *German Law of Tort*, 213–15; and Peter E. Quint, "Free Speech and Private Law in German Constitutional Theory," 48 *Maryland Law Review* 247 (1989).

68. *Bundesverfassungsgericht Decision of 25 February 1975*, 39 BVerfG E 1. English translation: *The Abortion Decision of February 25, 1975, of the Federal Constitutional Court, Federal Republic of Germany*, trans. Edmund C. Jann (Washington, D.C.: Library of Congress, 1975) (hereafter Jann).

69. Jann, 60.

70. Jann, 58, 65–66.

71. Fifteenth Statute to Reform the Penal Law of May 18, 1976 (Bundesgesetzblatt I, 1297), translated in *Annual Review of Population Law, 1976* (1977), 49.

72. *Thornburgh v. American College of Obstetricians and Gynecologists*, 476 U.S. 747, 762 (1986).

73. *Olmstead v. United States*, 277 U.S. 438, 478 (1928).

74. *The Florida Star v. B.J.F.*, 109 S. Ct. 2603 (1989); *Cox Broadcasting Corp. v. Cohn*, 420 U.S. 469 (1975).

75. *Whalen v. Roe*, 429 U.S. 589 (1977).

76. See, for example, the decisions protecting the confidentiality of divorce records and medical records translated and discussed in Donald P. Kommers, *The Constitutional Jurisprudence of the Federal Republic of Germany* (Durham, N.C.: Duke University Press, 1989), 337–48.

77. The "Census Act case" is translated and discussed in Kommers, *Constitutional Jurisprudence,* 332–36.

78. Henry Maine, *Ancient Law* (London: Dent Dutton, 1954), 139–40.

79. Jean-Jacques Rousseau, "A Discourse on the Origin of Inequality," in *The Social Contract and Discourses,* trans. G. D. H. Cole (London: Dent Dutton, 1973), 45–53, 66–67.

80. Plato, *The Republic,* 388a, as translated by Martha C. Nussbaum in *The Fragility of Goodness: Luck and Ethics in Greek Tragedy and Philosophy* (Cambridge: Cambridge University Press, 1986), 200.

81. Rousseau, "Discourse on Inequality," 50, 59; Hobbes, *Leviathan,* 105.

82. Rousseau, *The Social Contract,* 166.

83. Locke, *Two Treatises,* 218.

84. Aristotle, *The Politics,* trans. Carnes Lord (Chicago: University of Chicago Press, 1984), 37.

85. Ibid.

86. Karl Marx "On The Jewish Question," 41.

87. *The Limits of State Action,* trans. J. C. Coulthard, ed. J. W. Burrow (Cambridge: Cambridge University Press, 1969). The book was not published in a complete form until 1852, seventeen years after von Humboldt's death. The first English edition (titled *The Sphere and Duties of Government*) appeared in 1854.

88. Ibid., 16, 20–21.

89. James Barron, "Demystifying a Landmark Citation," 912.

90. See Klaus-Berto v. Doemming, Rudolf Werner Füsslein, and Werner Matz, "Entstehungsgeschichte der Artikel des Grundgesetzes," 1 *Jahrbuch des Öffentlichen Rechts der Gegenwart* 54–62 (1951).

91. Federal Constitutional Court decision of July 7, 1970, translated in Donald P. Kommers, "Liberty and Community in Constitutional Law: The Abortion Cases in Comparative Perspective," 1985 *Brigham Young University Law Review* 371, 403.

92. Kurt Sontheimer, "The Importance of the Principle of Human Dignity in the Constitutional Life of the Federal Republic of Germany," in *Germany and the Basic Law: Past, Present, and Future,* ed. Paul Kirchhof and Donald Kommers (Baden-Baden: Nomos, forthcoming).

93. Mill, *Utilitarianism, Liberty,* 82.

94. Ibid., 154.

95. On Rousseau's notions of self-sufficiency, see Joel Schwartz, *The Sexual Politics of Jean-Jacques Rousseau* (Chicago: University of Chicago Press, 1984).

96. See, generally, Mary Ann Glendon, *The Transformation of Family Law: State, Law, and Family in the United States and Western Europe* (Chicago: University of Chicago Press, 1989), 227–38.

97. United Nations Universal Declaration of Human Rights, Article 16.3.

98. David Harris, *The European Social Charter* (Charlottesville, Va.: University Press of Virginia, 1984).

99. Geoffrey Blodgett, *The Gentle Reformers: Massachusetts Democrats in the Cleveland*

Era (Cambridge: Harvard University Press, 1966), 21. On Mill's influence on Holmes generally, see Patrick J. Kelley, "Oliver Wendell Holmes, Utilitarian Jurisprudence, and the Positivism of John Stuart Mill," 30 *American Journal of Jurisprudence* 189 (1985).

FOUR The Missing Language of Responsibility

1. *Prosser and Keeton on the Law of Torts,* 5th ed., ed. W. Page Keeton (St. Paul, Minn.: West, 1984), 375.
2. People for the American Way, *Democracy's Next Generation* (Washington: People for the American Way, 1989), 9, 11, 15.
3. In ordinary private law, a right is but a duty seen from the other end. K. N. Llewellyn, *The Bramble Bush: Our Law and its Study* (Dobbs Ferry, N.Y.: Oceana, 1973), 85.
4. *DeShaney v. Winnebago County Department of Social Services,* 109 S. Ct. 998 (1989).
5. E.g., *Handiboe v. McCarthy,* 114 Ga. Ap. 541, 151 S.E.2d 905 (1966) (no duty to rescue a child drowning in a swimming pool).
6. *Yania v. Bigan,* 397 Pa. 316, 155 A.2d 343 (1959).
7. The cases are collected in Annotation, *Duty of One Other than Carrier or Employer to Render Assistance to one for whose Initial Injury he is not Liable,* 33 A.L.R. 3d 301 (1970).
8. *Osterlind v. Hill,* 263 Mass. 73, 76, 160 N.E. 301, 302 (1928).
9. *Buch v. Amory Mfg. Co.,* 69 N.H. 257, 261, 44 A. 809, 811 (1897). See also, *Union Pacific Ry. Co. v. Cappier,* 66 Kan. 649, 72 P. 281 (1903).
10. *Chastain v. Fuqua Industries, Inc.,* 156 Ga. App. 719, 275 S.E. 2d 679 (1980).
11. *Prosser and Keeton on Torts,* 375.
12. Ibid., 376–77. See also Annotation, *Duty of One Other than Carrier,* 303.
13. *Prosser and Keeton on Torts,* 376–77.
14. Annotation, *Duty of One Other Than Carrier,* 308.
15. Special Committee on the Tort Liability System, *Towards a Jurisprudence of Injury: The Continuing Creation of a System of Substantive Justice in American Tort Law,* Marshall S. Shapo, Reporter (Chicago: American Bar Assn., 1984), 12-1, 12-5.
16. Annotation, *Duty of One Other Than Carrier,* 303. See also, Comment, "The Failure to Rescue: A Comparative Study," 52 *Columbia Law Review* 631, 632 (1952); *Prosser and Keeton on Torts,* 373.
17. Jean Limpens, Robert Kruithof, and Anne Meinertzhagen-Limpens, "Liability for One's Own Act," Chapter 2 of vol. XI *International Encyclopedia of Comparative Law: Torts,* ed. André Tunc (Tübingen: J. C. B. Mohr, 1979), 36.
18. *Prosser and Keeton on Torts,* 373.
19. Ernest J. Weinrib, "The Case for a Duty to Rescue," 90 *Yale Law Journal* 274 (1980).
20. Richard A. Epstein, "A Theory of Strict Liability," 2 *Journal of Legal Studies* 151, 200–201 (1973).
21. *Prosser and Keeton on Torts,* 376.
22. André Tunc, "The Volunteer and the Good Samaritan," in *The Good Samaritan and the Law,* ed. James M. Ratcliffe (Gloucester, Mass: Peter Smith, 1981), 43, 46. For a general survey of these statutes, see the essay in the same volume by

Aleksander W. Rudzinski, "The Duty to Rescue: A Comparative Analysis," 91.
23. Kristen A. DeKuiper, "Stalking the Good Samaritan: Communists, Capitalists, and the Duty to Rescue," 1976 *Utah Law Review* 529 (1976). Limpens, Kruithof, and Meinertzhagen-Limpens say in their comparative survey that tort law is "in a state of evolution" on this point, "Liability for One's Own Act," 43.
24. Tunc, "The Volunteer and the Good Samaritan," 56–62; Gilbert Geis, "Sanctioning the Selfish: The Operation of Portugal's New 'Bad Samaritan' Statute," 1 *International Review of Victimology* (1991).
25. Tunc, "The Volunteer and the Good Samaritan," 43, 63.
26. D'Amato, "The 'Bad Samaritan' Paradigm," 802. Cf. Martin Golding's argument that "other-affecting duties" need not always entail corresponding rights, "The Primacy of Welfare Rights," 1 *Social Philosophy and Policy* 119 (1984). Golding points out that Jewish law imposes a duty to rescue someone in danger of losing his life, but does not create any right to be rescued.
27. James Fitzjames Stephen, *Liberty, Equality, Fraternity,* R. J. White, ed. (Cambridge: Cambridge University Press, 1967), 159–60.
28. See, generally, Mary Ann Glendon, *Abortion and Divorce in Western Law* (Cambridge: Harvard University Press, 1987), 125–34.
29. Oliver Wendell Holmes, Jr., "The Path of the Law," 10 *Harvard Law Review* 457, 458–59 (1897).
30. Ibid.
31. Oliver Wendell Holmes, Jr., "Natural Law," 32 *Harvard Law Review* 40, 41–42 (1918).
32. Holmes, "The Path of the Law," 464.
33. *Olmstead v. United States,* 277 U.S. 438, 485 (1928) (Brandeis, J., concurring).
34. Marc A. Franklin, "Vermont Requires Rescue: A Comment," 25 *Stanford Law Review* 51, 58 (1972).
35. Geis, "Sanctioning the Selfish," 12–15; Hans Zeisel, "An International Experiment on the Effects of a Good Samaritan Law," in *The Good Samaritan and the Law,* 209.
36. Henry Kaufmann, "Legality and Harmfulness of a Bystander's Failure to Intervene as Determinants of Moral Judgment," in *Altruism and Helping Behavior,* ed. J. Macauley and L. Berkowitz (New York: Academic Press, 1970), 77–81.
37. *Prosser and Keeton on Torts,* 377. Massachusetts, for example, imposes a reporting duty on bystanders at the scene of certain violent crimes. Mass. Gen. Laws Ann. Ch. 268, § 40 (West Supp. 1990).
38. These statutes are classified and analyzed in Comment, "Good Samaritan Laws— The Legal Placebo: A Current Analysis," 17 *Akron Law Review* 303 (1983).
39. Vt. Stat. Ann., tit. 12, § 519 (1973) (Supp. 1989) provides for a maximum $100 fine for violation of the following:

    A person who knows that another is exposed to grave physical harm shall, to the extent that the same can be rendered without danger or peril to himself or without interference with important duties owed to others, give reasonable assistance to the exposed person unless that assistance or care is being provided by others.

    There are no reported decisions on the question of whether violation of this statute could also ground an action in tort.
40. Minn. Stat. Ann. § 604.05 (West Supp. 1990).
41. *Jackson v. City of Joliet,* 715 F. 2d 1200 (7th Cir. 1983).

42. A sociological study of the police department of one good-sized (500,000 pop.) American city suggests that police officers' decisions and behavior are often deeply affected by their personal sense of having significant obligations to their fellow citizens. William K. Muir, Jr., *Police: Streetcorner Politicians* (Chicago: University of Chicago Press, 1970).

43. E.g., *Williams v. State,* 34 Cal. 3d 18, 23, 664 P. 2d 137, 139 (1983).

44. Ibid., 34 Cal. 3d at 24, 664 P. 2d at 140.

45. *Warren v. District of Columbia,* 444 A. 2d 1, 3 (D.C. 1981).

46. Ibid., 4, 8–9.

47. *Prosser and Keeton on Torts,* 1043–69.

48. Civil Rights Act of 1871, 42 U.S.C. § 1983 (1). Actions under § 1983 may also be brought in state courts.

49. *Jackson v. City of Joliet,* 715 F. 2d 1200, 1202 (7th Cir. 1983).

50. Ibid.

51. Ibid., 1203.

52. Ibid., 1204.

53. Ibid., 1203–04.

54. Ibid., 1205.

55. *DeShaney v. Winnebago County Department of Social Services,* 109 S. Ct. 998 (1989).

56. *DeShaney v. Winnebago County Department of Social Services,* 812 F. 2d 298 (7th Cir. 1987).

57. *DeShaney v. Winnebago County Department of Social Services,* 109 S. Ct. 998, 1003 (1989).

58. Ibid., 1004.

59. Ibid.

60. Ibid., 1007–8.

61. Ibid., 1011.

62. Ibid., 1003.

63. Ibid.

64. See Michael Kammen, *A Machine that Would Go of Itself: The Constitution in American Culture* (New York: Knopf, 1986).

65. *DeShaney v. Winnebago County Department of Social Services,* 109 S. Ct. 998, 1006 (1989).

66. Aviam Soifer, "Moral Ambition, Formalism, and the 'Free World' of *De-Shaney*," 57 *George Washington Law Review* 1513 (1989).

67. Wisc. Stat. Ann., § 893.30(3) (1983).

68. Marc Landy, "Citizens First: Public Policy and Self Government," *Responsive Community,* Spring 1991, 56, 60.

69. See, generally, Peter Schuck, *Suing Government: Citizen Remedies for Official Wrongs* (New Haven: Yale University Press, 1983), 199.

70. Gerhard Casper, "Changing Concepts of Constitutionalism: 18th to 20th Century," 1989 *Supreme Court Review* 311, 328.

71. Ibid., 331. Some of these prior notions are of very long standing. See, for example, the French Constitution of 24 June 1793, Art. 21: "Public aid is a sacred obligation. Society owes subsistence to unfortunate citizens, either by finding them work, or providing the means of subsistence to those who are unable to work." *Les constitutions de la France de 1789 à 1870* (Paris: La documentation

française, 1988), 12; *Allgemeines Landrecht für die Preussischen Staaten von 1794* (Frankfurt: Metzner, 1970), Part II, Title 13, Articles 2 and 3. The author of a recent monograph on the protection of human rights in Finland found it quite natural to begin his discussion by alluding to the solemn oath that kings of Sweden have taken since ancient times to protect their subjects, rich and poor alike. Tore Modeen, *La Protection des Droits de l'Homme* (Helsinki: Institute of Public Law, 1989), 1. See, generally, Bertrand de Jouvenel, *Sovereignty: An Inquiry into the Political Good,* trans. J. F. Huntington (Chicago: University of Chicago Press, 1957).

72. See, generally, Casper, "Changing Concepts"; and David P. Currie, "Positive and Negative Constitutional Rights," 53 *University of Chicago Law Review* 864 (1986).

73. Kurt Sontheimer, "The Importance of Human Dignity in the Constitutional Life of the Federal Republic of Germany," in *Germany and the Basic Law: Past, Present and Future,* ed. Paul Kirchhof and Donald Kommers (Baden-Baden: Nomos, forthcoming).

74. See, generally, Erhard Denninger, "Constitutional Law between Statutory Law and Higher Law," in *Law in the Making,* ed. A. Pizzorusso (Berlin: Springer-Verlag, 1988), 103, 108–110.

75. For developments under state constitutions, see Burt Neuborne, "Foreword: State Constitutions and the Evolution of Positive Rights," 20 *Rutgers Law Journal* 881 (1989). Some state constitutions make the provision of basic social assistance a duty of the state. E.g., "The aid, care and support of the needy are public concerns and shall be provided by the state and by such of its subdivisions, and in such manner and by such means, as the legislature may from time to time determine." N.Y. Const. art. XVII, § 1. New York's highest court held in 1977 that this provision not only proclaimed a public goal, but imposed an affirmative duty upon the state to aid the needy. *Tucker v. Toia,* 400 N.Y.S. 2d 728, 730–31, 371 N.E. 2d 449, 451–53 (1977).

76. E.g., *Goldberg v. Kelly,* 397 U.S. 254 (1970) (welfare rights may not be terminated without opportunity for hearing).

77. See the fascinating article by David Howes comparing the songs composed in various countries as part of efforts to raise funds for Ethiopian famine relief, and arguing that each country's constitution had an important effect on the types of moral argument implicit in their respective songs. Howes concludes that constitutions deserve more attention than they have thus far received in cultural studies since they not only inform production of legislation, but "production" in other realms of social life. David Howes, " 'We are the World' and its Counterparts: Popular Song as Constitutional Discourse," 3 *International Journal of Politics, Culture, and Society* 315, 337 (1990).

78. E.g., The "Declaration of the Rights of Man and of the Citizen" states that it is to serve as a constant reminder to citizens, not only of their rights, but also of their duties, *Constitutions et documents politiques,* 2d ed., ed. Maurice Duverger (Paris: Presses Universitaires de France, 1960), 3. The inclusion of the word "citizen" signifies that the enumerated rights are not just those of individual "men" to life, liberty, and property, but "citizens," members of the body politic aspiring toward fraternity.

79. William Blackstone, *Commentaries on the Laws of England,* Book I, *88.

80. Roosevelt's "second bill of rights" was contained in his 1944 State of the Union message. It is reproduced in Cass R. Sunstein, "Constitutionalism After the New Deal," 101 *Harvard Law Review* 421, 423 (1987).

81. Martin Luther King, Jr., *Strength to Love* (Philadelphia: Fortress Press, 1981), 33–34.

82. Mark Mellman, Edward Lazarus, and Allen Rivlin, "Family Time, Family Values," in *Rebuilding the Nest,* ed. David Blankenhorn, Steven Bayme, and Jean Bethke Elshtain (Milwaukee: Family Service America, 1990), 73, 83.

83. Mary Ann Glendon, *Abortion and Divorce in Western Law,* 83–91.

84. Timothy M. Smeeding and Barbara B. Torrey, "Poor Children in Rich Countries," *Science,* 11 November 1988, 873.

85. Alfred J. Kahn and Sheila B. Kamerman, "Social Assistance: An Eight Country Overview," 8 *Journal of the Institute of Socio-Economic Studies* 93, 104 (1983–84).

FIVE The Missing Dimension of Sociality

1. *Bowen v. Gilliard,* 483 U.S. 587, 632 (1987) (Brennan, J., dissenting).

2. Claude Lévi-Strauss, *The Savage Mind* (Chicago: University of Chicago Press, 1966), 1.

3. On the idea of a contemporary *Kulturkampf,* see George Weigel, *Catholicism and the Renewal of American Democracy* (New York: Paulist Press, 1989), 4–6.

4. *Local 1330, United Steelworkers of America v. United States Steel Corp.,* 631 F. 2d 1264 (6th Cir. 1980).

5. Benjamin Aaron, "Plant Closings: American and Comparative Perspectives," 59 *Chicago-Kent Law Review* 941 (1983).

6. A recent study of the restructuring of the steel industry in Western Europe finds that, while strong laws regulating layoff practices may have slowed restructuring of that industry, they also generated important social benefits, including community stability and a broader distribution of the risks and costs of economic change than would otherwise have occurred. See Susan N. Houseman, *Industrial Restructuring in the European Community: The Case of European Steel* (Cambridge: Harvard University Press, 1991).

7. *Sierra Club v. Morton,* 405 U.S. 727, 755–56 (1972) (Blackmun, J., dissenting).

8. *Hodel v. Irving,* 107 S. Ct. 2076 (1987).

9. Ibid.

10. See, generally, Julius Getman, "The Courts and Collective Bargaining," 59 *Chicago-Kent Law Review* 969, 977 (1983); Thomas C. Kohler, "Setting the Conditions for Self-Rule: Unions, Associations, Our First Amendment Discourse, and the Problem of *De Bartolo,*" 1990 *Wisconsin Law Review* 149.

11. *Federalist* No. 55.

12. Edmund Burke, *Reflections on the Revolution in France* (New York: Doubleday Anchor, 1973):

> To be attached to the subdivision, to love the little platoon we belong to in society, is the first principle (the germ as it were) of public affections. It is the first link in the series by which we proceed towards a love to our country and to mankind. (59).

13. Alexis de Tocqueville, *The Old Regime and the French Revolution,* trans. Stuart Gilbert (New York: Doubleday Anchor, 1955), xiii.

14. Alexis de Tocqueville, *Democracy in America,* trans. George Lawrence, ed. J. P. Mayer (Garden City, N.Y.: Doubleday Anchor, 1969), I, 70.

15. Ibid., 63.

16. Emile Durkheim, *The Division of Labor in Society,* trans. George Simpson (New York: Free Press, 1964), 28.

17. James Gleick, *Chaos: Making a New Science* (New York: Viking, 1987), 46 (Henri Poincaré "was the first to understand the possibility of chaos [science].")

18. "An Interview with Czeslaw Milosz," *New York Review of Books,* 27 February 1986, 34.

19. Robert Bellah, "The Invasion of the Money World," in *Rebuilding the Nest,* ed. David Blankenhorn, Steven Bayme, and Jean Bethke Elshtain (Milwaukee: Family Service America, 1990) 227, 228; Christopher Lasch, *Haven in a Heartless World* (New York: Basic Books, 1977).

20. Tocqueville, *Democracy in America,* I. 93–94.

21. *Ibid.*

22. Scholars in many fields, especially those with a sociological orientation, are beginning to make this point. See, especially, Alan Wolfe, *Whose Keeper? Social Science and Moral Obligation* (Berkeley: University of California Press, 1989). Wolfe has insisted that the "recovery of sociology and its moral tradition" is essential for the health of liberal politics:

    Markets and states have gotten people fairly far along the road to a better life, offering greater freedom on the one hand and a recognition of obligations to others on the other. But they have done so by taking real people living in specific social situations and removing them from the process by which morality is understood. (188).

    See also Robert Bellah et al., *Habits of the Heart: Individualism and Commitment in American Life* (Berkeley: University of California Press, 1985); Amitai Etzioni, *An Immodest Agenda* (New York: McGraw-Hill, 1983); Nathan Glazer, *The Limits of Social Policy* (Cambridge: Harvard University Press, 1988).

23. Like many others, I have found ecology a useful concept in dealing with contemporary social phenomena. See, Bellah et al., *Habits of the Heart,* 283 ("social ecology"); Urie Bronfenbrenner, *The Ecology of Human Development* (Cambridge: Harvard University Press, 1979); Clifford Geertz, *The Interpretation of Cultures* (New York: Basic Books, 1973), 3 ("cultural ecology"); Mary Ann Glendon, *The Transformation of Family Law* (Chicago: University of Chicago Press, 1989), 306 ("family ecology"); Alan Wolfe, *Whose Keeper?,* 256.

24. Brigitte Berger and Peter L. Berger, *The War Over the Family* (New York: Doubleday Anchor, 1983), vii.

25. *Griswold v. Connecticut,* 381 U.S. 479, 486 (1965).

26. *Eisenstadt v. Baird,* 405 U.S. 438, 453 (1972).

27. Laurence H. Tribe, *American Constitutional Law,* 2d ed. (Mineola, New York: Foundation Press, 1988), 1416.

28. *Moore v. City of East Cleveland,* 431 U.S. 494 (1977).

29. *Borough of Glassboro v. Vallorosi,* 16 Family Law Reporter 1190 (New Jersey Supreme Court, 1990).

30. Many states now provide a simple speedy form of divorce for childless couples who meet certain other requirements, while establishing more rigorous systems of judicial supervision of the economic aspects of divorces where minor children

are involved. See Mary Ann Glendon, *The Transformation of Family Law* (Chicago: University of Chicago Press, 1989), 189.

31. The presence or absence of children is often a key factor in determining whether partners in a nonmarital cohabitation should be treated as having agreed to property-sharing. See Glendon, *Transformation of Family Law*, 252–90.

32. Compare *Moore v. City of East Cleveland,* 431 U.S. 494 (1977), with the Court's decision approving an ordinance that excluded groups of three or more unrelated individuals, *Village of Belle Terre v. Boraas,* 416 U.S. 1 (1974).

33. "Code Blue," *New York Times,* 9 June 1990, A24.

34. People for the American Way, *Democracy's Next Generation* (Washington: People for the American Way, 1989), 27.

35. Ibid., 15.

36. Ibid., 45.

37. Ibid., 67.

38. Ibid., 69.

39. Ibid., 9,

40. Michael Oreskes, "Profiles of Today's Youth: They Couldn't Care Less," *New York Times,* 28 June 1990, A1, D21.

41. Tocqueville, *Democracy in America,* 315.

42. *Ibid.*

43. *Ibid.,* 589.

44. Urie Bronfenbrenner, *The Ecology of Human Development* (Cambridge: Harvard University Press, 1979), 3.

45. Emmy E. Werner, "Children of the Garden Island," *Scientific American,* April 1989, 106–11. See also, Emmy E. Werner and Ruth S. Smith, *Vulnerable but Invincible: A Longitudinal Study of Resilient Children and Youth* (New York: McGraw-Hill, 1982); Emmy E. Werner, "High-Risk Children in Young Adulthood: A Longitudinal Study from Birth to 32 Years," 59 (1) *American Journal of Orthopsychiatry* 72 (1989). All quotations in the text are from the *Scientific American* article.

46. Spencer Rich, "Troubled Children Assessed" (interview with Dr. Emmy Werner), *Washington Post,* 17 April 1990.

47. At the end of the second decade of the study, the researchers found that only a small proportion of the resilient children had had contacts with social service agencies, and these contacts were typically related to obtaining temporary financial assistance. None of the resilient children had sought or obtained any help from mental health professionals. Werner and Smith, *Vulnerable but Invincible,* 96–97.

48. Louis Roussel, "Démographie: deux décennies de mutations dans les pays industrialisés," in *Family, State, and Individual Economic Security,* ed. M.-T. Meulders-Klein and J. Eekelaar (Brussels: Story Scientia, 1988), I, 27–28.

49. Nathan Glazer, *The Limits of Social Policy* (Cambridge: Harvard University Press, 1988), 3.

50. "The Talk of the Town," *New Yorker,* 30 August 1976, 22.

51. Select Committee on Children, Youth, and Families, *U.S. Children and Their Families: Current Conditions and Recent Trends, 1989* (Washington, D.C.: U.S. Government Printing Office, 1989), 52.

52. "24% of U.S. Children Live With Just One Parent," *New York Times,* 28 January 1988, C8.

53. Select Committee, *U.S. Children*, 110.
54. *Who Cares for America's Children? Child Care Policy for the 1990s*, ed. Cheryl D. Hayes, John L. Palmer, and Martha J. Zaslow (Washington, D.C.: National Academy Press, 1990), 17.
55. Edward F. Zigler and Patricia Kilkenny, "An Agenda for the 1990s: Supporting Families," in *Rebuilding the Nest*, 237, 242.
56. Glazer, *Limits of Social Policy*, 155.
57. Michael Walzer, "The Communitarian Critique of Liberalism," 18 *Political Theory* 6, 11–12 (1990). According to Stephan Thernstrom, transiency was a part of the American way of life at least since the beginning of the nineteenth century. In what was "not a frontier phenomenon, or a big-city phenomenon, but a national phenomenon," people came and went from villages, towns, and cities at "a rapid and surprisingly uniform rate." *The Other Bostonians: Poverty and Progress in the American Metropolis 1880–1970* (Cambridge: Harvard University Press, 1973), 227.
58. Walzer, "The Communitarian Critique," 15.
59. Ibid., 18.
60. See Jean Bethke Elshtain, "The Family and Civic Life," in *Rebuilding the Nest*, 119.
61. See Richard C. Flathman, *The Practice of Rights* (Cambridge: Cambridge University Press, 1976), 2, 188. As former Justice Brennan once observed, "certain kinds of personal bonds have played a critical role in the culture and traditions of the Nation by cultivating and transmitting shared ideals and beliefs; they thereby foster diversity and act as critical buffers between the individual and the power of the State." *Roberts v. United States Jaycees*, 468 U.S. 609, 618–19 (1984).
62. Felicity Barringer, "Census Report Shows a Rise in Child Care and its Costs," *New York Times*, 16 August 1990, A20.
63. "A Huge Gain in the Poverty War," *New York Times*, 31 October 1990, A24.
64. Peter Berger and Richard John Neuhaus have long contended that if intermediate "institutions could be more imaginatively recognized in public policy, individuals would be more 'at home' in society, and the political order would be more 'meaningful.' " *To Empower People: The Role of Mediating Structures in Public Policy* (Washington, D.C.: American Enterprise Institute, 1977), 3. For a comparative study illustrating the variety of ways in which other countries have drawn on the voluntary sector to provide social services, see Ralph M. Kramer, *Voluntary Agencies in the Welfare State* (Berkeley: University of California Press, 1981).
65. E.g., the "community action programs" established under Pub. L. 88–452, 78 Stat. 516, 42 U.S.C. §2781 et seq. (1964), amended in 1967 and repealed in 1981.
66. Pub. L. No. 97–35, 95 Stat. 578 (1981), codified at 42 U.S.C. §300z et seq. (1982). The Act built on a predecessor, the Adolescent Health Services and Pregnancy Prevention and Care Act of 1978, Pub.L. No. 95–626, 92 Stat. 3595, 42 U.S.C. §300 (a) (21) et seq. (1978). See, for a critical appraisal, Janet Benshoof, "The Chastity Act: Government Manipulation of Abortion Information and the First Amendment," 101 *Harvard Law Review* 1916 (1988).
67. 42 U.S.C. §300z (b) (1)–(4).
68. 42 U.S.C. §§ 300z–3(b)(1) and 300z–10(a). An exception is provided for referral

for abortion counselling where such referral is requested by a pregnant adolescent and her parents.

69. S. Rep. No. 97–161, 97th Cong., 1st Sess., 15–16 (1981).
70. 42 U.S.C. § 300z (a) (10 (c).
71. 42 U.S.C. § 300z–5(a) (21).
72. *Bowen v. Kendrick,* 108 S. Ct. 2562 (1988).
73. The court left open for consideration on remand whether the statute, as applied, violated the Establishment Clause.
74. The reference is to the three-part test announced in *Lemon v. Kurtzman,* 403 U.S. 603 (1971) for determining whether a statute violates the establishment clause: Does it have a valid secular purpose? Is its primary effect to advance religion? Does it foster excessive entanglement between government and religion? To be constitutional, a statute must pass all three parts of the test.
75. *Bowen v. Kendrick,* 2571.
76. Ibid., 2573.
77. Ibid., 2574.
78. Ibid.
79. *Bowen v. Gilliard,* 632.
80. *Corporation of the Presiding Bishop v. Amos,* 483 U.S. 327, 342 (1987).
81. Charles Taylor, *Sources of the Self: The Making of the Modern Identity* (Cambridge: Harvard University Press, 1989), 3.
82. Learned Hand, "The Spirit of Liberty," in *The Spirit of Liberty,* ed. Irving Dilliard (New York: Alfred A. Knopf, 1960), 189–90.
83. R. George Wright, "The Interests of Posterity in the Constitutional Scheme," 59 *Cincinnati Law Review* 113 (1990).

SIX Rights Insularity

1. Fernand Braudel, *The Mediterranean and the Mediterranean World in the Age of Philip II,* trans. Siân Reynolds, vol. II (New York: Harper and Row, 1976), 764.
2. Warren E. Leary, "2 Superpowers Failing in Geography," *New York Times,* 9 November 1989, A20.
3. *New State Ice Co. v. Liebmann,* 285 U.S. 262, 311 (1932) (Brandeis, J., dissenting). Justice Brandeis stated that it is one of the "happy incidents of the federal system that a single courageous State may, if its citizens choose, serve as a laboratory; and try novel social and economic experiments without risk to the rest of the country." Id.
4. See Harold J. Berman, "Toward an Integrative Jurisprudence: Politics, Morality, History," 76 *California Law Review* 779, 799 (1988):
   In the process of international economic and cultural unification there is developing a universal body of legal norms and processes, and even a common world-wide legal consciousness, connected with [activities in the areas of commerce, science, technology, scholarship, literature and the arts, medicine, tourism, sports, and so on.]
5. *Dudgeon v. United Kingdom,* 3 European Human Rights Reports 40 (1980).
6. Convention for the Protection of Human Rights and Fundamental Freedoms, 4 November 1950, effective 1953, in Council of Europe, *European Convention on Human Rights: Collected Texts* (Strasbourg: Council of Europe, 1974), 4–5. The article cited in the text illustrates the general pattern of the Convention: each

right is set forth in a first paragraph, while a second paragraph states what restrictions are permitted.

7. *Dudgeon v. United Kingdom,* 4 European Human Rights Reports 149 (1981). The Court reached a similar conclusion in a later case involving a challenge to the homosexual sodomy laws of the Irish Republic. *Norris Case,* Judgment of 26 October 1988, Publications of the European Court of Human Rights, Series A, vol. 142.

8. *Hardwick v. Bowers,* 760 F.2d 1202 (11th Cir. 1985).

9. *Bowers v. Hardwick,* 478 U.S. 186, 191 (1986).

10. *Dudgeon v. United Kingdom,* 4 European Human Rights Reports 149, 186–87 (1981) (Walsh, J., dissenting in part).

11. One *amicus curiae* brief did cite (inaccurately) the earlier decision by the Commission. Anthony Lester, "The Overseas Trade in the American Bill of Rights," 88 *Columbia Law Review* 537, 560 (1988).

12. One member state, Malta, has ratified the Convention but has not accepted the Court's jurisdiction.

13. Northern Ireland since 1972 had been under interim direct rule from Westminster.

14. *Dudgeon,* 161–62.

15. Ibid., 160, 161, 163–64, 168.

16. Ibid., 164–65.

17. Ibid., 181.

18. Lord Devlin, quoted in Ibid., 182.

19. Ibid., 185.

20. *Bowers v. Hardwick,* 478 U.S. 186, 194 (1986).

21. Ibid., 194.

22. Ibid., 199 (Blackmun, J., dissenting, quoting Brandeis, J., dissenting in *Olmstead v. United States,* 277 U.S. 438, 478 (1928)).

23. Ibid., 208.

24. Ibid., 197 (Powell, J., dissenting). In 1990, retired Justice Powell said in a speech that he "probably made a mistake" in *Bowers v. Hardwick,* but that he regarded the case as "of little or no importance" because no one had actually been prosecuted. "Retired Justice Alters View on Gay Privacy," *New York Times,* 26 October 1990, A21.

25. Al Kamen, "Vote Switch Kept Sodomy Law Alive, Sources Say," reprinted from *Washington Post* in *St. Louis Post-Dispatch,* 14 July 1986.

26. See H. Patrick Glenn, "Persuasive Authority," 32 *McGill Law Journal* 261 (1987) for an illuminating discussion of important nonbinding resources for legal reasoning.

27. *Thompson v. Oklahoma,* 108 S. Ct. 2687, 2716 n. 4 (1988) (Scalia, J., dissenting).

28. Baron de Montesquieu, *The Spirit of the Laws,* trans. Thomas Nugent (New York: Hafner, 1949) I, 6.

29. See Guido Calabresi's discussion of this point in *Ideals, Beliefs, Attitudes, and the Law* (New York: Syracuse University Press, 1985), 109.

30. *Roe v. Wade,* 410 U.S. 113 (1973), discussed in Chapter Three above.

31. *DeShaney v. Winnebago County Department of Social Services,* 109 S. Ct. 998 (1989), discussed in Chapter Four above.

32. James Boyd White, *Justice as Translation* (Chicago: University of Chicago Press, 1990), 224.

33. Ibid., 224–25.

34. *Poe v. Ullman,* 367 U.S. 497, 545–46 (1961) (Harlan, J., dissenting).

35. As to Fourth Amendment "balancing," see White, *Justice as Translation,* 160–202.

36. James Michael, "Civil Rights: Homosexuals and Privacy," 138 *New Law Journal* 831 (1988).

37. J. G. Merrills, *The Development of International Law by the European Court of Human Rights* (Manchester: University Press, 1988), 6. The Court normally sits in panels of seven judges, but in certain cases raising serious questions of interpretation of the Convention, a plenary session is called, as happened in *Dudgeon.*

38. See Helmut Coing, "Europäisierung der Rechtswissenschaft," 15 *Neue Juristische Wochenschrift* 937–41 (1990); and Patrick Glenn, "Persuasive Authority," 296. For the past several years, the Chief Justices of European constitutional courts have been meeting on a regular basis to discuss common cases and problems.

39. Lester, "The Overseas Trade," 541.

40. The U.N. Covenants on Civil and Political Rights, and on Economic, Social and Cultural Rights, notably, have been ratified or acceded to by about 90 countries, including almost all of the European and Latin American nations. See Chapter One, note 14.

41. It was not always thus. For accounts of the use of foreign law in the U.S. in the nineteenth century, see M. H. Hoeflich, "Transatlantic Friendships and the German Influence on American Law in the First Half of the Nineteenth Century," 35 *American Journal of Comparative Law* 599 (1987); M. H. Hoeflich, "Roman and Civil Law in American Legal Education and Research Prior to 1930: A Preliminary Survey," 1984 *University of Illinois Law Review* 719 (1984); M. H. Hoeflich, "John Austin and Joseph Story: Two Nineteenth Century Perspectives on the Utility of the Civil Law for the Common Lawyer," 29 *American Journal of Legal History* 36, 75 (1985); Peter Stein, "The Attraction of the Civil Law in Post-Revolutionary America," 52 *Virginia Law Review* 403 (1966).

42. President Robert Badinter, "Constitutionalism and the Separation of Powers," (paper delivered at the Harvard Law School Conference on "Constitutionalism: The American Experiment in a Wider Perspective," Cambridge, Mass., 8 April 1989).

43. John Greenwald, "A Gift to All Nations," TIME, 6 July 1987, 92.

44. *Constitution Makers on Constitution Making,* ed. Robert A. Goldwin and Art Kaufman (Washington, D.C.: American Enterprise Institute, 1988), vii.

45. Ibid., 175.

46. Andrzej Rapaczynski, "Bibliographical Essay: The Influence of U.S. Constitutionalism Abroad," in *Constitutionalism and Rights: The Influence of the United States Constitution Abroad,* ed. Louis Henkin and Albert J. Rosenthal (New York: Columbia University Press, 1989), 406–8.

47. See Albert P. Blaustein, "The Influence of the United States Constitution Abroad," 12 *Oklahoma City University Law Review* 435 (1987).

48. Franz Wieacker, "Foundations of European Legal Culture," 38 *American Journal of Comparative Law* 1, 29 (1990).

49. See Chapters Two, Three, and Four above.

50. Mauro Cappelletti, "The 'Mighty Problem' of Judicial Review and the Contribution of Comparative Analysis," 53 *Southern California Law Review* 409 (1980); " 'Constitutional Justice' and the Overcoming of the Antitheses 'Equity-Law' and 'Natural-Positive Law,' " in *Conflict and Integration: Comparative Law in the World Today* (Japan: Chuo University, 1988), 10.

51. See John H. Merryman, *The Civil Law Tradition,* 2d ed. (Stanford University Press, 1985), 34–38.

52. *Law Society of Upper Canada v. Skapinker* [1984] 1 S.C.R. 357, 366–67 (Estey, J.).

53. Chief Justice Thomas Finlay, *The Constitution Fifty Years On* (Dublin: Round Hall Press, 1988), 5: ("Reliance [on American constitutional law] is now quite common"); James Casey, *Constitutional Law in Ireland* (London: Sweet and Maxwell, 1987), xii, (Foreword by Justice Brian Walsh); Michael Forde, *Constitutional Law of Ireland* (Dublin: Mercier Press, 1987), 84–85.

54. Jochen Frowein, "Recent Developments Concerning the European Convention on Human Rights," in *Laws, Rights, and the European Convention on Human Rights,* ed. Jacob Sundberg (Littleton, Colo.: Rothman, 1986), 27.

55. *Marbury v. Madison,* 5 U.S. (1 Cranch) 137 (1803).

56. *Dred Scott v. Sandford,* 60 U.S. (19 How.) 393 (1856).

57. See Chapter Two above.

58. *R. v. Morgentaler* [1988] 1 S.C.R. 30.

59. Ibid., 51.

60. Canadian Charter § 7.

61. *Morgentaler,* 75.

62. Daniel O. Conkle, "Canada's *Roe:* The Canadian Abortion Decision and its Implications for American Constitutional Law and Theory," 6 *Constitutional Commentary* 299, 311 (1989).

63. *Morgentaler,* 46.

64. Id. at 53 (quoting *In Re B.C. Motor Vehicle Act* [1985] 2 S.C.R. 486, 498) (Lamer, J.).

65. Ibid., 51.

66. Ibid., 45, 46.

67. Ibid., 46.

68. Ibid., 127.

69. Ibid., 112.

70. Ibid., 167.

71. Ibid., 171.

72. Dale Gibson, *The Law of the Charter: General Principles* (Toronto: Carswell, 1986), 81.

73. See, for an excellent discussion, Roderick A. Macdonald, "Procedural Due Process in Canadian Constitutional Law: Natural Justice and Fundamental Justice," 39 *University of Florida Law Review* 217 (1987).

74. Seymour Martin Lipset, "North American Labor Movements: A Comparative Perspective," in *Unions in Transition: Entering the Second Century,* ed. S. Lipset (San Francisco: ICS Press, 1986), 421, 442–43. See also the articles in the special issue of *Daedalus,* "In Search of Canada", especially John Conway, "An 'Adapted Organic Tradition,' " 117 *Daedalus* 381 (1988).

75. Canada Act of 1982, Canadian Charter of Rights and Freedoms, § 33. Article 33 permits federal or provincial legislatures to shield their laws from judicial review

under specified rights provisions of the Charter, by expressly declaring the intent to legislate "notwithstanding" the Charter. Any law adopted pursuant to Article 33 automatically ceases to have effect after five years, but may be renewed by following the procedure again. This "check" on judicial power to set aside legislation, balanced by the sunset provision, modifies the regime of legislative supremacy without permitting the courts to completely supplant the legislative process.

76. Canadian Charter §§ 2, 23, 25, 29, 35.
77. Ibid., § 27.
78. Paul Weiler, "Rights and Judges in a Democracy: A New Canadian Version," 18 *University of Michigan Journal of Law Reform* 51, 73–74 (1984).
79. *Webster v. Reproductive Health Services,* 109 S. Ct. 3040 (1989).
80. Kammen, *A Machine That Would Go of Itself,* 10–11.
81. Andrew L. Kaufman, "Judges or Scholars: To Whom Shall We Look for Our Constitutional Law?" 37 *Journal of Legal Education* 184 (1987).
82. See Alan Watson, *Legal Transplants: An Approach to Comparative Law* (Charlottesville: University of Virginia, 1974), for several entertaining examples.
83. *The Federalist Papers,* ed. Clinton Rossiter (New York: New American Library, 1961), 33.

SEVEN Refining the Rhetoric of Rights

1. *Whitney v. California,* 274 U.S. 357, 375 (1927) (concurring opinion).
2. See Charles Taylor, *Sources of the Self: The Making of the Modern Identity* (Cambridge: Harvard University Press, 1989), 9.
3. Robert N. Bellah et al., *Habits of the Heart: Individualism and Commitment in American Life* (Berkeley: University of California Press, 1985), 20.
4. Ibid., 27–51.
5. Christopher Lasch, "The I's Have It for Another Decade," *New York Times,* 27 December 1989, A23. See, generally, Lasch, *The Culture of Narcissism* (New York: Warner, 1979) and *The Minimal Self* (New York: Norton, 1984).
6. Lasch, "The I's Have It."
7. People for the American Way, *Democracy's Next Generation: A Study of Youth and Teachers* (Washington, D.C.: People for the American Way, 1989), 14–17. A similar national study by the Times Mirror Center is described by Michael Oreskes, "Profiles of Today's Youth: They Couldn't Care Less," *New York Times,* 28 June 1990, A1, D21.
8. See Barbara Whitehead, "Reports from the Kitchen Table: The Family in an Unfriendly Culture," 3 *Family Affairs* 1 (1990).
9. Abraham Lincoln, *Selected Speeches, Messages, and Letters,* ed. T. Harry Williams (New York: Rinehart, 1957), 34.
10. Stephen Macedo, *Liberal Virtues* (Oxford, England: Clarendon Press, 1990), 34, 41.
11. Ibid., 46.
12. Ibid., 71.
13. Wilson Carey McWilliams, "American Pluralism: The Old Order Passeth," in *The Americans, 1976,* ed. Irving Kristol and Paul Weaver (Lexington: D.C. Heath, 1976), 293, 315.

14. Robert E. Rodes, Jr., "Greatness Thrust Upon Them: Class Biases in American Law," 1983 *American Journal of Jurisprudence* 1, 6.
15. Carl E. Schneider, "State-Interest Analysis in Fourteenth Amendment Privacy Law: An Essay on the Constitutionalization of Social Issues," 51 *Law and Contemporary Problems* 79, 109 (1988).
16. John Stuart Mill, "On Liberty," in *Utilitarianism, Liberty, and Representative Government* (New York: E. P. Dutton, 1951), 163–67.
17. The data in this paragraph are from Jonathan Tasini, "Labor and the Media", 3 *Extra!* (Summer 1990), 1–13.
18. Mary Ann Glendon, *The New Family and the New Property* (Toronto: Butterworths, 1981).
19. See Marc K. Landy, Marc J. Roberts, and Stephen R. Thomas, *The Environmental Protection Agency: Asking the Wrong Questions* (New York: Oxford University Press, 1990), 3–17.
20. Vaclav Havel, "New Year's Day Address," Foreign Broadcasting Information Service, Eastern Europe, 90–001, 2 Jan. 1990, 9–10.
21. Ibid., 10.
22. Ibid.
23. Timothy Garton Ash, *The Uses of Adversity: Essays on the Fate of Central Europe* (New York: Random House, 1989), 48, 191, 203.
24. George Weigel, *Catholicism and the Renewal of American Democracy* (New York: Paulist Press, 1989), 5.
25. See James Gleick, *Chaos: The Making of a New Science* (New York: Viking, 1987).
26. Vaclav Havel, "New Year's Day," 10.

Index